2/9 - Chapter 3.
2/16 Chapter 4, 5

Accent
on Learning

Improving Instruction
and Reshaping the Curriculum

✳✳✳✳✳✳✳✳✳✳✳✳✳✳✳✳✳✳✳✳✳✳✳✳✳✳✳✳✳✳✳✳✳✳✳✳✳✳✳

K. Patricia Cross

✳✳✳

ACCENT
ON
LEARNING

 Jossey-Bass   Publishers
San Francisco · Washington · London · 1977

ACCENT ON LEARNING
Improving Instruction and Reshaping the Curriculum
by K. Patricia Cross

Library of Congress Catalogue Card Number LC 75-24003

International Standard Book Number ISBN 0-87589-269-8

Manufactured in the United States of America

JACKET DESIGN BY WILLI BAUM

FIRST EDITION
First printing: January 1976
Second printing: December 1976
Third printing: March 1977

Code 7524

The
Jossey-Bass Series
in Higher Education

Preface

For the past quarter of a century, America has introduced each decade with a new theme for higher education. In the 1950s, the theme could have been "accent on selection." In the 1960s, it was "accent on access." For the 1970s, it is *Accent on Learning.* In the 1950s, colleges measured their prestige by the number of Merit Scholars and average admissions test scores. In the 1960s, it became fashionable to brag about how many minority and low-income students there were on campus. Today, the talk of educators turns to one of two themes—accent on learning or possibly accent on austerity. Perhaps the two are connected. If colleges cannot devote their creative energies to expansion—more students, more buildings, more faculty, more research—then they must look to improving what they have.

Administrators and faculty in every type of college and university today are looking for ways to improve their present resources. They are seeking valid indicators of "teaching effectiveness," and faculty-development programs abound. The emphasis is clearly on better teaching; but, more important, the measure of better teaching is determined by better learning on the part of students. It is nice to have faculty enthusiastic about updating their lecture notes and keeping abreast of their field, but there is not much evidence that lecturing is related in important ways to student learning. It is discouraging to discover that "students carry away in their heads and in their notebooks not more than 42 percent of the lecture content" (McLeish, 1968, p. 9). This was the conclusion of a research study conducted in England under most favorable conditions. Students were told that they would be tested immediately following the lecture; they were permitted to use their notes; they were given a prepared summary of the lecture. The test for immediate understanding was bad enough, but when students were examined one week later without the use of their notes, they could recall only 17 percent of the lecture material. There must be more efficient ways to teach and to learn. *Accent on Learning* explores some alternatives.

This book is addressed to faculty members who want to know more about teaching and learning. It is also addressed to administrators in higher education at campus, state, and federal levels who are interested in providing options and alternatives that have good potential for motivating and exciting students about learning. I started this book thinking primarily about young people who are "turned off" by their past exposure to school learning. The much-ballyhooed "access to college" is not going to do much for students who hated high school if college learning proves to be more of the same. As I complete the book, and the two years of study that have gone into its preparation, I conclude that what is good for New Students—students who would not be in college except for open-admissions policies—is good for all students. Nevertheless, New Students represent a serious challenge to teaching, and they provide the focal point for this book.

I tried to do a number of things in writing this book. I did not accomplish them all, but these goals were constantly before me:

I wanted the book to be a positive statement, with the emphasis on constructive suggestion rather than criticism. Sometimes I think that we in academe value perceptive and sharp criticism beyond its real contribution to the improvement of society. I have no quarrel with good criticism, and this book is not free of criticism of present teaching practices. But I hope that the academic critics of society can take on the much more difficult task of suggesting solutions. This I have tried to do, but in humble recognition that the problems are clearer than the solutions.

I wanted the book to be grounded *in* research rather than grounded *by* research. I tried for a balanced mix of information and imagination. There is not enough solid knowledge about the teaching-learning process to lay out *the* guidelines. To be sure, we do not teach as well as we know how; but, on the other hand, we have been very conservative about the use of imagination and experimentation, adhering to an old-fashioned concept that the appropriate research and development model is the linear model: research-development-dissemination-implementation-evaluation. Had we insisted on that model in devising our present educational program, we would be waiting still. Precious little of what we now do in education has ever been demonstrated valid through research. Some of our conservatism is due to the recognition that we are striving to influence people's lives in education and therefore must be very careful not to do damage. True and admirable. But I believe that our present education is not as benign and safe as is sometimes assumed. Without doubt, it has done considerable damage to young people who spend the most formative years of their lives in the bottom third of the class. We need not fear that we will be departing from something very good if we apply good sense and judgment to instituting some changes as yet undocumented by research.

I have attempted to suggest, through the approach taken in this book, that a more workable model for planned innovation is to collect all the information we have at hand—from research, theory, practical experience, and evaluation; to synthesize such knowledge; to launch some reasonable hypotheses; and to ask researchers, scholars, evaluators, and practitioners to work together toward improvement. For that reason this book should not be interpreted as the dissemination of research findings. True, I have leaned heavily on research; I have reviewed

more than one thousand research studies and attempted to dis-
till the relevance of those findings. But *Accent on Learning* is
intended to be a starting point for the thinking of educators; it
is not a finishing point where the only task is to implement
some new programs.

I wanted the book to be concrete and specific—to provide
enough information so that educators could think about real
issues in a concrete model. Whether readers agree or disagree
with the suggestions made is not as important as whether they
are stimulated to make their own improvements and modifications or to use the ideas as springboards for their own action
programs.

I wanted the book to be interesting, readable, and substantive. Although I used research studies extensively, I have
sacrificed some of the precision and detail of research language,
assuming responsibility for making decisions about the relevance and limitations of research without spelling them out. To
balance possible errors of judgment on my part, I have been
overly conscientious about citing references where further detail
can be found.

Another practice with respect to the language of the
book should be mentioned. Use of the feminine and masculine
pronouns has become a real problem for authors who believe
that the language we use does shape our images and thinking. It
is awkward to use "he or she" or "s/he" or to convert everything to plurals to avoid the issue. I have followed the practice
of keeping the image of women teachers and learners on a par
with that of men by using a variety of approaches—plurals, both
masculine and feminine pronouns, or one or the other in random order.

The most difficult part of writing this book was making
constant decisions about what to omit. There is more on the
"cutting room floor" than in the pages of the final product.
Frequently, I pursued something for weeks, only to find that it
did not contribute constructively to this particular message.
That means that I left out some of my favorite innovations as
well as some of the favorites of readers. Many innovative teachers with workable methods for New Students will find no men-

tion of a learning program that works well for them. For this, I am sorry, but one book cannot—and should not try to—cover all of the interesting experiments in higher education today. Perhaps it will help if I make explicit my criteria for selecting the programs discussed.

First, the program should be useful or adaptable to the special needs of New Students as they were described in my 1971 book entitled *Beyond the Open Door*. Individual learning contracts, for example, are not discussed because, as important as I believe them to be, they are not appropriate for the *majority* of New Students, who lack the independence and motivation to be successful in this learning mode without an unrealistic amount of help from college staff.

Second, there should be information available about the effectiveness of the program. My strong preference was for programs with formal evaluation studies in existence, but since programs for New Students are relatively new phenomena, I occasionally settled for programs that lacked research evaluations if there was some experience with them in the field. It should be noted that the "field" is rich with experimentation today, especially in community colleges.

Third, I used some criteria that are idiosyncratic to *Accent on Learning*. The programs included had to fit the pluralistic model described in Chapter One. This model is not the only model of education for New Students, or even the best model. It is *a* model that illustrates the issues that I think people should be thinking about. While the presentation of the model offers the advantages of a conceptual—and I hope thought-provoking—framework, it has the disadvantage of excluding discussion of some fine programs. For example, I am convinced that cooperative education is an exceptionally promising program for New Students, and indeed for all students (Cross, 1973). But choices had to be made, and adherence to a framework with a message seemed more challenging to thought than an encyclopedia of unconnected but worthy approaches.

Authoring a book is never the solitary scholarship that it seems when the author's name goes on the spine. Although I wrote every word of the first as well as the final copy and therefore must accept responsibility for errors of fact as well as judgment, my debt of gratitude to many people is very great. A grant from Carnegie Corporation supported the project, and my two employers, Educational Testing Service and the Center for Research and Development in Higher Education of the University of California at Berkeley, were consistently helpful and encouraging, granting me complete freedom combined with the intellectual stimulation of a community of scholars concerned about the improvement of education.

I am especially appreciative of the assistance of the two women who worked most closely with me on the project. Margaret Elliott, my secretary at Educational Testing Service for the past five years, carried full responsibility for the demanding job of referencing all cited materials and for the typing of the manuscript from beginning to end. Her commitment, her identification with the book, and her patience with a sometimes irascible author are sincerely appreciated. Suzanne B. McMillan, who served as research assistant for the first crucial year and a half of the project, carried major responsibility for the search, collection, and organization of the vast numbers of documents that constitute the data base for this report. Her energetic search, her unfailing interest in the project, and her intellectual challenges are reflected in the final product.

My special thanks go to colleagues and friends across the country who took time out from busy schedules to give me the benefit of their experience and expertise. The following people reviewed one or more chapters, and their insights and suggestions were very helpful to me: Paul Breen of San Francisco State University; JB Lon Hefferlin of Jossey-Bass Publishers; Nancy Hoddick of the State Department of Education of New York; Frank Hodge and Kay Martens of the Two-Year College Development Center, State University of New York at Albany; Barbara Kirk, University of California, Berkeley, emeritus; James Kulik of the Center for Research on Learning and Teaching, University of Michigan; Karen Nelson of Harvard University; Isabel Peard, Cornell University, emeritus; J. Gilmour Sherman of the Center for Personalized Instruction at Georgetown University; Walter Sikes of the Center for Creative Change in

Higher Education, Yellow Springs, Ohio; Patricia Thrash of the North Central Association of Colleges and Secondary Schools; Dale Tillery of the University of California, Berkeley; Barbara Uehling of Illinois State University; Dyckman Vermilye of the American Association of Higher Education; Urban Whitaker of San Francisco State University; and Herman Witkin of the Educational Testing Service. In addition, I am grateful to educators everywhere who, knowing of my interest, sent materials and talked with me about problems and possible solutions.

Berkeley, California   K. Patricia Cross
December 1975

Contents

✹✹✹✹✹✹✹✹✹✹✹✹✹✹✹✹✹✹✹✹✹✹✹✹✹✹✹✹✹✹✹✹✹✹✹✹✹✹✹

Accent
on Learning

Improving Instruction
and Reshaping the Curriculum

❋❋❋❋❋❋❋❋❋❋❋❋❋❋❋❋❋❋❋❋❋❋❋❋❋❋❋❋❋❋❋❋❋❋❋❋❋❋

PART I

THE NEED FOR A NEW MODEL

Beyond Education for All—Toward Education for Each

✳✳

American higher education has worked hard for the past quarter of a century to achieve educational opportunity for *all*. It looks very much as though we shall spend the remaining years of this century working to achieve education for *each*. So obsessed were we, throughout the 1950s and 1960s, with the problems of attaining minimal educational rights for everyone that we gave little attention to maximizing learning for each individual. Access and remediation are laudable goals. But the *minimal* education implied by those concepts can hardly be what we have in mind when we invite those previously excluded from higher education into the academy. Educational opportunity means more than the right to meet minimal standards; it means the right to develop one's talents to maximum effectiveness.

3

Students who have not done well in school have often
not had the opportunity to develop high levels of competence
in any realm. They rarely attain mastery over their school work,
and no concerted educational effort is available to help them
develop other talents. The central thesis of this book is that
education has the obligation to offer *all students the opportunity for high level achievement.* Attaining this goal requires
some improvement of instruction and some reshaping of the
curriculum.

New Students

In the late 1960s, I undertook a research description of
the characteristics of students who were gaining access to higher
education through open admissions. The New Students described in *Beyond the Open Door* (Cross, 1971) are "new" to
higher education because only in an age of open admissions
would they be considered "college material." They were labeled
New Students (initial letters capitalized) if they ranked in the
lowest third of the high school graduates on traditional tests of
academic achievement. In the years since *Beyond the Open
Door* was published, people have spoken of new students—and,
more recently, of nontraditional students—as all learners who
were previously underrepresented in higher education: adults,
students from lower socioeconomic levels, ethnic minorities,
and women. And, of course, these students are "new" to higher
education and nontraditional in the sense that they differ demo-
graphically from traditional college students; however, I had a
specific purpose in reserving the term *New Students* for students who, for a variety of reasons, have difficulty with schoolwork. I consider the failure syndrome experienced by young
people who are not successful at what society considers their
major task—going to school—a social injustice and a personal
tragedy for many young people. It is these low performers who
present the major challenge to educators. Black students who
do well in school, for example, and working adults with strong
aptitudes and motivation for academic study are a *social* challenge—to see that they have access to education. But they are

not New Students by the definition used here and in *Beyond the Open Door*, and they are not an *educational* challenge in the sense that traditional instruction does them an injustice through handicapping and blocking their learning.

Almost everyone is in favor of equal educational opportunity—as long as it does not clash with other values. The painful dilemma these years is how to offer equal educational opportunity to students whose poor academic accomplishments threaten cherished values of academic excellence. Most of today's professors made their professional commitment to education in the 1950s, when "academic excellence" was *the* goal of all reputable institutions of higher education. Thus, the rapid change from the call for academic excellence to the cry for equal opportunity presents an especially poignant clash of values.

Widespread alarm now exists about the drop in academic aptitude test scores and the simultaneous rise in high school and college grade point averages (American College Testing Program, 1975; College Entrance Examination Board, 1975; Maeroff, 1973). If poorer students are getting better grades, and that appears to be the case, what is happening to academic standards? Some critics charge that open-admissions colleges are perpetuating the educational fraud of poor-quality high schools —passing students on when they have served their time, whether they know anything or not. The college degree is being cheapened, these critics complain; and some of the critics are found among New Students, who are no more enthusiastic about cheap degrees than college professors are.

Other critics allege that too few, rather than too many, are getting through the educational system. According to these critics, the fraud exists when we open the college doors to everyone but then narrow the exit gate so that only those who fit the traditional mold—mostly whites from the higher socioeconomic levels—pass through; in short, college standards preserve preferential treatment for the privileged classes. Furthermore, although a college degree is the entrée to better jobs in our credentialed society, these critics point to evidence that college performance has little or no relationship to later success in life (Hoyt, 1965; McClelland, 1973; Munday and Davis, 1974). Are we justified, they ask, in imposing an apparently arbitrary set of standards as the funnel to success and the gatekeeper to status in society?

Another phase of the argument over open admissions concerns the permissible balance between the successes and failures. Although no one seems to know just how many New Students are getting through college with reasonably good academic skills, it is clear that some of them are making adequate to excellent progress. If we can take pride in the 10 to 20 percent of lowest-third high school graduates who succeed, how are we to feel about the 80 to 90 percent who fail? Did they have equal opportunity?

These are not simple questions. The issues they raise are enormously complex. Fifteen years ago, John Gardner (1961) asked, "Can we be equal and excellent too?" We sometimes seem no closer to an answer today than we were then, but I believe that an affirmative answer is possible. We can have educational equality and excellence for all if we can provide maximum opportunity for *each* student to develop fully his or her talents. The rest of this book constitutes a plan to this end. Let us begin with a snapshot of the New Students.

Two thirds of the New Students described in *Beyond the Open Door* (Cross, 1971) are first-generation college students; their parents have never attended college. Over half of them are Caucasians, about 25 percent are black, and about 15 percent are other minorities. One of the most persistent misunderstandings of the educational community as well as the broader society is that most New Students are members of minority ethnic groups. That is not true: the *majority* of high school graduates ranking in the lowest academic third are white. Concern about the lack of academic preparation of ethnic minorities, however, is well justified. Black Americans are overrepresented among the New Student population: about two thirds of the blacks entering two-year colleges fall among the lowest academic third of the entering students. Mexican Americans and American Indians are also overrepresented. Although New Students tend to come from the lower socioeconomic levels, not all New Students are from disadvantaged homes. About one fourth of the low-achieving students entering open-door colleges are the children of fathers who have attended college. Despite their socioeconomic advantage relative to the majority of New Students, their sense of school failure is just as personally destructive as that of their financially disadvantaged peers.

One of the most vivid lessons learned in school is one's relative standing in life. New Students learn gradually that they are "below average," and many learn that they are "failures." Research shows that they are more likely than successful students to adopt passive attitudes toward school learning, to state that they feel nervous and tense in class, and to protest that teachers "go too fast" with lessons. If given a list of activities and asked to check those on which their performance is "above average," many of them find no activity—in school or out—that they can say they do well (Cross, 1971).

Fundamentally, New Students find themselves in college because of the rising educational expectations of the society. For the majority of students, the motivation for college arises not from the anticipation of the joys of learning or from intellectual curiosity but from the recognition that education is the way to a better job. Conservative and suspicious of "innovative" education, they want from college what they have seen others obtain—better jobs, more money, higher social status. They are pragmatic and realistic enough to know that the degree per se, not necessarily the knowledge, is the entrée to a higher socioeconomic status than that of their parents. A problem that neither they nor we have faced squarely is the possible devaluation of the college degree when most people have one. How possible is it to extend elitist privileges—those valuable *because* of their scarcity—to the masses? It looks now as though the emphasis must shift from the value of the credential to the value of the knowledge and skills gained through college.

Access and Remedial Models

Throughout the 1960s and into the 1970s, the nation concentrated on *access models*—the removal of obstacles—to bring about equality of educational opportunity. Federal and state policies moved steadily and effectively toward lowering the financial barriers to a college education; financial aid to students increased 6000 percent from 1954 to 1974. The explosive growth of community colleges and open-admissions practices virtually eliminated poor educational preparation as a barrier to college access. Special recruitment programs worked steadily toward reaching the uninformed and unmotivated. As a result, during the 1960s college enrollments increased 124 percent (Carnegie Commission, 1971). Although some of this increase could be attributed to population increases, some of it was clearly the result of efforts to ease the routes of access. The proportion of high school graduates entering college increased from one third in 1960 to more than half today. And most of the increase has come from the second and third quartiles of academic ability (Cross, 1971).

We should be delighted with our success, but the high optimism of the 1960s has faded into disillusionment in the 1970s. Although we have proved that we can deliver on our promise to open the doors of access to college, we have not demonstrated that we can deliver an education that is attractive and useful to the majority of the American public—the kind of education that develops *individual* talents. The kind of education that develops only a limited range of human abilities will advance those who possess the "right" talents and penalize those with other kinds of talents that may be of equal value to society. In short, the access model has been quite successful in doing what it was designed to do—increase the availability of higher education for previously excluded segments of the population; but it is an incomplete model and, by itself, will not bring about the equal opportunity that it promises.

Recognizing the limitations of the access model, educational and political leaders have worked hard to devise and support *remedial models*—programs and services that make access more than a hollow victory for those whose backgrounds prevent full utilization of the opportunities newly won. These efforts to overcome educational deficiencies through remediation, discussed in Chapter Two, have helped some people, mostly those on the borderline of acceptable academic performance, to pass into the academic mainstream. But we have not found any magic key to equality of educational opportunity through remediation. Although remediation efforts help us to keep up with the demands of an advanced society for larger numbers of educated people, they offer no assurance of improving the *relative* position of the lower classes through education. In short, the remediation model—like the access model—offers only a partial solution, necessary but not sufficient. Both models have operated on the procedural fringes of the higher education enterprise; they have not penetrated into the instructional core.

An Instructional Revolution

It appears that what started as a simple approach to equality through lowering the access barriers to colleges has turned into an educational revolution involving all of higher education. The revolution has reached the heart of the educational enterprise—the instructional process itself. Chapters Three, Four, and Five of this book describe some of the changes in teaching techniques that are taking place as a result. Most of these new teaching methods are taking place across the broad spectrum of higher education, not just in classrooms where New Students are present. But the pressure to "invent" the new methods comes from an increasing awareness that the old methods are no longer adequate to our needs.

One of the few definitive results of the scientific study of human behavior is the demonstration of individual differences; yet we have ignored that simple and obvious fact. Research psychologists frequently regard individual differences as a nuisance that introduces "error" into the search for the general laws of learning. Practitioners attempt to simplify their teaching and administrative jobs by minimizing individual differences and working with groups of students who are doing the same thing at the same time in as much the same manner as possible. In individual classrooms as well as in the total system of education, *individuals* are taught as though they were a homogeneous group: "Too often we have carried the academic lockstep into each individual course, meeting classes faithfully three times every week, giving the same assignments to every student, treating each student exactly the same in the interest of fairness" (McKeachie, 1969, p. 202).

A critical challenge to the academic lockstep at the college level came when open admissions greatly increased the range of individual differences in the entering classes. Our initial reaction to that shock to our educational system was to organize remedial programs whose mission was to change the newcomers so that they would fit the requirements of traditional institutions. We did not, in the beginning, give comparable attention to changing institutions so that they would fit the needs of the new learners. (See Cross, 1975.)

There is some evidence that the *instructional* programs of colleges were protected from change throughout most of the 1950s and 1960s by the imposition of buffer zones between the "regular" faculty and "remedial" students. Subject-matter specialists in the community colleges patiently waited for remedial programs to get students ready for their courses; four-year-college faculty were protected from the impact of the New Students by the buffer zones of the two-year colleges. The data from my 1970 and 1974 surveys of college practices (Appendix A) paint a clear picture of our initial attempt to grant access to New Students with a minimum of discomfort to the traditions of the system. By the time of the 1970 survey, the majority of community colleges had instituted *administrative* procedures and programs to help New Students adapt to colleges. Most colleges offered a variety of specially designed recruitment programs, financial-aid packages, counseling programs, and remedial courses. While these special programs catered to the needs of the New Students, they also had the inadvertent effect of accepting New Students into a buffer zone that was different from "real college."

My data indicate that the *psychological* acceptance and absorption of New Students into academe did not take place until the early 1970s, when the community colleges made dramatic moves toward deemphasizing differential treatment for New Students. The practice of *requiring* remediation for certain students declined from 79 percent of the colleges in 1970 to 59 percent by 1974. At the same time, degree credit for remedial courses rose from 32 percent to 53 percent of the colleges. Teacher attitudes apparently changed, too; and colleges were able to limit remedial faculty to those expressing interest (from 47 percent to 56 percent) and to offer faculty on-campus training in remedial education (from 16 percent to 27 percent).

While there is evidence that New Students are being absorbed into the college mainstream, the data from *Beyond the Open Door* (Cross, 1971) showed that New Students differ in significant ways from traditional college students. The combination of the two conclusions, drawn from research, suggests that attitudes and teaching styles have probably changed to accommodate the learning needs of New Students. And there are data to support that hypothesis. Indeed, the changes are so clear that it is no exaggeration to say that we are witnessing the beginning of an instructional revolution.

The surveys presented in Appendix A clearly show that the dramatic changes in community college programs between 1970 and 1974 occurred in the instructional areas. The use of programmed instruction increased from 44 percent of the colleges in 1970 to 74 percent in 1974; the use of self-paced learning modules increased from 31 percent to 68 percent; and skills centers spread from 36 percent of the colleges in 1970 to 67 percent by 1974. Ironically, the influx of large numbers of New Students into colleges has brought about individualization of instruction. "Mass education," it turns out, is not the inevitable route to "education for the masses." Indeed, the very diversity of the masses calls for the abandonment of mass approaches to education.

The speed with which individualized programs of instruction have been adopted is one sign of the instructional revolution. The upsetting of traditional ways of thinking about education is another indicator. Mastery learning is the revolutionary concept that lies at the heart of the new teaching strategies. Simply stated, mastery learning permits all students to learn to the same high level of achievement regardless of the time required. Traditional education, on the other hand, permits the level of *attainment* to vary while the amount of *time* is per-

ceived as a constant across the group of learners. Thus we turn
out students who are well educated and those who are not, but
all have spent the same amount of time at the task—surely a
meaningless measure of education. Our grading system does not
solve the problem; it just acknowledges that some students
learned a lot in the time specified and received A's while others
learned little and received D's and F's. If Bloom, Bruner, and
other scholars are correct in their assertion that anyone can
learn a subject to mastery if given adequate time and appropriate help, then we have a breakthrough that permits us to provide for individual differences through holding *attainment* constant and letting *time* vary.

The introduction of mastery learning solves two major
problems for egalitarian education. It gives New Students some
experience with high achievement in school work, and it speaks
to those concerned about the erosion of academic standards.
There is no compromise with standards when every student
masters the material he has studied.

The educational merit of mastery learning is substantial,
but mastery learning is not a panacea. Although many New Students will experience the satisfaction of mastery over school
assignments for perhaps the first time in their lives, that does
not mean that they will become accomplished academicians.
Yet society and individuals are ill-served if the educational
system is geared only to the production of academicians.
Beyond the instructional revolution that demands changes in
the *methods* of instruction lies a reshaping of the curriculum
that calls for new *missions* in education.

Reshaping the Curriculum

Over the centuries, we have refined our definitions of
learning to mean a certain kind of *school* learning, and educational systems have been geared to nourish a narrow range of
human talent. Although Taylor (1968) has estimated that the
ability to manipulate the abstractions of academe calls for
approximately one tenth of the known human abilities, we are
nonetheless obsessed with the importance of our restricted con-

cept of learning. We seem to forget that other kinds of learning are equally important to our individual and collective welfare.

By this time we know that there are individual differences along the narrow dimension of *academic* ability. Exactly how much of what we call academic aptitude is due to environment and how much to heredity is a question that defies our methods at present. But the issue may not be that important. It is only important under the assumption that people with high academic ability are more worthy of our educational efforts and more valuable to the society than those with talents in other areas; there is just no evidence to support that assumption. If we persist in thinking that the ability to perform academic tasks is the measure of the ability to deal with a variety of socially important tasks, then we face the prospect of creating an undernourished society and a new group of "disadvantaged," consisting not necessarily of minority groups or poor people but of all those from any stratum of society with below-average academic aptitude. We must look beyond academic ability as the sole determiner of human contribution.

Harvard's Jerome Kagan (*Saturday Review*, 1973, p. 43) goes so far as to advocate that children be "rank-ordered on the basis of humanism as we rank-order on the basis of reading and mathematics." He claims that schools exist to serve the needs of society and that the greatest need now is to restore faith, honesty, and humanity: "I am suggesting in deep seriousness that we must, in the school, begin to reward those traits as the Spartans rewarded physical fitness." While I agree with Kagan that we must reward the characteristics that are valued by society, I don't think we make progress by replacing one unidimensional system with another.

It is a statistical fact that on any single dimension of human ability, half of the people in the nation will be below average—by definition. Naive egalitarians have the notion that working with the bottom half will somehow raise them to equal status with the top half. At least part of the failure of remedial and compensatory programs can be attributed to the impossible task assigned them. They were expected to raise everyone above the mean. Unfortunately, status in the society is relative, and on any single measure there will always be a lower half. There is, however, a way to reduce the number in the lower half, and that is to expand the number of dimensions along which talent is measured. If talent is measured on two independent dimensions, the statistical probability is that 75 percent will be above average on one or the other dimension. If three independent talents are assumed, the statistical probability is that 87.5 percent will be above average on one of the three dimensions.

The notion that IQ is an all-pervasive measure of innate ability—that IQ determines one's competency to deal with a wide variety of tasks—is a myth that seems exceptionally difficult to dispel. People insist that the individual who stands at the top of one measure of talent will probably also stand at the top of any other socially important talent. Thus, they say, the individual who makes good grades in school will turn out to be the one who has talent in other areas and who becomes a success in life. The myth has been repeatedly shown false by research, but McClelland (1973, p. 2) describes the tenacity of the belief:

> Researchers have in fact had great difficulty demonstrating that grades in school are related to any other behaviors of importance—other than doing well on aptitude tests. Yet the general public—including many psychologists and most college officials—simply has been unable to believe or accept this fact. It seems so self-evident to educators that those who do well in their classes *must* go on to do better in life that they systematically have disregarded evidence to the contrary that has been accumulating for some time. In the early 1950s, a committee of the Social Science Research Council of which I was chairman looked into the matter and concluded that while grade level attained seemed related to future measures of success in life, performance within grade was related only slightly. In other words, being a high school or college graduate gave one a credential that opened up certain higher-level jobs, but the poorer students in high school or college did as well in life as the top students. As a college teacher, I found this hard to believe until I made a simple check. I took the top eight students in a class in the late 1940s at Wesleyan University where I was teaching—all straight-A students—and contrasted what they were doing in the early 1960s with what eight really poor students were doing—all of whom were

getting barely passing averages in college (C— or below). To my great surprise, I could not distinguish the two lists of men 15-18 years later. There were lawyers, doctors, research scientists, and college and high school teachers in both groups. The only difference I noted was that those with better grades got into better law or medical schools, but even with this supposed advantage they did not have notably more successful careers as compared with the poorer students who had had to be satisfied with "second-rate" law and medical schools at the outset.

High achievement in the traditional curriculum is not *the* key to later success. I suspect, however, that learning to achieve and to capitalize on one's best talents may have a great deal to do with self-fulfillment, and perhaps with success.

A major conclusion arising out of my research on the characteristics of New Students was that they had some talents that were not being developed in the traditional curriculum (Cross, 1971). *Beyond the Open Door* ended with the suggestion that we gear education to the needs of society by matching the cultivation of individual talents to societal needs in a three-dimensional model patterned after the skills needed in occupations as they are defined in the *Dictionary of Occupational Titles*. The United States Employment Service, after devoting years of research to the effort, has determined that the world's work can be described by three major functions: work with data, work with people, and work with things. Most jobs consist of combinations of the three functions, and each is classified in the *Dictionary* according to the level of skill required in each of the three areas.

These three skills—specific knowledge, interpersonal skills, and the ability to work with objects and materials—are necessary, it seems to me, not only to occupations but to life in our society. We all need knowledge about the increasingly complex world in which we live. We need to be able to read, to understand what we hear, to express ourselves orally and in writing, to have some understanding of quantitative concepts and of science. In other words, we all need those skills typically taught in school. But in addition we need to know how to get along with people. Few of us can avoid working with people, although some of us enjoy interpersonal relations more, and are more skillful at it, than others. And finally, the technological revolution has made it imperative that everyone have some understanding of how things operate.

Specifically, in *Beyond the Open Door* I proposed a pluralistic model in which the task of education would be to develop the student's greatest talent to the point of excellence and also to prepare him or her to live in today's world by developing adequacy in the other two areas. Students who have interest and ability in the manipulation of ideas would pursue academic excellence, but they would also be required to develop adequate skills in working with things and people. The development of interpersonal skills would no longer be left to extracurricular activities and to chance but would be consciously developed so that future counselors, receptionists, and social workers could pursue excellence in human relations. Future sculptors and future auto mechanics would pursue excellence in the manipulation of tools and materials, but they would also develop basic adequacy in traditional academic subject matter and in working with people.

Educational pluralism casts a new light on remedial education. All of us—not just the so-called disadvantaged—have weaknesses, and all of us need remediation. Consider, for example, the popular, academically oriented son of a surgeon who is totally dependent on others to tell him how things work. He is disadvantaged when it comes to working with things, and he has many of the symptoms of the academically disadvantaged. His life circumstances cast him in a situation where his father knows nothing about mechanics and lacks even a basic vocabulary to help his son learn. Just as there are few good books in the homes of educationally disadvantaged, so there are few good tools in the homes of the mechnically disadvantaged. Remediation for this high-risk mechanic need not consist of his learning to fix his own car if he has no interest or talent in that direction. But he might well be exposed to some remediation in learning about how things work. A college professor whose total dependence on others to tell him what goes on under the hood of his car is just as disadvantaged as the poorly educated person who cannot understand the cost of buying on credit. Neither is equipped to make informed decisions about important realities.

Remediation in any area need not extend beyond the basic competencies needed to prevent handicapping disabilities. The correction of weakness can be overdone, and it probably has been overdone in our present "deficiency" perceptions of New Students. The important contribution of a *pluralistic model* is that it emphasizes the development of *strengths* rather than the correction of deficiencies. Not only New Students but all of us need to develop skills that set us apart from the crowd. We all need the opportunity to excel at something that is important to people. Equal opportunity means more than the opportunity to develop mediocre competence in the area of someone else's strength. It means the opportunity to develop one's own talents to the point of excellence. Most people today speak of education *for* diversity as though it were education *by* diversity. We are willing to entertain the idea that people can learn the same things by different methods or in differing amounts of time—although we are slow to implement even those obvious facts. Even when we do implement them, it is with the implicit understanding that some students will take to traditional academic learning like a duck to water, while others will struggle to remain afloat. Never mind that our sinking duck can run like a gazelle or fly like a swallow. What we are not yet ready to concede is that running and flying are as good as swimming and that our world is better for the existence of all three talents, appropriately used.

The pluralistic model consists of three major programs—excellence in people, ideas, and things—and three minor programs—adequacy in people, ideas, and things. Minimum requirements for graduation are a major in one area of excellence and minors in the other two areas. An exceptionally energetic student might elect to pursue three majors of excellence, but no one would graduate without meeting rigorous standards in his or her major, and no one would graduate without knowing enough about his fellow human beings and about the world of ideas and about the technological world to be able to function effectively in this society. The model calls for ratings of quality in the area of excellence (through grades, competencies, or levels of accomplishment) and for minimal threshold adequacy measures in the minor fields. A transcript notation of pass/no record seems appropriate here.

Although it would be easy to suggest that the student striving for adequacy would take the more elementary courses in the curriculum designed for excellence, adequacies should not be distorted into watered-down versions of the courses in the areas of excellence. As anyone acquainted with physics for nonmajors knows, the course content is something other than elementary physics. Similarly, learning how to get along with one's coworkers and family (adequacy in human relations) suggests some *different,* not just lesser, learning experiences from those required for a career as a counselor. Nevertheless, most learning has a sequential nature, and there are some core concepts and principles that must be learned by everyone. The principle of levers in physics and a sensitivity to the feelings of others, for example, are basics that must be mastered by everyone if we are to avoid a "tracking" system in which people are locked into early choices. The adequacy minors must be substantive enough so that anyone can move into an excellency major upon completion of the minor. Fortunately, the concept of lifelong learning, and the increasing flexibility of colleges in permitting learners to move in and out of educational programs throughout lifetimes of learning, makes early choices less serious than when education was considered something to be completed *before* beginning a career.

The goal of the pluralistic model is to help every college student achieve excellence in a career area and to achieve adequacy in dealing with the challenges of life. At the same time, the goal is to close no doors to opportunity. Adults returning to college should be able to build new excellency majors—to change from excellence in working with people as a social case worker, for example, to excellence in working with ideas as a college teacher of social work. Or they should be able to pursue their original excellency major in greater depth—to move from working as a visiting case worker to employment as a supervisor of a regional office of case workers, still pursuing excellence in human relations but requiring a somewhat different set of skills.

While it would be nice to develop a full-blown implementation for the pluralistic model by presenting curricular and instructional ideas for all three adequacy minors and all three excellency majors, such an ambitious task is beyond the scope of one book. Some choices had to be made, and I made my choices on two criteria: (1) I wanted to give major attention to the areas that offer the greatest potential for improving education for New Students. (2) I hoped to direct attention to relatively neglected areas—topics not being addressed by other educators and scholars. Higher education has concentrated on *academic* excellence for hundreds of years. While much remains to be done for both New and traditional students, there is no lack of attention to improvements such as independent study, honors courses, learning contracts, and interdisciplinary studies. Most faculty members are acquainted with such reforms, and I can add little to the ample literature and the generally strong support that exists for these reforms within the academic community. The individualized approaches covered in Chapters Three, Four, and Five of this book are, of course, *one* approach to academic excellence, but my primary reason for addressing these concepts in detail is their promise for helping New Students with academic skills and with a positive reorientation to school learning through the concept of mastery learning.

Excellence in working with things, like excellence in working with ideas, has had considerable attention over the years. While vocational education is not quite synonymous with my concept of "working with things," government and industry have supported this important area of education with some generosity. Its greatest problem lies in *acceptance* by the educational community, and my contributions to that admittedly serious problem seemed potentially less productive than attention to the greatly undernourished realm of educating for interpersonal effectiveness.

Our ability to deal with human problems is our primary problem as a society. We need to explore every possibility for educating a cadre of "experts" to work with people through human services careers. Almost no attention has been given to this critical area by higher education, and almost any attempt to utilize present knowledge to deal with the question will make some contribution. That is what I have attempted to do in Chapters Seven and Eight. Furthermore, as Chapter Five suggests, New Students may represent an untapped national resource for excellence in working with people.

Almost as important as the curriculum for *excellence* in human relations is the curriculum for *adequacy* in interpersonal skills. People are telling us in all kinds of ways that they feel inadequate in their personal lives to relate appropriately to coworkers, family, and friends. Participation in "personal-growth" seminars and in interpersonal-relations workshops is unprecedented. The potential for helping all students, New and traditional, to improve interpersonal skills is very great. Although most of the research shows that college students do gain in interpersonal skills throughout their college careers, their education in this area is more by accident than design. It appears to be the result of group living and close acquaintance with a variety of people. Strong trends toward *non*residential education may decrease even the present feeble attempts to help people relate to people. Thus, it is imperative that we give conscious attention to both adequacy and excellence in the development of interpersonal skills.

In summary, my work in this book is directed toward developing the curriculum and teaching methods for adequacy in working with ideas and for both adequacy and excellence in working with people. The remaining blanks in the model, excellence in working with ideas and excellence and adequacy in working with things, are being or should be tackled by others.

Curricular Evolution

There are signs, especially in the community colleges, that the curriculum is being reshaped to fit the needs of New Students. In fact, the prestige curriculum of the traditional academic disciplines may be facing problems similar to those faced by the classical curriculum at the turn of the last century. To be sure, it will be a long time before new curricula make dramatic inroads on higher education. Curricular changes are made ever so slowly. After all, George Washington proposed that agriculture should be included in the curriculum of a national university in his second presidential message, but it took nearly one hundred years for Congress to get the message that farming could be improved through formal learning. And when Congress finally passed the first land-grant college bill, in 1860, it was promptly vetoed by President Buchanan. Two years later, however, the Morrill Act recognized the legitimacy of teaching "applied" subjects in college. Even today applied subjects are still slowly working their way into the academic pecking order. We are forced to admit that there is some truth in the statement attributed to a university faculty member: "When an engineer gets up to speak in the university senate on a matter of educational policy, you can still hear a groan once in a while, but nothing like it used to be" (Cheit, 1975, p. 28).

If history repeats itself, and it surely will, college curricula will slowly respond to the changing learning needs of the nation. There will be no revolution; it will look more like continuing evolution. But with the exponential pace of change today, we may see a substantial reshaping of the college curriculum by the year 2000. That is, the traditional academic disciplines will not be diminished, but the social sciences, in particular, may be reshaped by the new emphases on experiential learning.

The national needs in the last century were to upgrade the knowledge of farming and the "mechanical arts" so that they could *produce* for the burgeoning nation. The achievement of higher education in carrying out this national assignment is one of the great success stories of all time. The national needs of the final quarter of this century are people-related. There are urgent problems—crime in the streets, morality in government, increasing dependence on drugs (legal and illegal), a rising divorce rate, the civil rights of minorities, job dissatisfaction for the majority of workers, paralyzing labor strikes, a bumbling confusion and lack of knowledge regarding social reform. But there are also promises of richer lives through greater leisure, lifelong education, and cultural revitalization. The need for improved knowledge about human relationships in our times must be as obvious as the need for better farming was in the 1800s. And the resistance to expanding higher education to meet the needs must be at least as great. Much as agriculture was held to have no intellectual content because it was done by people without education, so the subject of applied human relationships is held to be noncollege material because it is done every day by people without much knowledge about the subject.

For thousands of years, we assumed that farmers learned farming by growing up on a farm. How unnecessary it seemed to people two hundred years ago for a farmer to go to college to learn what he had been doing, apparently reasonably adequately, all his life. We assume today that people learn to work with people by growing up in a family. To be sure, some people don't grow up in a very adequate family; some people learn their subject better than others; and some discover through trial, and sometimes painful error, their own solutions. Who two hundred years ago could have dreamed that a formal curriculum in agriculture would improve farming? Who among us today can imagine how the improved practice of human relations might change our world? The Morrill Act did not bring a full-blown, sophisticated agriculture curriculum into instant reality, but it enabled the intellectual leadership to study the issues, and it also legitimized the commitment of people to work toward steady progress. Similarly, there is no full-blown, sophisticated curriculum for helping people develop personal adequacy and career excellence in interpersonal relations. But there are many people who are committed to pushing at the frontiers of knowledge—through study, through research, and through practice. There is no lack of intellectual challenge in the human relations curriculum. Indeed, one of our problems is that the subject is so complex that it has defied our attempts to study it. But education has not made progress through shrinking from challenge.

The Morrill Act changed more than the curriculum of colleges. It changed the posture of higher education from one of isolated scholarship to active involvement through applied research, extension, and instruction of the children of the workers. Once again there is a call for colleges and universities to become involved with the issues of our times. To date, most of the study of human relations has been "academic" rather than experiential, "pure" rather than applied, and "consultative" rather than involved. The social sciences do not have a laboratory comparable to the university farm of an earlier era. Just as it is hard to imagine improving farm production without growing experimental crops, so it is hard to imagine improving human relations without experiential learning in people-populated laboratories.

Chapters Six, Seven, and Eight do not present a sophisticated curriculum that will gain academic respectability overnight. But they do show that a start is being made, and they may encourage readers to study the issues and to move ahead by building upon knowledge from the past.

Accent on Learning emphasizes two needs for the education of New Students: instruction in the traditional curriculum must offer opportunities for mastery, and the total educational experience must offer opportunities for the development of excellence in work considered valuable by society.

Remedial and Developmental Education: Historical Perspective

✳✳✳✳✳✳✳✳✳✳✳✳✳✳✳✳✳✳✳✳✳✳✳✳✳✳✳✳✳✳✳✳✳✳✳✳✳✳✳

American higher education has had almost a century of experience with remedial education. Contrary to popular opinion, it is not a new phenomenon brought into being by the press for civil rights and equal educational opportunity. As best I can determine, the first course in remediation for academic deficiencies was introduced at Wellesley College in 1894. The notion that colleges bear some responsibility for helping students overcome weaknesses in academic backgrounds and skills has been a part of the American college scene ever since. In the historical analysis of the literature on remediation, two issues stand out. First, the perceived "causes" of poor academic performance have changed over the years, with one or another of the causes tending to be predominant at certain periods in history. Second, evaluation of the effectiveness of remedial efforts has undergone three phases of development.

Perceived Causes of Poor Academic Performance

There appear to be five perceived causes of poor academic performance; and, as one would expect, these causes are linked to admissions policies and the nature of the students served by the colleges of a given era. In the early years of higher education, the perceived cause of poor academic performance was poor study habits. Considering the fairly aristocratic college system and the puritan work ethic of that time, it is easy to imagine that the sons and daughters of "good" families were seen not as stupid, or the products of poor elementary training, but as immature and in need of discipline in planning and organizing their study. A typical how-to-study course was that offered by Stanford University (Sharp, 1943). It was a voluntary noncredit course developed as a student service by the office of the dean of men. The course sought to promote good study habits through attention to such things as the proper distribution of time, efficient procedures in note taking, tests and how to study for them, the proper study atmosphere, and appropriate health practices.

These how-to-study courses lasted until changing circumstances called for additional steps in helping students to cope more effectively with college studies. Specifically, in the late 1930s and early 1940s, remedial reading projects were introduced and frequently added to the existing how-to-study courses (Charters, 1941; Triggs, 1942). Thus, the perception of the problems of low academic achievers was broadened to include inadequate development of fundamental academic skills in reading speed, comprehension, vocabulary, and other so-called mechanics of reading. Students in need of remedial reading were usually identified by low test scores, but critical cutoff scores appeared to be as much a function of how many students could be handled in the program as of any clear rationale for who needed the assistance (Charters, 1941). The treatment in these early courses seemed to follow the somewhat mechanistic pattern set by the courses in study habits. Tests were given, eye movements analyzed, and diagnoses made of vocabulary, skimming skills, and organizational ability. Instruction was of the informal workshop variety, with plenty of practice in reading simple materials such as *Scholastic,* high school texts, and trade books for adolescents (Charters, 1941). Evaluation was sparse and inadequate, usually consisting of testimonials from students and instructors. A vivid example of the lack of rigor of evaluation at the time is given by Charters' (1941, p. 117) assertion that "The most striking characteristic of the projects is that they seem to be uniformly successful; *at least no respondent said that they were not*" (emphases added).

By the postwar years of the 1950s and 60s enrollment pressures were on, and state universities that had formerly been nonselective were looking for ways to make room for a tremendous expansion in the number of students. Remediation was undertaken in earnest as public institutions sought to assure themselves and their publics that students attending the university were making good use of their opportunities. There was a certain lack of sympathy with the "undeserving" (low-achieving) student who was taking space that might better be used by a more promising candidate. The University of Iowa, for example, required students with poor high school records and low test scores to make satisfactory progress in a summer session devoted to remediation if they wished to enter the university in the fall (Goodstein and Crites, 1961). Rather rapidly, the major public universities moved to selective admissions and into the heyday of the educational meritocracy.

An overzealous attempt to determine which students had the greatest academic promise, and could therefore use the limited resources to the greatest advantage, led to the third major historical approach to poor academic performance. There was now considerable effort to determine *which* students could profit from remediation. It was assumed that students of "low ability" should be separated from the "underachievers," who were usually defined as those with good ability (as measured by test scores) but poor motivation and inadequate study habits (as reflected in poor grades). Some of the writing of the era was pretty blunt: "During these times, the great importance of not allowing conditions to deteriorate to a point where qualified instructors are forced to dissipate their energies on undeserving students can hardly be overemphasized. . . . A college can

hardly do very much for students of low academic ability"
(Pittman, 1960, p. 426).

Not everyone was ready to give up quite so easily on the
student with "low academic ability," but it is probably fair to
say that most of the remedial efforts during the educational
meritocracy were directed toward salvage of underachievers,
who were assumed bright but not using their talent effectively.
By the mid-1960s the concept of remediation had become more
sophisticated, and treatment of the "underachiever" was likely
to be comprehensive, demonstrating less concern with symptoms and more with underlying motivational and sociopsycho-
logical problems. For example, the twenty-nine analytical
papers in the massive book on underachievement edited by
Kornrich (1965) are listed under the subheading "Psycho-
dynamic and Sociocultural Factors." This categorization shows
a more complex perception of the phenomenon of underachievement than did the mechanistic approaches that stressed
study habits and eye movements.

There are, then, five perceived causes of low academic
achievement as the subject is revealed in the literature: poor
study habits, inadequate mastery of basic academic skills, low
academic ability or low IQ, psychological-motivational blocks
to learning, and sociocultural factors relating to deprived family
and school backgrounds. Although each "cause" seems to have
been predominant at a given time in history, each new generation of treatment specialists has perceived the problem as more
complex than did the preceding generation. As a matter of fact,
the historical trends in diagnoses appear additive; the latest
emphasis on sociocultural factors is thought to include most of
the earlier problems. That is, students growing up in sociocultural settings which are antithetical to school achievement are
likely to have problems with study habits, basic skill development, and motivation. Perhaps because of this hierarchical complexity, there are few isolated courses today on how to study.
The trend is toward remediation or developmental efforts embedded in a total *program* that includes cognitive, social, and
emotional components.

Until the era of open admissions, remedial efforts were

low-key projects of concern to a limited number of students, parents, and educators. The nation as a whole was certainly not concerned with the problem, and even colleges as institutions gave little attention to the isolated efforts that were usually launched by student personnel offices and counseling services. Remediation moved to center stage in higher education with the advent of open admissions, when students who previously would have been eliminated on the basis of poorly developed academic skills entered college in staggering numbers. Roueche (1968a) presents a number of statistics from various college programs to demonstrate the enormity of the problem faced by open-door colleges. For example, almost 70 percent of the freshmen entering California community colleges in 1965 failed the qualifying examination for English 1A; and 75 percent of the students enrolled in mathematics courses in 1964 were taking mathematics courses similar to those offered in the high schools. California was not unique. At Forest Park Community College in St. Louis, nearly half of the on-campus students were having academic difficulties. The problems were not only broad, in the sense that they were widespread, but they were deep as well, in the sense that some students were *seriously* behind in skill development. Teachers at Bakersfield College found that they had to start at about the fifth-grade level to build academic skills. And 25 percent of the students admitted to the four-year colleges of the City University of New York (CUNY) scored below the ninth-grade level in reading comprehension (Lavin, 1971); the proportion was higher in the community colleges. Informed sources estimated that, nationally, about half of the students in two-year colleges required remediation in reading in order to prepare them for college work.

When remediation was catapulted into national prominence in the 1960s, it was with the clear perception of socioeconomic factors as "cause." Other causal factors that had surfaced from time to time were forgotten in the urgency of the times to do something about the inadequate educational experiences of students from disadvantaged backgrounds. It was assumed that the way to correct for "not enough" skill development was to provide "more." Remedial courses in English and mathematics proliferated. Remedial instruction moved from counseling and other specialists to the regular faculty, who were subject-matter specialists with no training and sometimes little sympathy for the learning problems of eighteen year olds reading at the level of eight to ten year olds. Not surprisingly, many faculty reacted with alarm, and some with desperation, to the flood of "unqualified" college students. Almost no teacher specializing in an academic discipline with the notion of teaching at the college level had any background to cope with the learning problems of their New Students. Some administrators found that teachers trained for elementary and secondary school teaching were better able to cope with the vast range of ability in the community college population than were the subject-matter specialists that formed the backbone of traditional college faculties.

Gradually, as faculty gained experience with the learning problems of the New Students, greater sophistication was brought to bear on remedial education. Some of the lessons learned earlier about psychological and motivational barriers to learning were recalled, and more integrated approaches began to replace the academic drill and skill sessions. My surveys of community college practices (Appendix A) show that between 1970 and 1974 "total-push" programs increased from 20 percent to 36 percent in the community colleges. These were usually federally funded programs emphasizing a unified approach of recruitment, counseling, and financial aid, combined with carefully designed remedial efforts under the direction of a full-time director. During the same time period, special counseling programs designed for New Students increased from 61 percent to 72 percent, and remedial or developmental courses increased from 92 to 98 percent. The trend was clearly toward broader and more integrated approaches, and that was characteristic of remedial *courses* as well as of college programs.

A good illustration of the kind of program change taking place in the early 1970s is provided by LaGuardia Community College (1974). After the remedial program there had been in existence for a year, the faculty and administrators discovered that the program did not meet the needs of skills-deficient stu-

dents. There were two major problems: the achievement scores
of entering freshmen continued to drop in the early 1970s, so
that more and more help was required; and even after remediation, many faculty felt that some of the students were
unable to meet the demands of "regular" college courses. The
new program, called Basic Skills, has the following characteristics: (1) The basic objective is to help students develop the reading, writing, studying, and mathematics skills they need to
achieve educational and career goals. (2) Teachers, counselors,
tutors, and laboratory technicians function as a team, and student progress is monitored by counselors. Counselors also work
intensively with students, individually and in groups, on personal, vocational, and academic concerns. (3) Classroom instruction is supplemented by extensive tutoring by instructors, professional tutors, and peer tutors. (4) Content-oriented, college-
level coursework is included in each student's program during
the first quarter to stimulate motivation. (5) The content and
methods of basic skills courses are specifically designed for low
achievers; that is, they are not repeats of high school courses or
watered-down college courses.

At the same time that some educators were developing
more sophisticated approaches to "remediation," others were
beginning to talk about a new concept, called "developmental
education." The distinction between the two approaches is elab-
orated by Roueche and Wheeler (1973, p. 223): " 'Remedial'
implies the remediation of student deficiencies in order that the
student may enter a program for which he was previously ineli-
gible. Typically, such work consists of noncredit courses in
English, mathematics, or study skills taken as prerequisites to
credit courses. 'Developmental' or 'compensatory,' on the other
hand, refers to the development of skills or attitudes and may
not have anything to do with making a student eligible for
another program. Under these latter approaches, curricular
materials are frequently modified to begin credit work where
the student is, and the academic calendar is modified so that the
student can move at his own pace in acquiring mastery of a
course."

I am not certain whether the above definition has helped

or hindered people in making the distinction between developmental and remedial education. In the literature, as well as on campuses across the nation, *developmental* is frequently used as a euphemism for *remedial* in a dim awareness that *developmental education* is the more enlightened term to use. The Roueche-Wheeler definition suggests that the distinction between remedial and developmental education lies in the pedagogical sophistication of the approach. In my view, a more useful distinction is to be found in the *purpose* or goal of the program. If the purpose of the program is to overcome *academic deficiencies,* I would term the program remedial, in the standard dictionary sense in which remediation is concerned with correcting weaknesses. If, however, the purpose of the program is to develop the diverse talents of students, whether academic or not, I would term the program developmental. This book, for example, is broadly concerned with *developmental* education. Its mission is to give attention to the fullest possible development of talent and to develop strengths as well as to correct weaknesses. Remediation in academic skills areas is, I think, a legitimate part of developmental education. In fact, Chapters Three, Four, and Five discuss some promising approaches to remedial education. In brief, I do not consider *remediation* a "bad" or an old-fashioned term. It is simply an incomplete concept and it has been overdone with respect to New Students. We have for the past three decades concentrated on correcting weakness without giving equal time to developing strength. I suspect that therein lies the reason for the negative connotations attached to "remedial education."

Historical Trends in Evaluation

There are three distinct periods in the history of the evaluation of remediation in higher education. Until about 1960, investigators generally reported "positive" results. Entwisle (1960, p. 250) concluded her review of the research of the 1940s and 1950s with the euphoric statement "The uniformly favorable results as reported are striking, when one considers the wide variation in kind of course leading to improvement,

and the disparate kinds of students enrolled." My own evaluation of the literature of that period is not as optimistic as Entwisle's. While it is true that many investigators were drawing
positive conclusions, it is also true that the research of the
period was quite inadequate. The criteria for the success of the
programs were poorly formulated, the research designs were
naive, and the data interpretations and implications for improvement were weak. Robinson (1950), for example, reviewed
nearly one hundred studies of remedial reading and found that
less than a dozen specifically concerned the effect of reading
programs on scholastic improvement. Since the avowed purpose
of most study skills programs of that era was to improve grades,
the lack of attention to whether or not they accomplished their
purpose is hard to explain.

The lack of adequate control groups was another problem
in the research of the 1940s and 1950s. Investigators were likely
to report that students who signed up for study skills courses
made better grades than students with equally poor prognoses
who did not. Since we now know that student motivation is
probably one of the most influential factors in student success
(Entwisle, 1960; Lesnick, 1972; Meister, Tauber, and Silverman,
1962; Roueche, 1973), it is not surprising that students who
wanted to succeed enough to seek help made better grades than
those who were in academic difficulty but less motivated to do
something about it.

Another research error, repeated all too frequently, was
the measurement of improvement from pretest to posttest on,
say, a standardized reading test. This approach has two problems: (1) Although remedial reading may have helped to improve reading test scores, such test-taking skills may not have
transferred to other coursework. For example, people frequently improve reading speed with a little practice, but speed
and comprehension are not necessarily related; furthermore, a
student's reading speed on a test may be totally unrelated to his
reading speed when studying history. (2) There is a statistical
artifact known as "regression toward the mean" in which
people who make extreme scores (either high or low) on the
first testing will tend to make scores closer to the average on the

second testing on the basis of chance alone. High scorers may have had a lucky day the first time, and low scorers may have had a bad day. In any event, if low scorers are separated out on the basis of test scores, there is a strong probability that their average scores will be better on the second testing—regardless of what kind of activity took place in the interim. Investigators using a pretest, posttest design without adequate control groups frequently attributed the gain of the low scorers to the remedial course.

Although the poor research of the 1940s and 1950s seems to be the result of a general lack of research sophistication, some valiant attempts were made to institute the proper controls (McDonald, 1957; Mouly, 1952; Robinson, 1950). Such attempts were only partially successful, however. Mouly (1952), for example, found his grand design for control groups frustrated by the refusal of many students with low test scores to enroll in the remedial courses. Although required by the university to take the three-hour-per-week noncredit course, many students found ways to avoid or postpone it. It is significant that, generally speaking, the better-designed studies showed less glowingly positive results than the simpler but less adequate research studies.

The research of the 1940s and 1950s was typically conducted in universities with at least partially selected student populations. The issue of the *ability* of the student to do the work was not a primary concern in those days, and the courses were frequently offered as a "student service." While those directly concerned with helping distressed students to improve their academic performance were presumably interested in evaluation and improvement, remedial education was not an issue of widespread concern, in or out of the university. No one was demanding accountability of the programs. If evaluations were conducted, they were typically small projects conducted by those working with the program, who were usually inexperienced and unsophisticated in research. The widespread concern with remediation and its effectiveness came later, with the rise of open admissions and especially with the concern for equal opportunity for ethnic minorities.

Two important events were taking place in higher education in the 1960s—the drive for civil rights and the rapid expansion of open-admissions colleges. Perhaps because of this temporal contiguity, many people assumed that the need for remediation in the community colleges was occasioned by the influx of (largely) blacks into higher education. Research clearly demonstrates, however, that the overwhelming majority of low achievers who gained admission to colleges through open-door policies were *not* ethnic minorities. They were predominantly the white sons and daughters of blue-collar workers (Cross, 1971). Nevertheless, many people, on and off the campuses, had the inaccurate notion that remedial classes were established *for* ethnic minorities. However understanding people may have been about the social and educational deprivation of ethnic minorities in this country, a real problem developed as people began equating the need for remediation with skin color. The perceptual problem was exacerbated when many of the remedial programs were placed under the auspices of federally funded programs for the "disadvantaged"—which usually meant ethnic minorities. The result was a tremendous pressure to "prove" that a little remedial or compensatory education was all that was needed for ethnic minorities to join the mainstream of higher education.

If anything, the research of the 1960s was even worse than that of the 1940s and 1950s because evaluation was approached not as a research question (Are the courses effective?) but as a highly emotional question (Do ethnic minorities have academic potential?). The fires of emotionalism were further kindled when Arthur Jensen, in an article in the November 1969 issue of *Harvard Educational Review,* maintained that blacks are *innately* less able than whites to learn the content of the school curriculum. Most people, white or black, who were responsible for remedial education in the 1960s felt called upon to defend the thesis that blacks *are* able to do college-level work. Instead of looking for inadequacies of the programs, many of the "evaluation" reports put out by institutions in those years (usually by the project director) turned out to be— understandably, I think—a defense of the program and of the students rather than an evaluation. If any evidence for the viability of remediation was offered, it was likely to be in the form of testimonials from students. Somewhat more objective were the studies showing that retention was improved with the introduction of remedial programs. Very few studies attempted to evaluate the academic performance of the students. As Roueche (1973, p. 26) observes, critics charged that "community college leaders deliberately did not evaluate remedial programs because they knew beforehand how disastrous the results of such an evaluation might be." In the context of the emotionalism of the times, the critics were probably correct. An unfavorable evaluation would be disastrous in two respects: it might indicate that the new community colleges could not do the job assigned to them by society, and it might indicate that "remediation" would not enable ethnic minorities to succeed in college.

It was clear that *no one* knew how to design educational experiences that would compensate for the "disadvantaged" student's lack of adequate education. But instead of working together to find the answers through development of new approaches and solid research evaluations, the unhappy approach was to make the remedial courses look as much like "regular school" as possible and to claim success in the outcome. People who suggested that the efforts were *not* successful were likely to be put down as "racists" who were criticizing the capacity of the students to learn, rather than as constructive educators who were criticizing the capacity of the colleges to teach. Criticism of remedial education was bound to be unpopular in the mid-1960s. Most people, especially educators, wanted to see both the New Students and the new colleges succeed. To imply that either was not fulfilling the ideals of instant egalitarianism was to ask for trouble.

Finally, more objective analyses began to emerge. As early as 1966, Gordon and Wilkerson (p. 157) observed: "Where evaluative studies [of compensatory programs] have been conducted, the reports typically show ambiguous outcomes affecting unknown or amorphous educational and social variables." Two years later, Roueche (1968b, p. 47) came out with his hard-hitting charge: "There is a paucity of research on the efficacy of remedial programs in the junior college. Indeed, with few exceptions, community colleges neither describe nor evaluate their endeavors in this critical area. Available research will not support the contention that junior colleges offer programs that in fact remedy student deficiencies. Programs are certainly offered, but the entire issue of remedying deficiencies has not been sufficiently researched to date. Those few junior colleges that have evaluated the success of their remedial programs found that their programs were not remedying student deficiencies to a point where remedial students could enter regular college credit courses upon completion of the remedial course." In the late 1960s, then, people were willing to admit that remedial programs could work but that most of them were not working very well. Better planning, better evaluation, and greater knowledge about learning and motivation were clearly called for.

By the early 1970s those responsible for remedial programs were able to get down to the hard work of seeking new and better alternatives. Racial tensions had subsided; ethnic minorities were making their way into the mainstream of education and of society. Attention shifted from concern over the question of *whether* ethnic minorities would make it in college to *how* all students could be helped to gain more from their education. It is apparent that there are good academicians and poor academicians among blacks just as there are among whites, and that academic achievement is not a racial issue but an individual matter. Because of this widespread realization that individuals, not "races," require treatment, both the design and the evaluation of remedial programs have improved substantially in the 1970s.

Research Findings

Despite the limitations of the research, there are some lessons that can be learned. Whether a remedial program is judged "successful" or not depends on the criteria used. Robinson (1950, p. 83) takes a strong position on what he considers valid criteria. "Academic performance is clearly the sine qua non for the validation of remedial courses. . . . In the final analysis remedial instruction must necessarily stand or fall on the basis of this single criterion." The validating criteria for this academic-performance model of remediation are not especially complicated; they consist of easily quantifiable indices of grades, test scores, and performance in the next-level course. Many researchers have used these three criteria because of their perceived importance and convenience. Yet it is not easy to package the results and present a succinct summary of our knowledge.

We must make the usual research equivocations about the effectiveness of remedial courses in raising grades. In a recent review Santeusanio (1974) concludes that evaluations of remediation using grade point averages (GPA) as the criterion give inconsistent results. He cites eleven studies with positive results and thirteen studies that show no relationship between grades and enrollment in a reading-study skills course. He questions many of the findings on the grounds of inadequate research design and concludes that the "effectiveness of CRSS [college reading-study skills] programs is not well established and a great many CRSS programs are not serving their purpose" (p. 267). If the purpose of remediation is to raise GPAs, evaluations to date offer no assurance that improved grades are a likely outcome of standard skills training directed toward a group of low-scoring young adults.

Other academic-performance criteria of improved test scores and better performance in the next-level class do not show any more promise than GPAs. Sharon (1972), in a well-designed study, found that low-scoring students who went directly into regular English without remedial English fared almost as well as those who had taken the remedial course. The nonremedial students were just as likely to complete the course as those who had spent a semester preparing for it, and they appeared to be as well satisfied with the course and with their performance in it. The remediation did, however, result in slightly improved grades for the remedial group, and thus some case can be made for the usefulness of remedial English. But on the other side, Howard University abolished its remedial English course because grades in it bore no relationship to grades in the subsequent course in English I (Tinker, 1969). The story is the same for improved test scores as a result of remediation. There are positive findings, no-difference findings, and "yes" on some tests and "no" on others.

The lack of well-designed remedial programs coupled with the ambiguity of research evaluations has divided educators into pessimists and optimists with regard to the educability of the *majority* of New Students. (Almost everyone admits that a certain *minority* of New Students can be helped.) Since New Students have no documented evidence (grades or test scores) to indicate their intellectual capacity to deal with the abstractions of academe, much of the controversy has raged around the issue of whether remediation is worthwhile for students with limited intellectual ability. Evans and Dubois (1972, p. 41) present a good statement for the pessimists: "First, there is the individual who is an underachiever because of limited intellectual capacity. He is below normal in intelligence and because of a slower growth rate will be, at any specified age and grade level, retarded in his level of intellectual development. Often called 'slow learners,' such individuals are properly described as mentally immature and generally unable to attain, before termination of their formal educational experience, sufficient abilities to satisfy the intellectual demands of higher education. . . . Typically, a test of academic performance shows a general retardation in all areas as opposed to deficiencies in particular areas of content or skills."

This position implies that such students should not be in college. Some faculty members quickly perceive that the best way to maintain academic standards is to admit only those students that present little risk of embarrassment to the institution. On the other hand, there is now a well-articulated national commitment to provide two years of postsecondary education to all who wish it. To many, the resolution of the conflict lies in making a distinction between "postsecondary programs" for the "noncollege material" and "higher education" for those with a proven track record in the academic curriculum. But respected

academicians such as Jerome Bruner and Benjamin Bloom believe that most young people are intellectually capable of learning the abstract subject matter that forms the core of the college curriculum. Bloom (1971b, p. 51) maintains that "95
percent of the students . . . can learn a subject to a high level of
mastery (for example, an A grade) if given sufficient learning
time and appropriate types of help."

The optimists and the pessimists may not be as far apart
as they appear on the surface. The difference, it seems, is not
over the *existence* of individual differences in learning ability.
Rather, it is over how to deal with such differences. Bloom
(1971b, p. 49) readily admits, for example, "that 'individual
differences' between learners exist is indisputable," and Evans
and Dubois (1972) make clear that their conviction about the
futility of remediation for low-ability students applies to short-
term remedial courses, such as those typically taught in mathematics or English. Despite concessions on each side, it is clear
that Evans and Dubois are generally pessimistic about the
potential of remediation to enable low-ability students to profit
from standard college courses, whereas Bloom and his followers
are optimistic. Bloom would be the first to admit, however, that
if success is to be achieved, great changes are needed in the
instructional process, and his work forms the background for
some important instructional innovation. (See Chapters Three
and Four.)

As is common in the ambiguous world of research, both
the optimists and the pessimists regarding the potential of remediation have research evidence to support their point of view.
Dimichael (1943) found that a how-to-study course proved of
greatest benefit to students in the middle ranges of mental ability and that those in the lowest quarter in intelligence did not
profit noticeably from the course. In fact, he concluded that
the improvement made by the lowest-quarter groups would not
be sufficient to enable them to compete successfully with students in the next-highest quarter who had not been given special
instruction. Working along similar lines, Tresselt and Richlin
(1951) attempted to construct a hierarchy of the stubbornness
of various problems with respect to remediation. Classifying

students as above average or below average in ability, personality adjustment, and study techniques, they found that students with poor study techniques were the easiest to help and that those with low ability were the most difficult regardless of other positive attributes; students with severe personality problems were also very resistant to treatment by the how-to-study course. Very early, Bird (1931) had suggested that remedial efforts would benefit a student in direct proportion to his ability, provided that help arrived before academic defeat became an expectation. Dimichael (1943), however, found that high-ability low achievers were almost as hard to help as low-ability students. But his results might be explained by the Tresselt-Richlin hypothesis; this hypothesis holds that low performance combined with personality maladjustments is very difficult to treat.

Researchers from the mastery learning school are generally optimistic about remediation for students of modest academic ability. After reviewing some forty major studies, Block (1971a, p. 8), for example, concludes that "three fourths of the students learning under mastery conditions have achieved to the same high standards as the top one fourth learning under conventional, group-based instructional conditions." The general thesis of mastery learning is that standards of performance should remain constant for all students and that time and process should become the changing variables. Conventional education, of course, has treated *time* as a constant and has permitted the *level of achievement* to vary. Thus, slow learners inevitably accomplish less in a semester geared to the learning rate of average students; they end up knowing less and falling further and further behind because they lack the background skills that form the foundation for future learning. It would be far better, say the advocates of mastery learning, to make sure that each student has mastered the basic skills before he proceeds to subsequent learning, however long it may take.

The newer approaches to remediation build upon the concepts of mastery learning, recognizing the need for more skillful and individualized instruction for New Students, but they also face up to the additional time needed for slow learners. Carroll (1971b, p. 31) concludes: "A number of re-search studies suggest that the bottom 5 percent of the students will take about five times as long as the top 5 percent of the students." By extrapolation we could surmise that if a highly able student deficient in certain academic skills could compensate for his background in a one-semester course, a low-ability student might require two and a half years. Even where the time required for learning is compared in the moderate ranges of ability, we may find that some students take two or three times as long to learn as others.

McCausland and Stewart (1974) found that students learn how much time they need to spend in order to accomplish the aspirations they set for themselves. When students were divided into four groups on the basis of test scores on the American College Test Composite (ACT), they seemed to divide into two groups with respect to academic aspirations. Groups 3 and 4 had low test scores and below-average aspirations; but students in Group 4 worked harder to meet these minimal standards than did students in Group 3, who had somewhat more ability as measured by ACT. The same phenomenon occurred with Groups 1 and 2, composed of students with above-average aspirations and higher test scores; students in Group 2, who had lower ability than those in Group 1, worked harder than the Group-1 students to meet these above-average aspirations. In other words, this study showed that students seem to gear their aspirations and their study habits to their ability level.

Our present knowledge regarding the role of academic ability as a "cause" of low academic achievement leads to two important conclusions: (1) Academic ability *is* an important variable in the time required for learning traditional academic subject matter. (2) A very large proportion (85-90 percent) of the population *can* learn traditional subject matter, given appropriate time and treatment. We can probably assume that anyone who has made it to college can, with varying amounts of individual and institutional effort, master the college curriculum. There are limits of practicality, however. It might be quite foolish, for example, to expend huge amounts of effort and time in helping students with limited academic abilities attain a college

degree on the grounds that it represented educational opportunity and that since it *could* be done, it *should* be done. It may
be extremely important, on the other hand, for low-ability students to master certain reading skills necessary for survival in a
highly verbal society. Both the optimists and the pessimists,
then, are correct in their assessment of the prognosis for remedial efforts. We probably *can* prepare most New Students for
the traditional college curriculum, given enough time, money,
and staff commitment. But a thesis of this book is that academic ability per se has been greatly overvalued. Do we really
want to press a student with limited *academic* ability to pursue
the traditional academic curriculum while other possibly excep-
tional talents atrophy and die for lack of nourishment?

Conclusions

A synthesis of the literature of the last thirty years reveals five major conclusions, which can be stated as recommendations for the future.

1. Skills training must be integrated into the other college
experiences of the student. We have known for years that
"transfer of training" does not take place automatically. Bridges
must be consciously and carefully built, so that the communications skills learned in remedial English, for example, carry
over to the term paper for social studies.

2. Cognitive skills training must be integrated with the
social and emotional development of the student. Reading spe-
cialist Maxwell (1971) writes: "We are very doubtful that exposure to a reading-improvement course, to a pacer or tachisto-
scope or to study techniques—without intensive counseling—will
change these students' habits or enhance their chances of succeeding academically" (p. 361) and "The college reading spe-
cialist needs to understand the dynamics of personality, motivation, and interpersonal relationships and should possess counseling skills if he is to be effective in helping students acquire the
insights which must precede and accompany any changes in
their reading and study skills behavior" (p. 422). In short, academic achievement or lack of it is not a purely cognitive matter.

The faculty member who claims that his or her responsibility is limited to the "mind" of the student should not be working with New Students. Indeed, such a parochial view of the teaching function is so unrealistic in the light of everything we know about human learning that it is hard to defend even for highly motivated graduate students.

3. Staff working with remedial students should be selected for their interest and commitment as well as for their knowledge about learning problems. Education generally, and community college education in particular, has come a long way in recognizing the multiple causes of poor academic performance. In five years' time, Roueche and his associates (Roueche, 1968b; Roueche and Kirk, 1973) found a great difference in the characteristics of faculty members working with remedial students. In 1968, inexperienced teachers with low status in the departmental pecking order generally were assigned the "onerous" task of teaching New Students. By 1973, many experienced faculty members, committed to working with the whole student, were gaining satisfaction from—as one psychology instructor put it—"working with those students who have never done well before" (Roueche and Kirk, 1973, p. 63). Even committed faculty, however, cannot do the job without knowledge and skill. The need for the special skills of the counseling staff cannot be overemphasized. In some phases of the developmental program, the counseling staff will assume primary responsibility. In other phases they will need to work closely with individual faculty members and departments in the development and continuing improvement of a viable program that takes account of the whole student.

So far, we have talked primarily about the integration of the work of two educational specialists—teaching faculty and counselors. Increasingly, community colleges are beginning to combine these functions and to develop specialists in remediation. My 1970 survey indicated that half of the community colleges had specialists in remediation on the staff; by 1974, 61 percent of the remedial teachers had special training for working with underprepared students (Appendix A). Frequently these specialists are present or former teaching faculty from the fields of English and mathematics who have assumed most of the responsibility for working with New Students on skill development. The unique value of these specialists is obvious. They represent most vividly our awareness of the need for integration of cognitive and social-emotional dimensions of students. Increasingly, they are likely to have specialized training in counseling and remediation as well as in their academic discipline.

4. Degree credit should be granted for remedial classes. The students most in need of remediation are those who have found little meaning and little satisfaction in education. Initially at least, the major "reward" that education has to offer these students is college credit. Ultimately, all students may come to appreciate the personal satisfactions of learning; until then, New Students, more than other students, need the immediate and tangible reward of credit. The defense of no credit for remedial education is made on the grounds that to grant credit for below-college-level work is to lower standards and to cheapen college degrees. But we may be protecting standards that do not exist. We already know that what is senior-level performance in one institution is below the level of acceptable freshman performance in another; furthermore, it is highly unlikely that A and B students have been or will be hurt by the granting of credit for remedial courses. While college credit for below-college-level work may threaten institutional egos, it should not threaten the egos of *educators* whose task it is to help students learn. In any event, the trend is toward credit, and most of the recent literature advocates granting credit for remedial or developmental courses. In 1970, less than one third of the community colleges were granting degree credit for remedial courses; by 1974, 53 percent were granting degree credit and 42 percent were granting nondegree credit (Appendix A).

5. Remediation should be approached with flexibility and open-mindedness. There is still much that we do not know. We do not even know which skills developed to what level are important to academic survival. Present definitions are arbitrary, consisting primarily of normative measures of what most college freshmen can do. Furthermore, our knowledge is frustratingly inconsistent. Some very slow readers, for example, get

high grades in college; and some students with all the skills presumed necessary for success fail miserably. We do know that self-confidence is a major ingredient of success, and remedial courses have the potential for building or destroying self-confidence. Showing a student that he can develop skills to a high level of mastery may be more worthwhile for its impact on affect than for its cognitive results. At the same time, an overemphasis on the importance of skill development may do considerable damage by convincing some students that even with all the help and kindness in the world they do not accomplish academic tasks at a pace or level comparable to those of their classmates. We need to determine the kind and level of academic skills that are essential to life in our complicated society, and to try to help each student accomplish these basics—which are probably much less complicated than we presently assume. But beyond that, we might do better to create valid alternatives to the traditional academic curricula—alternatives that will enhance the contributions of individuals and add diversity to our international talent bank.

PART II

THE INSTRUCTIONAL
REVOLUTION

✳✳✳ 3 ✳✳✳

Individualizing Learning

✳✳✳✳✳✳✳✳✳✳✳✳✳✳✳✳✳✳✳✳✳✳✳✳✳✳✳✳✳✳✳✳✳✳✳✳✳

Throughout the history of education, there has been tension between behaviorists and humanists. Behaviorists stress the application of scientific principles to improve the teaching-learning process, whereas humanists emphasize the need for personal attention and human warmth. Markle (1970, p. 297) sees the two positions as divisive. There is, she says, "a basic divergence in point of view between the tough-minded empiricism of the product-oriented programming fraternity and the tender-minded idealism irrespective-of-evidence of the process-oriented educational philosophers." In the strong movement toward individualized instruction in the 1970s, there are signs that the most promising approaches are neither coldly scientific nor permissively humanistic. Rather, the technologists seem to be personalizing their approaches, while the humanists are adding structure to theirs. (See Chapters Four and Eight.)

At the present time, however, the behaviorists are clearly dominating the educational scene. Faculty are busy writing behavioral objectives, and educational researchers are promoting the application of such behavioristic principles as immediate

49

reinforcement and small packages of clearly specified learning tasks. Brand names proliferate: Personalized System of Instruction (PSI), Computer-Assisted Instruction (CAI), Individually Prescribed Instruction (IPI), Programmed Instruction, and Audio-Tutorial System. All of these formulas for increasing the effectiveness of learning are basically behavioristic, springing from the work of B. F. Skinner and his predecessors. But, within this cluster of behavioristic approaches to learning, the trend has been away from the "coldly scientific" and toward the "personal touch."

Chronologically, programmed instruction is the grandfather of the newer approaches, and it is the most rigidly behavioristic in design. Modeled after the teaching machine, it uses small units of learning with immediate feedback and reinforcement. It is obviously and unabashedly a product of the animal laboratories of psychology: "The short and intensive history of programmed instruction illustrates an oversimple, overmanaged, and overcontrolled use of reinforcement" (Erickson, 1972, p. 1). There is general agreement that programmed instruction per se is on the wane after having enjoyed a rather brief period of enthusiasm in the late 1950s.

The newest approaches in higher education are the audio-tutorial method promoted by S. N. Postlethwait, a biologist, and the Personalized System of Instruction (PSI) advocated by psychologists Fred Keller and J. Gilmour Sherman (Chapter Four). Both of these systems, which are built on the basic principles of programmed learning, make a special point of adding provisions for personal contact. And PSI, which is ten years younger than the audio-tutorial system, moves most strongly into the need for the *personalization* of learning: "The . . . possibly most important feature in the Personalized System of Instruction is the reliance on undergraduate students to serve as peer tutors . . . for it is through their unique contribution to the instructional process that PSI gains its truly 'personalized' aspect" (Ruskin, 1974, pp. 13-14).

Although the dominant movement now is toward personalizing a behavioristic approach to learning, the more dedicated Skinnerians are not giving up their faith in the ultimate power of science to program "personalized" instruction. Thus, we have computer-based instructional management systems that are programmed to perform some of the tasks presently performed by the peer tutors in PSI. Miami-Dade Community College, for example, has introduced a computer-managed system in which the computer analyzes student test performance, diagnoses problem areas, and prescribes appropriate assignments in a personal letter to the student.

No doubt the tug of war between the behaviorists and the humanists will continue. Behaviorists will continue to insist that human behavior that is completely understood can be duplicated by science. Humanists will continue to emphasize the distinctively human aspects of people. And the world will continue to profit from the insights of both schools of thought, as long as they continue to coexist in creative tension. University of Michigan psychologist Wilbert McKeachie exemplifies the stance of many working through data-based research to improve education. After a comprehensive review of the contributions of hard research data to the psychology of learning, he remarks "I still have some sense that the most important focus of instruction is a living, breathing, seeking, human being" (McKeachie, 1974, p. 162).

With this overview as background, we shall look at the development of some major approaches to individualizing instruction. From our perspective in the mid-1970s, the chronological progression of the various approaches appears to be the logical progression also. Later models build on earlier models, correcting weaknesses and emphasizing strengths. Indeed, it is heartening to look at these developments historically to assure ourselves that the general movement is forward, albeit with many false starts and tangential diversions. The advancement of knowledge, however, is not so orderly that I can arrange the descriptions of the major developments neatly by date of introduction. There are branches that divide only to merge again later, and there are branches that divide to spawn new progeny. Nevertheless, insofar as possible, I shall try to present the approaches to individualizing instruction so that the developmental sequence is apparent.

Characteristics of Individualized Instruction

All methods of individualized education begin with five basic principles that are widely accepted today as essential ingredients for effective learning.

1. The student must be active rather than passive. All individualized approaches emphasize the active mental involvement of the student, and many stress physical manipulation of learning materials as well. The goal is to have students take major responsibility for their learning. The teacher assumes the role of manager; he or she prepares materials, diagnoses, prescribes, motivates, and serves as a resource for the student. The emphasis is on learning rather than teaching. The shift is well illustrated by the maxim "You can no more say that something has been taught when nothing has been learned than that something has been sold when nothing has been bought." It has been painfully obvious for years that students have not bought much of what we thought we were selling. In fact, there is good evidence that many New Students have developed sales resistance to much of education (Cross, 1971).

2. The goals of learning must be clear and must be made explicit to the student. It is futile to seek the active involvement of learners if they are unaware of what they are trying to accomplish. Activity without direction is little more than the spinning of wheels. There are many who claim that the new emphasis on stating behavioral objectives for all learning units will improve education because it will help teachers clarify their own instructional goals. The value of learning, of course, depends upon the significance of the objectives. One can have clear-cut measurable objectives that are not worth pursuing, and the blind faith in behavioral objectives as a cure-all for poor instruction has been justifiably taken to task (Atkin, 1968; Flanagan, 1971; Huther, 1973). Nevertheless, both logical analysis and research evidence do support the notion that students, especially New Students, will experience greater satisfaction and achievement if they have a clear idea of what is expected of them (Cross, 1971; Huck and Long, 1973). Furthermore, in these days of concern for the consumer, colleges have an obliga-

tion to tell students what they will be able to do when the course is completed satisfactorily. The day may come when discriminating consumers will demand a look at course objectives. The time may also come when students, looking at some of the objectives provided today, will reject them as trivial and not worth the price in money, time, and energy.

3. Very closely related to the need for course objectives is the desirability of small lesson units (frequently referred to as learning modules) dealing with a single concept. This precept comes directly from the work of the behaviorists, who stress the need for immediate reinforcement of the correct learning behavior. Various individualized approaches differ greatly in their interpretation of "immediate" and, therefore, in the size of the learning unit advocated. The unit for programmed instruction, for example, is the "frame," and a course may consist of thousands of them. Some of the newer approaches, on the other hand, advocate roughly fifteen units per semester course. There is general agreement, however, that the work covered over a semester or a quarter is too long and complex and must be divided into smaller units in which objectives can be specified and reinforcement can be provided.

4. Effective learning requires feedback and evaluation. This is simply another way of stating the reinforcement principles that have predominated in learning psychology. Learning can hardly move forward unless correct responses are recognized and rewarded. Small learning units and frequent testing are the rule. The mid-term and final examinations of traditional college courses frequently permit the student to proceed through critical learning sequences with an inadequate or incorrect understanding of the concepts involved. By the time he receives the evaluation, it is too late to be effectively utilized in learning.

5. Recognizing the enormous individual differences in rate of learning (not only do individuals differ from one another, but most of us differ from time to time and from task to task in our own learning efficiency), all approaches to individualized instruction feature self-pacing—permitting the learner to control, to a greater or lesser degree, the pace of the presenta-

tion. This feature is basic to the concept of mastery learning, and its significance for the New Student or the "slow" learner cannot be overemphasized. Block (1972) reports a fascinating study in which he found that students who learned one task well took significantly less time to learn a related task than those who had not learned the initial task to a high level of mastery. Is it any wonder that students who get off to a poor start in school fall further and further behind? (See Coleman and others, 1966, for evidence that they do.)

All individualized learning systems accept the above five principles of learning, although each system has its own distinctive contributions and emphases. Audio-tutorial schemes, for example, emphasize variety in presentation, using many media to provide for the different learning styles of students; PSI emphasizes the personal-social needs of students; mastery learning pays particular attention to individual differences in rate of learning. Whatever their unique emphases, the goal of all advocates of individualized instruction is to present instructional materials in a way that is maximally useful to the individual.

The concept behind this approach to education is that what the student is doing in the learning event is more important than what the teacher is doing. Milton (1973, p. 123) reminds us that there is no simple and direct correlation between "what a faculty member does—for example, how clearly and vividly concepts are explained—and what the students learn." This does not imply that how the faculty member manages the learning situation is not important. Indeed, that function is all-important. The advocates of individualized instruction are interested in shifting the emphasis from teacher as central figure in the learning event to student as central actor. No one indicates that, in theory or in practice, the demands on the teacher are less in individualized instruction. Ideally, the instructor is constantly observing and adapting to the progress of the learner—a task calling for considerably higher-level teaching skills than the more traditional task of presenting information to a group of students and hoping that a majority are attending to the presentation and understanding what is said.

Let us turn now to an analysis of the development of

some of the more prominent approaches to individualized instruction.

Programmed Instruction (PI)

Programmed instruction has not fulfilled its early promise at the college level, but no one should underestimate the contribution that the concepts behind PI have made to successors in the movement. The credit for the initial idea of applying behavioristic concepts to education is generally accorded to S. L. Pressey, the inventor of a rather primitive type of teaching machine. In the 1920s, Pressey applied the "laws of learning" to teaching. In his teaching machine, the program moved on to the next frame as soon as the student had given the correct answer twice in succession. This procedure assured efficiency and prevented overlearning, and it also implemented the three laws of learning: the law of recency, wherein the last answer must always be the correct answer; the law of frequency, which holds that the right response should be made most often; and the law of effect, which says that responses that are rewarded will be repeated.

The next step in the attempts to move from the research laboratory to the classroom came with the work of B. F. Skinner in the 1950s. Skinner is the most controversial figure in psychology today, not so much for his research, which is universally admired, but for his ideas about the meaning of the research and how it should be applied to the world in which we live. Although Skinner started his work with rats and pigeons, he soon related his concepts to the teaching of people. His research convinced him and his followers that an animal—or a human being—can be made to learn whatever the experimenter desires by the appropriate use and timing of reinforcement. Specifically, reinforcement should be immediate, it should take the form of reward rather than punishment, and it should be directly associated with the act. To effect this direct association, Skinner (1958) emphasized the importance of small steps arranged in sequence: "In acquiring complex behavior, the student must pass through a carefully designed sequence of steps.

... Each step must be so small that it can always be taken, yet in taking it the student moves somewhat closer to fully competent behavior. The machine must make sure that these steps are taken in a carefully prescribed order."

Programmed instruction consists of a series of "frames" that are carefully arranged to successively "shape" the desired behavior. Test questions are embedded in the program, and these provide the immediate reinforcement and feedback concerning the desired response. The learner can control the rate of the presentation, and the program is carefully sequenced so that foundation concepts are learned before later ones are tackled. The *rate* of learning, however, is almost the only thing that is controlled by the learner. True to Skinnerian notions about the control of the environment, the *designer* of the program has virtually complete control of what will be learned, how it will be learned, and when criterion performance has been attained.

Problems. Much of the criticism of PI is directed toward the rigidities of the method. Once the program is made, there is nothing for the student to do except to proceed through it as predetermined by the programmer. In the linear program, the student makes a response and the correct answer is provided. Whether the response is right or wrong, the student moves to the next frame in the program. Thus, every student sees the same sequence of material, although not necessarily at the same rate. Recent refinements add "responsive" or "branching" programs, which respond to wrong answers as well as to correct ones. If the student makes an error or shows incomplete understanding, he is directed to a sequence of frames designed to correct his particular problem. In like manner, students for whom some sections would be superfluous can be directed to skip them. Branching programs provide for greater individualization because the response of the student determines which series of frames will be presented next. In this sense the program is "individually responsive" to the learner.

Branching, however, is an extremely complicated process, requiring people highly skilled in the logic of the subject matter as well as in the diagnosis of student learning. An estimated 50 to 75 hours of programming are required for each student hour presented, even for the so-called "simple" skills associated with military and industrial training (Markle, 1970). Thus, it is hardly surprising that there has been an extreme shortage of programmed materials ever since PI was introduced. Neither should it surprise us, given the enormous expense involved, that many of the materials have not been subjected to pretesting before they were placed on the market. In 1965, 40 percent of the programs produced for schools had never been pretested—and by 1967 as much as 70 percent of the programs had not been prevalidated (Licklider, 1970).

Because of the time and expense involved, programmed instruction has not proved very practical to implement on a wide scale, but even more disappointing has been its failure to validate a scientifically rigorous approach to learning. There are, by this time, well over one hundred studies comparing programmed instruction with more traditional approaches, and there are also a number of excellent reviews of the research (Campeau, 1974; Jamison, Suppes, and Wells, 1973; Lange, 1972, Silberman, 1962; Zoll, 1969). While a slight edge might be given to programmed instruction in terms of student achievement, research findings fall short of justifying the investment of the money, time, and personnel that is required to create programs of high quality.

Another serious problem with present forms of programmed instruction is the boredom that is experienced by many students. Research indicates that the monotony of programmed frames leads to decreased interest after the initial novelty has worn off (Jamison, Suppes, and Wells, 1973). Most programmed materials require a limited kind of action that may involve the muscles without fully engaging the mind. There is a kind of deadly passivity that can enter into the programmed text or machine. When students are relieved of making decisions or raising questions, they can hardly be called "active" learners.

Appropriate Uses. Despite the criticisms, programmed instruction can be helpful when it is used well for what it can accomplish. There is fairly consistent evidence that students learn the facts and skills presented by programmed instruction in less time than is required by other means. Despite occasional

forays into more imaginative uses, it is probably fair to conclude that, at the present time, the teaching of facts and skills is
what programmed instruction does best. One of the reasons for
the popularity of PI in the skills centers of community colleges
relates to the inadequate skill development of most New Students. The highly structured, directive, concrete tasks presented
by programmed instruction may be very helpful to students
who have never been given the kind of direction and opportunity for practice that are needed to develop basic skills.

At the college level, most programmed material is in
fields such as mathematics and spelling, where presentations can
be made in short sequential units and where there is a "right"
answer. Relatively little experimentation has been done in using
programmed instruction for teaching concepts, interrelationships, and applications. Thus, many people see programmed
instruction as stifling student initiative and creativity rather
than encouraging it. But Crutchfield (1965) has shown what can
be done with programmed instruction by imaginative design. He
uses a variation of programmed instruction to teach creativity
to fifth and sixth graders. Children using his lessons containing
detective puzzles and other problem-solving exercises show a
"marked superiority" over control children in their ability to
generate high quality and quantity of creative solutions. Crutchfield's work, however, is more the exception than the rule in
programmed materials today.

The effective use of PI would appear to involve the following precautions: (1) Not all students with weak skills will be
helped by programmed instruction, and the instructor needs to
check frequently with the student to determine progress and
personal reactions to the technique. Hartley (1968) found that
"anxious introverts" tended to complete programmed materials
whereas "stable extroverts" did not. (2) The effectiveness of
programmed instruction, like any other technique, will depend
heavily on the quality of the material. (3) Programmed materials are most effective in disciplines where learning tasks are
sequential and can be presented in small units which can be
reinforced by the "right" answer. (4) Instructors should utilize
programmed materials as long as there are no better alternatives

available. Changes are taking place rapidly today, and new and improved techniques are constantly in the process of development. We need not be satisfied with something that seems to work fairly well if something that works better can be found.

It now seems quite clear that the teaching machine will not replace the teacher and that programmed texts are not well used in independent solitary settings. They should be used as supplements and not as replacements for other forms of instruction. Our research evaluations of programmed instruction would probably be much more useful if, instead of comparing programmed *versus* conventional instruction, they would compare conventional *supplemented* with programmed instruction versus conventional alone. Hartley (1973) claims that eleven out of twelve research studies making this comparison showed superior results for the combination. The use of programmed instruction to teach facts and skills should relieve the teacher of routine tasks, making it possible for him or her to spend more time with the special problems of individual students—but only if the teacher views programmed instruction in this light.

In the long run, we may find that the greatest contribution of PI is not in its direct application in the classroom but rather in what it tells us about the process of learning. Some scientists contend that PI should be viewed not as a medium of instruction, such as television or audio cassettes, but rather as a *process* which can be used to design effective programs of all kinds. Most of our newest approaches to individualized instruction are, in fact, based upon the scientific principles that are illustrated concretely in programmed instruction. Stolurow (1969, p. 1020) pleads for attention to the lessons to be learned from the process as well as the application of PI. "The decision to use PI in and for education is not simple or easy, but any doubts about its permanence or effectiveness would have to stem from prejudice or ignorance. The only course of action for areas of application is how to use PI most effectively, and the only course for research is how to improve upon what little we now know so that we can begin to understand teaching and learning as they take place in schools, universities, and training establishments."

Two emerging branches of programmed instruction are attempting to correct some weakness of programmed texts. One approach, the use of learning modules, attempts to alleviate the mechanistic approach to learning and the consuming boredom that many students find in programmed instruction through the use of a larger learning unit than the "frames" of programmed instruction. The learning module can be used to present the concepts and interrelationships of higher-level learning, and students generally find modules more interesting and appropriate for college-level study. We shall look at this branch in Chapter Four. The second branch attempts to find some solutions to the management problems highlighted by programmed instruction. Even an initially homogeneous group becomes spread out through the self-pacing feature, thus creating such serious problems of "administration, scheduling, and guidance that only computer techniques as yet undevised and modes of school organization as yet only vaguely imaginable could be expected to cope with them" (Mesthene, 1971, p. 237). Computers might also be used to handle the extremely complex programs that are necessary for more individualized learning. The computer can present diagnostic tests, provide branched programs to accommodate individual needs, and furnish prescriptive assignments that might refer the student to a textbook, a laboratory experiment, or a consultation with the instructor. In other words, computers, far from ignoring individuality, have the potential for individualizing instruction to a greater extent than is possible with human teachers. Whether computers can provide personalized attention is another question that is addressed by other branches of the individualized instruction movement. The two primary computer-oriented programs arising out of programmed instruction are computer-assisted instruction (CAI) and computer-managed instruction (CMI). The latter is sometimes referred to as computer-based instructional management systems (CBIMS).

Computer-Assisted Instruction

Computer-assisted instruction (CAI) is one of those terms that has been corrupted by imprecise use to the extent that some writers use it to include any use of computers by educators, including data management. We shall limit the meaning of CAI to those programs where the computer is used to interact tutorially with the student as he or she moves through a self-paced program or course of instruction.

The student and computer ordinarily communicate through a teletypewriter; the computer types instructions, diagnostic questions, and feedback messages, and the student responds via the keyboard. The "messages" from the computer, however, need not be limited to words or simple concepts. Some systems, for example, use slide projectors or closed-circuit television or recordings of foreign languages. In like manner, student responses can be fairly complex; an electronic stylus, for example, can be used for pointing to places on graphs or maps. There are even systems where computers can detect the placement of objects such as blocks on a "manipulation board." The possibilities for variety in the communication modes between computer and student seem almost endless. Goodlad (1971, p. 91) describes the potential of computers for flexibility and variety: "The computer is a tireless, relentless, evaluating teacher which has several modes of instruction at its disposal: sound, sight, and touch. A properly programmed computer is able to present words to be spelled, sounds to be made, instructions to be followed, and so on. It is able to present images and symbols to be responded to by touch. It is able to evaluate pupil performance and to direct the student backwards, forwards, sideways, for appropriate learning activity."

The potential of the computer for individualizing instruction is enormous. Its patience, its memory, and its endless capacity for detail are assets that defy competition from ordinary human teachers. Although such characteristics undoubtedly cannot replace the charm of a Mr. Chips, there are times and situations and subjects where such "inhuman" virtues are undeniably important. Yet the use of computers for instructional purposes has not really caught on in education. My 1974 survey showed that CAI is used in only 16 percent of the community colleges. Many computer enthusiasts are disappointed in the slow acceptance of CAI, but they warn that we should not confuse the present reality of CAI with its potential. Baker

(1971, p. 51) observes that the "early conceptualization of CAI grossly underestimated both the complexity of the learning process and the level of computer-related equipment necessary for wide-scale implementation of CAI. As a result, many CAI systems were developed, but most demonstrated only the feasibility of CAI, not its practicality."

The computer has not really had time to demonstrate its practicality for instructional purposes. Early uses of computers for instruction date back to 1959, but only as recently as 1966 IBM announced the development of a system designed for instructional rather than business use. We need to remember that CAI and its cousins are only ten years old, so that its development is still immature, if not downright primitive. As Lawrence Stolurow has observed, "Projections based upon today's systems would have the same degree of fidelity as projections based upon the Wright brothers' first plane would have had for predicting the design of the supersonic transport" (quoted in Parkus, 1970, p. 75).

In full recognition of the extreme youth of CAI, it is still fair to ask why a technique with its apparent potential is not moving more rapidly into use. Enthusiastic endorsements such as that appearing in *American Education* (an official publication of the Department of Health, Education, and Welfare) shortly after the IBM instructional system was introduced are rarely seen today. According to that early endorsement, the CAI system would "never get tired . . . allow the individual to proceed at his own pace . . . make possible a daily tracking system . . . ensure the acquisition of basic skills . . . and provide a complete, instantly available record of each [student's] achievement and furnish information for course modification" (Hausman, 1967). We should be able to use those advantages effectively in educational programs; but, like any other new technique, CAI has some strengths, some limitations, and quite a few problems to be solved.

Strengths. As with programmed instruction, CAI seems to have its greatest advantage in the reduction of the time required for learning. The research to date shows that students who participate in CAI generally do at least as well as those in conventional classrooms in significantly less time. Rather remarkable results have been shown with very small amounts of CAI (five to fifteen minutes per day) added to the regular program (Atkinson, 1974; Suppes, 1966; Vinsonhaler and Bass, 1971). For subjects in which drill is required, CAI is at its efficient best. As Ornstein (1975, p. 396), discussing the teaching of foreign languages, points out: "While in an ordinary fifty-minute class a student is lucky to recite for five minutes, in CAI he must be almost constantly active. Massive amounts of drill, the lifeblood of language acquisition, are possible, so that live sessions of students and teacher can be devoted to liberated conversation, problem solving, and a salutary airing of complaints."

Students using CAI for drill express particular pleasure with the patience of CAI. There is no embarrassment, no feeling of delaying the teacher or other students, no awareness of being "slow" in accomplishing the task. While the computer has been charged with being impersonal, there is no evidence that students feel depersonalized by their practice sessions with the computer. In fact, in one study junior high school students considered the computer "fairer," "easier," "clearer," "bigger," more "likable," and "better" than the teacher (Hess and Tenezakis, 1971).

In the few colleges having experience with CAI, student reaction is described as varying from good to enthusiastic (Golden West College, undated; Hedges, 1973; Sax, 1972). We should, however, be mindful of Coulson's (1970, p. 206) warning: "Initially, almost all students exhibit a 'pinball machine' effect; that is, a motivational lift resulting from the novelty and the automation of the equipment. This effect cannot be expected to have permanence, however; the content material must have intrinsic interest beyond the mechanical gadgetry." Obviously, the teaching effectiveness of the computer will be no better than the program put into it; it possesses no magical ability to transform poor instruction into quality instruction. But given skillfully prepared programs, the computer brings some advantages to the task of instruction. And it has some special merit for New Students. (Other instructional uses of computers are especially useful with high-ability, creative students who seek problem-solving interactions with computers.)

There has been some question about whether low achievers possess the independence and reading ability to handle CAI (Reed, Ertel, and Collart, 1974), but students who have not responded well to conventional educational programs apparently react quite favorably to CAI. Golden West College (undated) found that students who expected a C or less in their courses were especially enthusiastic about CAI, and Rappaport (1974) reports that CAI resulted in significant changes in attitude toward subject matter on the part of low achievers. It has also been observed that the use of CAI in college physics truncates the distribution of lower grades; that is, not as many people make poor grades when CAI is used (Hansen, Dick, and Lippert, 1968).

Clearly, there are some real strengths in CAI; however, it is not a panacea that will solve all learning problems. Like programmed instruction, CAI should be combined with other learning activities; it should not replace them. Atkinson (1974) suggests that CAI should supplement classroom teaching by concentrating on those tasks in which individualization is critically important. The computer's great strength is individualization, and it makes good sense from an efficiency standpoint to utilize the tools of education where they do the most good. Ignoring this generally good advice has led to most of the features described as limitations of CAI.

Limitations. Even the advantages of CAI can turn into limitations when they are overused and abused. While the use of CAI for drill and practice seems thoroughly desirable, there is some concern lest the mere convenience of CAI encourage "drill" for subjects in which drill and memory work are not appropriate to the mastery of the subject matter. What political figure did what in which year may be one of the least important understandings to be gained from a course in political science; but if such information is on the computer and students and teachers come to enjoy the convenience of CAI, the content-laden curriculum may become even more entrenched.

Education as *content* versus education as *process* is per-

haps the most serious educational issue raised by CAI. Many of
the new technologies assume that the goal is to make present
education more efficient. Advocates seem to say that since the
learning of academic content is our major emphasis now, CAI is
an improvement because it can accomplish this task with greater
efficiency. Not necessarily so. Education that simply transfers
information from one receptacle to another is sterile, and the
danger of adding only efficiency to education through CAI is a
real danger, especially for New Students. De Lone (1971, p. 40)
puts it well: "Computer-assisted instruction becomes the ne
plus ultra of remedial education. And remedial education, too
often, can be defined as an effort to pour into a student in concentrate what he has already rejected in diluted form. Most
efforts at programmed learning, and their refinement into CAI,
seem to adopt wholesale this pernicious assumption."

Another example of a strength turning into a limitation
through unwise application is the extent to which the learning
task is defined for the learner. One of the strengths of CAI is
presumably the active involvement of the learner, but many
people are beginning to question how "active" the mind really
is when the learner simply responds to whatever appears on the
screen in front of him. There is a distinction between machine-
controlled programs and learner-controlled programs. At the one
extreme are the linear CAI programs, in which the student has
no choices except for the pace of learning; he simply proceeds
on a fixed path, which is controlled by the machine. At the
other extreme is the "randomized encyclopedia" model, where
the student has access to many content units with free choice of
frames and sequences (Newkirk, 1973). Bushnell (1970, p. 162)
has some sharp words of criticism for the machine-controlled
model: "If the learner's own interests and talents are stifled by
machine-directed learning or the imposed demands of the system, the results may be facts temporarily stored, but at the cost
of knowledge becoming irrelevant and curiosity being de-
stroyed. . . . As a rule of thumb, it is perhaps better to offer
opportunities or resources that the student cares about than the
particular body of information that the teacher happens to
know. At the very least, and no matter the discipline, if a stu-

dent is allowed to ask questions that matter to him, he soon learns the habit of self-generating inquiry." A major trend in the use of computers for instruction is the shift from machine to learner control. More attention is being given now to providing more options and more interaction between learner and computer. The goal is to make the computer more responsive to the commands and questions typed by the student, so that students can derive their own diagnoses and take more responsibility for directing their own learning (Zinn, 1972).

Some learning tasks are clearly inefficient, and nothing will be accomplished through trying to "program" such learning. "Much learning takes place on the hoof or in conversation with a more capricious responder than the computer. If we are to encourage the spirit of inquiry, we want students to go to the library, to putter about the shop; to prepare them for responsibility we want them to meet together to make plans for group activity, to take part in plays and in team games. That is, learning by doing is not dead, and there are some 'doings' that the terminal is unsuited for" (Hilgard, 1971, p. 128). Changes are gradually being made as teachers and students gain experience with the use of CAI, but there are still some difficult problems deterring widespread use of CAI.

Problems to be solved. Present difficulties in the use of CAI are both educational and administrative. Primary among the administrative problems has been cost. Many people still perceive cost as *the* deterrent to the adoption of CAI. But costs have been reduced markedly in recent years. When business computers were used for instructional purposes, the cost ran as high as $35-$40 per student hour; with the introduction of computers designed for instructional purposes, the cost was reduced to $3-$5 or less per hour (Hall, 1971). Some of the newer programs estimate costs at 35¢ per student hour, a figure well below the current community college average for instructional expenses (Hammond, 1972). Other projected costs are as low as 12¢ (Bitzer and Skaperdas, 1971) and 25¢ per student hour (Carroll, 1971a). One imaginative program proved that putting a computer into a mobile van and taking the program to the students was less costly than training students in an on-campus institute (Hall, Cartwright, and Mitzell, 1974).

The cost of software has followed the same pattern as that for hardware. In 1970, Coulson estimated that twenty hours of CAI material required two man-years to develop. But in the space of three years, the faculty of Golden West College, with the help of technical assistance from CAI programmers, developed 239 hours of instructional materials in twenty-one different subject areas (Golden West College, undated). Admittedly, that is a great success story, especially in the face of talk about faculty resistance to the use of CAI; but in these times of heightened consciousness about budgets, it is hard to imagine granting faculty all across the country "time off" to develop their CAI materials, and it is also probably unnecessary. At the present time, there is enormous waste in the CAI system. Sax (1972) located five colleges using CAI for teaching remedial English and mathematics to low achievers—and found not one instance of common use of materials. The proliferation of different CAI languages does not help the situation. As the use of CAI increases, the sharing of materials appears to be both a financial necessity and an educational advantage in obtaining materials of high quality.

It is understandably difficult to get faculty to accept materials developed by others unless they understand the technology well enough to do it themselves. Most faculty probably feel sure that they could write a better textbook than the one they use, but at least they know how to tell a good text from a poor one. The study by Sax (1972) revealed that many subject-matter specialists resist learning the computer language and resent being forced into computer-logical ways of thinking about their subject. Unless the institution takes specific steps to encourage understanding and use of CAI, it is almost a foregone conclusion that faculty will live up to their reputations as "resistant" to the new technologies.

A panel of educational leaders, polled via the Delphi Technique by the National Center for Higher Education Management Systems (NCHEMS), named the faculty as the group most resistant to the use of television, computers, and new technologies. Nevertheless, 97 percent of the members of the panel —which consisted of federal and state legislative and executive representatives, foundation leaders, university students, faculty, and administrators, and representatives from professional associations and agencies—said that, in their opinion, the use of the new technologies *should* occur and *would* occur by the end of the decade (Huckfeldt, 1972).

Actually, the state of North Carolina found it surprisingly easy to convert faculty to the use of computers. After a two-week workshop conducted for 136 teaching faculty in biology, business, chemistry, economics, music composition, political science, psychology, and sociology, the use of computers for instructional purposes went from 46 percent prior to the workshop to 70 percent a year later. Most of the 136 faculty members (45 percent) simply adopted materials already in existence, but a substantial number (31 percent) created their own materials, and 25 percent designed new courses (Denk, 1973).

There is evidence in various colleges across the country that faculty are not, as a group, resistant to using new teaching techniques when they understand them, and some faculties seem to have adjusted to the new role demands remarkably well. But as yet no one has given much attention to how faculty are using the time that is presumably freed by the use of the computer. One often-mentioned advantage of CAI is that scheduling the routine aspects of education on the computer leaves the teacher free to do those things that are uniquely human. But Goodlad (1971) questions whether we know how to utilize human beings effectively in education. What are the "uniquely human" things that can be accomplished by a teacher freed from the routine of instruction? And will teachers be able to do those things all day long? Goodlad notes that even teachers rated as superior devote an enormous amount of time to purely routine tasks and that people seem to need a considerable amount of routine between creative efforts. "How," he asks, "is the human teacher to establish and maintain a productive relationship with thirty other human beings and maintain it throughout five or six hours of an instructional day? Most teachers would be in a state of collapse at the end of such days" (p. 93). Goodlad refers primarily to elementary schools, but the question is a valid one. College students are presumably more independent than children, and college teachers are not confined to a room with "thirty other human beings" throughout the day. Nevertheless, a teacher whose days are spent in individual conferences with students, analyzing computer reports of progress, and "managing" the learning program has taken on a dramatically new role, and it would behoove us to learn more about the satisfactions and dissatisfactions of this new role.

In addition, we probably need to give more attention to what it is that human teachers can do uniquely well. Hilgard (1971) mentions three especially human functions: helping the student to initiate inquiry, helping the student to gain a favorable self-image, and helping the student toward effective participation with others. We do not know whether teachers using CAI are devoting more of their time to those high-level teaching functions. We do know that machines are poor substitutes for teachers in personalizing education. Students are not fooled by the attempts of computer advocates to "humanize" their machines by programming the machine to use students' first names (Schoen, 1972) or to provide verbal praise for correct responses (Majer, Hansen, and Dick, 1971). Students were pleased by the use of their names, and students who were praised by the computer took less time to complete the task, but there were no significant differences in achievement shown through this kind of personalization. If teachers are to provide the "uniquely human" touch to learning, we will need to redouble our efforts in educational research and staff development to help teachers work effectively with individual students.

A final problem that CAI and every other teaching technique will have to solve is that of unlocking the clues to a viable theory of instruction. Even in these years of scientific use of CAI, we have not pushed much beyond Crowder's analysis, made in 1960: "The person who creates a teaching machine might seem to be claiming that he understands human learning in sufficient detail and generality that he can set up, via the machine, those conditions under which efficient learning will inevitably occur. However, we . . . do not have access to any such educational philosopher's stone. Rather, we suspect that human learning takes place in a variety of ways and that these ways vary with the abilities and present knowledge of different students, with the nature of the subject matter, with a number of interactions between these sources of variation, and with other sources of variability of which we are not even aware."

Computer-Managed Instruction

Although both computer-assisted instruction (CAI) and computer-managed instruction (CMI) assign heavy educational responsibilities to the computer, the two systems are very different. In CMI, students do not interact on line with the computer. Rather, the computer is used to manage individualization, largely through diagnostic testing and prescriptive assignments tailored to individual needs. There is some agreement that CMI has greater promise for widespread adoption in the near future than CAI (Brudner, 1968; Cooley and Glaser, 1969). Not the least of its advantages is that it costs less than CAI (Brudner, 1968).

Brief descriptions of two CMI systems used at the college level will illustrate the method. One of the earliest systems was designed by Kelley (1968) to teach economics. His system is called Teaching Information Processing System (TIPS). Six to ten times a semester each student takes a diagnostic test (composed of ten to twenty-five items) and, a few hours later, receives information about his test score, the correct answers, his level of achievement, and a number of prescribed learning activities. Prescriptions might be a typical homework assignment, attendance at a lecture, or perhaps referral to a teaching assistant or help in a small-group setting. The professor and teaching assistants receive cumulative information about the class as a whole as well as information about the progress of individual students.

A similar system has recently been put into effect at Miami-Dade Community College in Florida, in a program called Response System with Variable Prescriptions (RSVP). Homebound students as well as on-campus students may participate in the program, since the computer sends individualized letters to students, with essentially the same type of information as that described for TIPS. For each module in the RSVP program, the student takes a ten-item multiple-choice "survey." RSVP analyzes patterns of responses and identifies for the student whether he missed a "main idea" or a question. The student therefore learns which concepts he failed to understand; he can then be directed to certain portions of a television documentary, pages in a textbook, or sections of a learning module.

In all CMI systems, the computer is used to score tests (or "surveys," as some prefer to call them), diagnose learning problems, prescribe appropriate assignments, and report results on an individual and cumulative basis. The enormous advantage of these systems lies in the *management* of self-paced or individualized learning. If self-paced learning works, it creates great diversity in a class. Students soon spread out across the range of the course to an extent not experienced in traditional education, where everyone must be at approximately the same point each time the class meets. If the class is large, a single instructor simply cannot handle the individual needs of students, and the attempt to individualize instruction through self-pacing breaks down. It may well be that CMI is a necessary accompaniment to widespread adoption of individualized instruction.

The system is a spectacular success in Miami-Dade's completely self-paced Open College, enrolling largely older, off-campus students. The students rated the RSVP feature more useful than *any* of the other components of Open College, including texts, study guides, telecasts, and broadcasts (Anandam, 1974). The RSVP program received especially high ratings on items related to the reduction of anxiety and the building of self-confidence. Seventy-three percent of the students felt strongly that RSVP had helped them stay with the course, and the same proportion felt strongly that they could not have performed as well in the course without RSVP.

Sophisticated systems of CMI are capable of performing a number of functions to assist in instruction (see Cooley and Glaser, 1969): (1) They can present to the student alternate goals and subgoals, making it possible for individuals to follow different learning paths. (2) They can diagnose and store information about the characteristics of the learner—long-term characteristics such as abilities, interests, and learning styles or short-term characteristics such as recent performance on a related study unit. (3) They can assign or suggest an appropriate method of study, even to the point of grouping students together for a discussion. (4) They can conduct continuous monitoring and assessment, including information about how much practice the student requires, how well she retains information, and what kinds of instructional alternatives she chooses or does well with. (5) They can provide the instructor with group and individual statistics to help in the revision and constant improvement of courses and materials.

It is difficult to fault the goals or the potential of the CMI systems. If self-paced learning is worth doing, it is worth doing well, and computer-managed systems aim to do just that. CMI, however, makes a number of assumptions about education, and these should be made explicit. (1) It assumes that the objectives of learning can be specified and that learning problems can be diagnosed through student responses to objective questions or sets of questions. (2) It assumes that useful prescriptions can be prepared for groups of students having common diagnoses. (3) It assumes that instructors receiving cumulative and individual information about educational progress will *use* the information to improve their instruction. In the hands of imaginative and creative educators, these assumptions may pose no difficulty; in the hands of lazy or pedantic educators, they can be troublesome.

The first assumption is not unique to CMI. Any system of individualized instruction starts with the assumption that the objectives of instruction can be stated and that we can determine through student response when the objectives have been achieved. Objectives can be narrow and unimportant, calling for little imagination in either specification or measurement; or they can be broad-based growth goals, calling for highly creative specification and measurement. Growth in areas that are not specified, however, will not be assessed. It is entirely possible to overlook important kinds of student performance, and it is also possible to overlook unintended but deleterious side effects. Students may, for example, be learning content very well, but they may be doing so at the cost of gaining experience in assuming initiative for their own lifelong education. Brudner (1968) makes a special point of the need to encourage student self-direction even with elementary school children. Teachers in the elementary pioneer program of IPI (Individually Prescribed Instruction) are available to guide and help students, but students are expected to proceed as independently as possible. This is an important point to make because the advocates of the use of computers for instructional purposes are usually busy defending themselves against charges of the cold impersonality of the computer. While one of the advantages of individualized instruction is surely to give personal attention when needed, oversolicitude and overprogramming can lead to dependence on learning activities that are developed by others.

The second assumption poses a problem for CMI, since it assumes that students making similar patterns of responses can profit from similar prescriptions. It is comparable to practicing medicine through a computer where common symptoms result in common prescriptions. If *all* relevant data are fed into the system, there is no reason why it should not work; but the prescription for a 250-pound man with cold symptoms appearing after exposure while on a hunting trip might be quite different from that for a 90-pound child with the same cold symptoms but with known allergies. Teachers, almost without recognizing it, make certain adjustments to individual situations; they decide, for instance, when to encourage and when to take the hard line, or when to help and when to put the student on his own. It is extremely difficult to program *all* of the relevant factors in student situations—the death or divorce of parents, for example. But then it is even more impossible for the instructor to provide individualized attention without the help of the computer. The reality is that very few teachers give any attention at all to individual diagnoses and prescription. Using the analogy to medicine, the present situation is more like giving identical prescriptions to a 250-pound man with a cold and to a 90-pound child with a broken leg. As long as that situation exists, CMI appears to be a distinct advantage, if not the final answer.

The third assumption underlying CMI is also reality-oriented. The fact that the computer *can* provide teachers with data about class and individual progress does not mean that people will use it wisely to revise and improve course plans or to seek out students with obvious learning problems. But once again, the problem is not with CMI systems—unless we begin to assume that once the technology is operative, it is self-sufficient. Faculty and staff training and development is an inevitable part of any technological advance in education—no less in CMI than in any other.

Conclusions

The individualization of learning lies at the heart of the instructional revolution. The movement is young, but it is accelerating rapidly now, so that almost every college in the country has been affected in some way by the phenomenon of self-paced learning. Programmed instruction, although still very popular in community colleges, is on the wane and is now more interesting for its historical contribution to knowledge about the learning process than for its use as a teaching technique. The principles demonstrated by PI have now found their way into a great variety of new applications. The newest applications tend to be *systems* of learning rather than techniques, and we shall be looking at these in Chapter Four.

The use of computers to help in the task of individualizing learning is a significant technological extension of PI. Computer-assisted instruction, as we have defined it in this chapter, is best understood as a sophisticated application of the learning process introduced by PI, but CMI is a technological tool that has considerable potential for managing the complexities of individualized instruction. If the instructional revolution is to have the dramatic impact that this book predicts, then the capacity of computers to "remember" highly individualistic learning needs may be a virtual necessity in managing the thousands of *individual* learners that will complicate the existence of educators in the 1980s.

Mastery Learning and Self-Paced Modules

✳✳✳

At the heart of the instructional revolution lies the self-paced learning module and its conceptual companion, mastery learning. Although, as we saw in Chapter Three, there is an evolutionary history behind the gradual improvement of programmed instruction and its progeny, the speed of adoption of self-paced learning modules across the country looks more revolutionary than evolutionary. Indeed, as Novak (1973, p. 4) observes, "The use of some form of modular instruction is probably the fastest-growing trend in the history of Western education." My 1974 survey (Appendix A) showed that almost three fourths of the community colleges reported some use of self-paced learning modules. And the vote of confidence given the approach makes it an unlikely candidate for faddism. When community college administrators were asked to name innovative approaches that they found especially effective, self-paced modules were nominated more frequently than any other technique.

The use of self-paced learning modules is also making a significant impact on university teaching, especially in the disciplines of biology, physics, engineering, and psychology. There are more than one thousand self-paced courses in psychology alone, and entire colleges and numerous departments have moved to modular instruction. College IV, a cluster college of Grand Valley State Colleges in Michigan, has a completely self-paced program, offering a wide array of courses to a broad cross section of students. The Center for Research on Learning and Teaching at the University of Michigan (University of Michigan, 1975, p. 1) proclaims, "It is our belief at CRLT that variations on the self-paced supervised study arrangement will become a long-lasting procedure for certain kinds of courses in many departments of the university."

While revolutions are characterized by suddenness and rapid spread of change (that is, *breadth* of influence), their more profound impact lies in their power to upset old ways of thinking (that is, in their *depth* of influence). The concept of mastery learning that underlies self-paced learning has an evolutionary history, but it is a revolutionary idea. If it attracts the broad constituency in the 1980s that it missed when it was first introduced in the 1920s, we will be into the instructional revolution. From this vantage point in 1975, it looks as though the powerful pedagogical linkage between mastery learning and self-paced learning modules may provide both the breadth and the depth to spark dramatic change in the way we think about and practice education.

Although many educators are familiar with the general concepts of learning modules and of mastery learning, it may prove helpful to define our terms before proceeding to a discussion of their role in the instructional revolution.

A *learning module* is a self-contained learning unit with well-defined objectives. Usually it consists of learning materials, a sequence of activities, and provisions for evaluation. Students may use the modules independently at their own rate and at times of their own choosing to replace or supplement the more traditional lectures, laboratories, and discussions. Aside from those rather general characteristics, there is considerable variety in the construction, emphases, and utilization of learning modules. We will return later to a detailed discussion of some of these variations.

Mastery learning refers to the pedagogical concept that learning must be thorough—one unit must be learned to a high level of competency before the next unit in the sequence is tackled. The concept of mastery learning is revolutionary because it upsets traditional ways of thinking about education. Those two stalwarts of the school system—grades and semesters—become almost meaningless when mastery learning is implemented. Ideally, all students would earn A grades, and they would take as long as necessary to accomplish this level of mastery.

Learning modules are the progeny of two reform movements in education. They most recently appear to stem from programmed learning approaches to instruction. They represent, however, a reaction against the small frames of PI. Many people, especially those in higher education, were dissatisfied with the mechanistic presentation of numerous small frames of learning material. The very small bits of learning presented by PI are deemed more appropriate for drill and practice than they are for the conceptual learning that educators hope characterizes college learning. Thus, there was a move to make the learning units larger than the PI "frame" but still smaller than the semester course.

Today's use of learning modules also arises out of the mastery learning movement, which has roots going back to the 1920s. Over fifty years ago, two programs incorporating the concept of mastery learning, the Winnetka Plan and the Morrison Plan, were launched in elementary schools in Illinois. Both plans had the major features of today's self-paced learning modules: educational objectives were specified, instruction was organized into learning units, diagnostic progress tests were administered after each unit, and mastery of one unit was required before the student could proceed to the next unit. For some reason, these early approaches to self-paced learning did not become widespread or generally accepted, and both disappeared in the 1930s; they resurfaced as corollaries of programmed instruction in the 1960s. Block (1971a, p. 4) suggests that the disappearance of mastery learning in the 1930s was due "to the lack of the technology required to sustain a successful strategy," but he may be too modest about his own contributions to the explication of a rationale for the concept of mastery learning. The work of scholars such as Block (1971b), Bloom (1971b), and Carroll (1963) has done much to place the needed foundations of research and theory under self-paced learning modules.

Mastery Learning

I believe that mastery learning is the critical missing link in the education of low achievers. Its advantages are both cognitive and affective: (1) It lays a foundation for future learning by insisting that one unit must be mastered before the student may proceed to subsequent learning; (2) it demonstrates to poor students that they are capable of doing good work. To most New Students, those two critically important experiences are missing from traditional education. New Students are perpetually at a cognitive disadvantage in school because they are rushed along to advanced learning before they have mastered the more elementary concepts. Students cannot gain anything from a study of algebra if they do not know the multiplication tables; they cannot readily grasp the significance of history if they lack an adequate reading vocabulary. To the extent that knowledge is cumulative and sequential, efficiency in learning depends upon mastering each step in turn. As children proceed through school and the gap between achievers and nonachievers increases, the bright get brighter and the dull get duller (Coleman and others, 1966). The widening gap is probably due to the efficiency factor in learning. Whereas achievers have the tools and the background to make good use of further education, the future learning of nonachievers is perpetually thwarted by their failure to master fundamentals. Block (1972) hypothesized an efficiency factor in mastery learning when he found that students who learned one unit to a high level of mastery took significantly less time to learn subsequent units.

Even worse than the cognitive handicaps wrought by traditional education's notion that everyone should move along with the group is the affective damage done to young people who are offered no alternative to doing "poor work." Rarely do New Students experience the satisfaction of doing schoolwork in which they can take pride. In my research on New Students (Cross, 1971), I was struck by the pervasiveness of the failure experiences of these students; repeated school failure had apparently eroded their self-concept and their self-confidence as learners. Not surprisingly, students who spend the most formative years of their lives in the bottom third of the class begin to think of themselves as "below-average" people. Glasser has been forthright in his charge that the schools *cause* the failure. In the introduction to his well-known *Schools Without Failure* (1969, p. xiii) he writes, "Much has been written on the difficulties of improving education in the central city. From personal experience, I believe that most people who write about these schools have not raised the critical issue. They have been so obsessed with the social, environmental, and cultural factors affecting students that they have not looked deeply enough into *the role education itself has played in causing students to fail, not only in the central city but in all schools.*" Later in the book, he makes the blunt assertion "Very few children come to school failures, none come labeled failures; *it is school and school alone which pins the label of failure on children*" (p. 26).

Bloom (1971a, pp. 14-15, 22) is not as incensed and angry as Glasser, but his conclusions are the same:

> In school, the likelihood is that each student will be judged many times each day in terms of his adequacy relative to others in his class, group, or school. No matter how well he does, if others do better, he must come to know it and to place himself accordingly. . . .
>
> We do not know what level of objective success or failure will be interpreted by the individual as success or failure. But, in general, we believe that to be in the top third or top quarter of his class group (grades of A and B) over a number of years in a variety of school subjects is likely to be interpreted by the student as adequate or as success. Also, we believe [that] to be in the bottom third

or quarter of his class group (grades of D and F) over a number of years must leave the individual with a negative self-view—at least in the academic area.

Torshen (1969) has summarized the studies showing relationships between self-concept and school achievement. While the correlation between *total* self-concept and school achievement is of the order of +.25, the correlation between *academic* self-concept and school achievement is about +.50. It is evident in these studies that the academic self-concept is relatively clearly defined by the end of the primary school period. These correlations indicate that for students at the extremes (upper and lower third) on academic achievement, the relationship between achievement and academic self-concept is very strong, with little overlap in academic self-concept between these extreme groups. That is, students in the lower third of the achievement distribution tend to have negative self-concepts while students in the upper third tend to have positive self-concepts.

Bloom (1971b) claims that 95 percent of the students can attain mastery of most school learning tasks if they are given sufficient time and appropriate types of help. Thus, 95 percent of the students should be able to attain A grades—if by an A grade we mean to certify that the student has mastered the learning task and not simply that he is one of the best in a particular class. A grading curve with mostly A's is completely sound educationally, but it is anathema to those who are accustomed to thinking of educational results measured by the bell-shaped normal curve. The normal curve, after all, is a statistical tool designed to reflect the result of *random* processes. If there are no factors operating *except* chance, then the normal curve is the result. To the extent that purposeful, directed influences are operating, the curve should depart from a chance distribution. Education is not a random process; the outcomes of successful education should push the grading curve away from anything resembling a chance distribution. Following this logic, Bloom (1971b, p. 49) points out that "our educational efforts may be said to be unsuccessful to the extent that student achievement is normally distributed."

Logical as Bloom's argument is, custom has made us so accepting of the normal grading curve that teachers who give more A and B grades than D and F grades are looked upon as "soft graders" instead of as effective teachers. Many people equate the preservation of the normal grading curve with the preservation of academic standards. Actually, standards are better served when students learn the material. And students do seem to learn the material under conditions of mastery learning. Bloom (1971b) reports on his experience in teaching a test theory course by traditional methods in 1965 and by mastery methods in 1966 and 1967. He found that 80 percent of the 1966 class and 90 percent of the 1967 class reached the level of mastery attained by only 20 percent of the 1965 class. This experience corresponds well with Block's (1971a) report on the results from forty major studies carried out in schools: three fourths of the students learning through mastery learning achieved as much as the top fourth using conventional group-based methods. Block reports equally positive affective outcomes in student interest and attitudes toward the subject matter. Ely and Minars (1973) corroborate the positive affective outcomes of mastery learning by showing improved scores on the Tennessee Self-Concept Scale for students learning under mastery conditions.

Paraphrased and abbreviated, the following practical suggestions for implementing mastery learning are taken from Block's (1971c) chapter on operating procedures for mastery learning.

1. Mastery learning is probably most effective when the learner can start learning for mastery in the elementary phases of the subject. This poses no problem since despite their college age, New Students have "mastered" very little of the school curriculum.

2. Mastery learning works best with subjects which are sequentially learned, such as reading and mathematics. Such subjects make maximum use of the idea that the learning of complex behaviors depends on the sequential learning of less complex behaviors.

3. Mastery learning demonstrates its potential most vividly in subjects emphasizing convergent rather than divergent thinking. It shares this characteristic with other approaches

emphasizing behavioral objectives. If teachers can define a finite set of ideas to be mastered and can specify the criteria for attainment, the outcomes of mastery learning are likely to be more advantageous.

4. An absolute (as opposed to relative) standard must be set for mastery. Teachers may set this standard by defining an objective competency that represents mastery or by transferring existing standards to the mastery situation. Block suggests, for example, that scores on final examinations which earned students in traditional classes an A or a B might be used as mastery criteria under mastery learning conditions. Once set, however, the standard must be the *sole* criterion for judging student performance. "Neither teachers nor administrators need feel they have gone 'soft' by giving perhaps almost all students A's under an absolute grading system compared to only 10 to 20 percent under a relative grading system" (Block, 1971c, p. 68).

5. Formative evaluation is of critical importance in mastery learning. Short instruments testing the skills that students must learn from a given unit should be used to frequently provide feedback on progress. These "formative" tests are for the student's guidance; they are *not* graded.

6. Diagnoses must be made through the formative tests and appropriate "correctives" or prescriptive assignments given so that students can profit from their errors. This is the type of function that might well be performed by the CMI techniques discussed in Chapter Three. Obviously, there should be a variety of correctives open to the student.

7. Students need to be oriented to mastery learning. Many New Students are convinced that they cannot learn to high levels of attainment, and thus they feel that attempting to get an A grade is futile and ridiculous. Plenty of time should be given in the very beginning to orientation, encouragement, support, and positive evidence of learning success.

Two impressive programs of learning, the audio-tutorial approach and the Keller Plan or PSI (Personalized System of Instruction), have emerged from self-paced learning modules and mastery learning. These two systems of learning have different philosophies and components, but they illustrate nicely the kind of branching progress that is made as improvements and corrections arise from experience to take us in new directions. The audio-tutorial approach emphasizes self-paced learning modules incorporated into a multimedia presentation. The Keller Plan builds heavily on the concept of self-paced mastery learning.

Audio-Tutorial

The audio-tutorial (A-T) approach to learning began as a remedial program in botany at Purdue University in 1961, when biology professor Samuel Postlethwait became aware that some of the students in his class of 380 freshmen were not ready for the material he was presenting in his lectures. As an experiment, he decided to tape a "remedial" lecture each week, so that students who felt the need for additional help could play and replay the tape at their convenience. After some experience with the tapes, Postlethwait concluded that the technology had greater potential than was being utilized by the mere presentation of supplementary lectures. He moved away from the lecture format of dispensing information and into the tutorial format of guiding students' learning. Thus, today the "message" on the tape is not a lecture but a guided program of learning activities for the student; it is, as the name implies, an audio-tutorial. The tape may present an introduction to the unit and then direct the student to turn off the tape and read a passage in the textbook or look at some slides or filmstrips or examine some objects that have been placed in the A-T booth or study carrel.

The A-T method is not a tool or a technique but might more appropriately be termed a learning system. It concerns itself with designing a *process* that will be effective and efficient for the learner. The tape, which gives audio-tutorial its name and which is its most distinctive characteristic, serves as a programming device. There is some tendency today for anyone using tapes in an independent study situation to refer to the method as audio-tutorial, but the term is usually reserved for the Purdue Postlethwait program, which has three distinguishing components: independent study sessions, the general assembly, and integrated quiz sessions (Postlethwait, 1974).

The *independent study session* takes place in a learning center that is open throughout the day and evening, so that students can work at their own pace and convenience. The center provides learning carrels equipped with various media. One of the features that distinguishes A-T from other forms of self-paced learning is its emphasis on multiple systems of communication—visual, audio, touch, and even smell. Proponents of A-T take explicit note of the existence of the multiple modalities through which students learn, and they also provide in this way for differences in learning styles of students. Students using the Purdue A-T pick up a mimeographed sheet of behavioral objectives upon their entrance to the laboratory and go directly to a booth, which may be equipped with up to four kinds of learning materials: (1) physical objects such as specimens, equipment, and models; (2) printed materials such as textbooks, study guides, and journal articles; (3) projection visuals such as slides, movies, and filmstrips; and (4) audio tapes. Materials too bulky or expensive to include in each booth are placed in a central position for use by all students. Through earphones, the student listens to the voice of the senior instructor suggesting a variety of learning activities. It is important to A-T that the student be an active learner, frequently physically as well as mentally. He or she may be told to pick up a physical object that has been placed in the booth or to leave the booth to conduct an experiment. Putting an experiment or observation in the independent study session has several advantages. Most important, it places the activity in the study sequence where it will be most meaningful; in addition, it permits encounters with other students and instructors, and it provides variety in the study activities. The Purdue laboratories are equipped with a room where students may take coffee breaks to relax and talk with other students.

The *general assembly* meets once a week and is used for activities best done in a large group—guest lectures, long films, major examinations. Attendance is not required except for special occasions.

The *integrated quiz session* takes place in small groups consisting of six to ten students and an instructor meeting once a week. In preparation for the session, each student is expected to prepare an explanation about each of the items in the study unit. This format has a number of advantages. It helps students integrate their knowledge by being required to "teach" it to others; it provides for the personal-social stimulation of discussion groups; it provides information for the continuing evaluation of course materials; and it gives instructors knowledge about the learning problems and strengths of individual students.

The system design of A-T departs from earlier attempts to apply science to education in that its emphasis is not on the development of a master machine that will do all things, but rather on the creation of a flexible master teaching system. The three types of learning sessions incorporated into A-T embody a number of educational principles. Postlethwait and his associates (Postlethwait, Novak, and Murray, 1969) point to seven ingredients of good learning conditions that they consider strengths of A-T:

1. Although *repetition* is necessary in education, the learner should be able to adjust the amount of repetition to his needs. The self-pacing feature of A-T permits students to repeat difficult concepts and to pass quickly over topics and skills that are easy for them.

2. Learning requires *concentration*. The A-T approach to learning permits students to select times when they are prepared to give full concentration and attention to the subject. Also, the private study carrel, with earphones shutting out other distractions, should be more conducive to concentration than the usual lecture or discussion class replete with distractions and opportunities to let the mind wander.

3. Meaningful learning requires *association*. The care given in A-T to planning the taped sequence of learning activities assures that students will have the appropriate background for incorporating new information. Furthermore, activities can be scheduled when they are most meaningful; for instance, the student can observe and handle a specimen or object as she

reads or hears about it, or she can conduct an experiment at the time when it has the most meaning in terms of the lesson to be learned.

4. The size of the *learning unit* should be adjustable to individual needs. As we shall see in the chapter on cognitive styles, some people are comfortable with large global concepts whereas others find small units more effective. While A-T offers no external reinforcement tied to learning units, such as the CAI reinforcement of "frames" or the mastery tests of learning modules, it does permit moderate self-pacing. The student performs the activities prescribed on the tape at her own pace, and the reinforcement occurs once a week in the weekly quiz sessions. In this sense, the "size" of the reinforced unit is relatively large—a week's work—and is the same for all students.

5. The form of *communication* should be adapted to the objective. Education has been heavily dependent upon the written and spoken word, but this exploits only a small portion of the spectrum of communication tools that we possess. Some things are done better by filmstrip, some are done best by manipulation of concrete objects, and so on. A-T places particular emphasis on using the media best designed to convey the message.

6. Because people differ in their responsiveness to media, A-T proposes a *multimedia* approach. Some people learn well through reading, others through listening, and still others through the manipulation of concrete objects. Provision is made in A-T for individual preferences for different kinds of activities and for the use of different sensory modalities.

7. The *integration* of learning activities is essential if meaningful learning is to occur. Postlethwait gives a great deal of attention to the importance of planning (and reworking) the sequence and proximity of various activities. Whereas conventional education may expose the student to a lecture on Monday, the lab on Wednesday, and textbook reading on Sunday evening, A-T permits an integrated sequence of activities that results in a synergistic effect.

In addition to these seven advantages specific to A-T, we should not forget that the A-T method shares the advantages of most modular learning systems. Since course objectives are clearly specified, teachers and students know what these objectives are and when competency has been attained. Learners are active participants in their own learning rather than passive observers of the teacher's activity. Finally, progress tests are given frequently, so that both student and teacher can evaluate performance.

While the advantages of A-T over conventional lecture classes are many, the A-T method also has some problems. Most of those cited by Postlethwait and his associates (1969) are attributed more to the inadequacy of the implementation than to the inadequacy of the method. Good objectives are, of course, necessary for all individualized instruction. The program of A-T will be no better than the programmer. If the tape consists of warmed-over lecture notes instead of a carefully planned sequence of learning activities, then A-T is not likely to be very effective (or very popular) with students. Likewise, if the learning materials (visuals, objects, experiments) are inadequate or inappropriate, A-T will fall short of its potential. The A-T method, properly used, has a built-in procedure for constant revision and improvement, and Postlethwait does not expect a first-generation A-T course to be optimally effective. Some faculty members, however, may lack the energy or initiative to continually improve their courses, just as some continue to use last year's lecture notes. "A poorly conceived course taught by the A-T method is still a poorly conceived course. A bad lecture put on tape is still just a bad lecture" (Ehrle, 1970, p. 103).

Some criticisms, however, are directed against the A-T method itself. Some claim that the step-by-step procedures of A-T rob the student of the initiative for learning how to plan his own study. This is a familiar complaint about all programmed instruction—whether it is the subject matter or student learning activities that are programmed. One answer, of course, is that A-T does force the student to take more responsibility for his own learning in terms of planning time. What it does not do is charge the student with the responsibility for the organization of his course time; that is done for him in the carefully programmed sequences of A-T. But one can argue that the organization of the subject matter is the responsibility of the teacher and that the integrated quiz sessions are the place for the student to practice organization and integration of the subject matter.

In any event, no one method is likely to meet all educational needs. A-T seems to have special advantages for use in the laboratory sciences, where it has had its greatest acclaim. In the natural sciences, where there is a body of factual knowledge to be learned and objects that can be manipulated, the use of such technologies as time-lapse photography and close-up visuals is of obvious merit. Although one can see appropriate uses for the method in the fine arts and the humanities, it will not come as close to "fitting" these disciplines as it does the sciences.

Another criticism directed against A-T is the impersonalization of the audio tape. Postlethwait (1971) specifically denies this charge, claiming that A-T actually enhances personal contact through more face-to-face conversations in the laboratory and quiz sessions. Indeed, one of the merits of A-T is that it helps to break down the anonymity of huge lecture classes. The advantages of A-T are undoubtedly greater for large classes than for small on grounds of both personalization and cost effectiveness. In small classes, teachers may be able to provide some degree of personal attention, and the costs and labor involved in setting up A-T may not be justified. Nevertheless, most proponents of A-T would insist that the work involved in stating objectives and sequencing learning and planning multimedia approaches is justified whatever the size of the class.

One of the criticisms that could be—and probably should be—directed at the promoters of A-T is the lack of evaluation and research on the method. Postlethwait and his colleagues have devoted most of their attention to describing A-T in considerable detail, even including suggested floor plans for the laboratory, procedures for record keeping, and instructions to new teaching assistants (Postlethwait, Novak, and Murray, 1969). Theirs is basically a pragmatic approach in which fairly widespread adoption, especially among fellow biologists, can be attributed largely to the existence of very explicit directions and testimonials about how well the program works. Little attention is given to known research and theory on learning, and what little research there is is at a fairly simple conceptual level. There is plenty of evidence that most students prefer the A-T approach (Doty, 1974; Morman, 1971; Richason, 1971; Wilson, 1972), and there is fairly good evidence that students learn as well as or better than they do in conventional classes (Morman, 1971; Richason, 1971; Wilson, 1972). What we do not know, after fifteen years of existence of A-T, is which students profit most from A-T, which students are not helped, and how A-T can be improved and made more broadly applicable. Is A-T just a more efficient method for learning facts which are soon forgotten? Are there side effects of A-T that we are not aware of? What is the relative merit of the various components of A-T?

Although it seems to work in selective universities, A-T has not yet made much impact on community college teaching. What happens when the method is transported to the much more diverse student population of the community colleges, where student motivation is a serious problem? In their use of A-T at the community college level, McDonald and Dodge (1971) admit that problems of student motivation come into sharp focus. A few interesting forays into the merit of A-T for New Students have been made. Wilson (1972), for example, found that freshmen students in an A-T course in mathematics at Florida Agriculture and Mechanical University felt that they were at least as good in mathematics as in other academic subjects (93 percent to 60 percent for the conventional approach to teaching mathematics), increased their confidence in their mathematical ability over the term (63 percent to 43 percent for the conventional), and were willing to take another course in mathematics (63 percent to 33 percent). Furthermore, students seemed to feel that A-T has special merit for students who usually have difficulty with mathematics. If Wilson's findings can be replicated in community college courses and locations, A-T and variations thereof would have enormous potential for use with New Students.

Personalized System of Instruction (PSI)

The personalized system of instruction (PSI), in contrast to A-T, is well grounded in the research and theory of learning, and its promise for adding to our understanding of the learning process is potentially very great. Whereas Postlethwait and his colleagues improve A-T courses primarily through concentrating on better organization of the subject matter, Keller and Sherman, two of the originators of PSI, improve PSI courses through the application of learning principles. The difference in orientation, no doubt, reflects the disciplinary orientation of the men. Postlethwait is a biologist interested in teaching his subject more effectively; Keller and Sherman are psychologists interested in the learning process. While PSI looks like A-T in some respects, the two systems are different in emphasis and rationale. PSI is a little younger than A-T, having been initiated at the University of Brasilia in 1964 and introduced broadly into this country through an address given by Fred Keller to the American Psychological Association (Keller, 1968). Today, the activities of the burgeoning PSI movement are coordinated through the Center for Personalized Instruction located at Georgetown University in Washington, D.C., and directed by one of the originators of PSI, J. Gilmour Sherman.

Before we discuss the features and rationale behind the Personalized System of Instruction, also known as the Keller Plan, it may prove useful to present a brief description of the procedures of a PSI course. Typically, the course is broken down into fifteen or twenty self-paced learning modules, with learning objectives clearly spelled out by the instructor in a study guide. Using the guide and traditional materials of education such as textbooks, articles, and other printed materials, the student masters each learning unit, taking as much or as little time as needed, studying wherever and whenever convenient. When she feels prepared, she presents herself to a student proctor, typically an undergraduate student who has already mastered the material, for testing. The test is a fifteen- to twenty-minute short-answer quiz which the student must pass at a high level of competence, indicating mastery of all the objectives of the learning unit. The test is graded immediately in the student's presence. If she fails to pass, the student proctor may quiz her further to determine areas of difficulty, may help her with special problems, or may refer her for further study. There is no penalty for failing to pass the mastery tests, but the learner may proceed to the next unit only after demonstrating mastery of prior units. Lectures and demonstrations are not required but are used to inspire and motivate. In fact, students must earn admission to the lectures, which are few in number, by mastering all the units required for a particular lecture.

This, then, is the basic outline of a PSI course of instruction. These procedures grow out of five fundamental characteristics of the PSI system.

1. The stress is primarily on the written word. Unlike A-T, which emphasizes a multimedia approach, PSI is fairly traditional as far as the tools for learning are concerned. Textbooks and other readings, supplemented by study guides which program the course into learning units, are the standard materials. While other media may be introduced, they are not of fundamental importance in PSI. Like A-T, however, PSI does place importance on defining clearly and explicitly the objectives of the course. Ruskin (1974, pp. 8-9) notes, "If the student doesn't know what is important for him to learn in a given area of content, and the instructor can't clarify what is important, then the learning process will be inefficient and ineffective."

2. Mastery learning is an essential concept in PSI. The student must demonstrate mastery of one learning unit before proceeding to the next. True to the principles of reinforcement theory, positive reward is a more powerful motivator for learning than punishment, and the learning of complex behaviors consists of mastering and shaping prior behaviors. Theoretically, PSI gives an A (reward) for mastery and would ignore or give an incomplete (avoidance of punishment) for failure to achieve mastery. Reinforcement theory, which is the backbone of PSI, demands that the appropriate response be elicited and that it be rewarded immediately and consistently. In the words of Keller (1974b, pp. 52-53), "From [reinforcement theory] it follows

that any 'learning situation' in which the task is not identified or is unclear, in which the critical behavior is or can be absent, and in which the rewards are not assured is not a learning situation in the proper meaning of the term. This eliminates from serious consideration as a teaching method the usual lecture, the usual classroom demonstration, the usual discussion group, and the usual assignment of a paper to be written. In none of these is the behavior guaranteed or optimal reinforcement provided, even when the tasks are well defined."

3. Self-pacing is an obvious and necessary accompaniment of mastery learning. Individual differences in learning academic skills do exist, and if the level of achievement is to be held constant at mastery, then the time for learning will have to vary. This is the revolutionary feature of mastery learning and the feature that makes incorporation of PSI into the traditional education difficult; it upsets accepted notions about semesters as the proper units of time and grades as the proper measures of achievement. Most individualized instruction systems find it necessary to compromise on self-pacing to some extent. PSI, however, gives considerably more latitude on time than does A-T, for example. Self-pacing in A-T is ordinarily by the week; that is, while students may pace themselves in their study carrel, they must all be ready for the integrated quiz session by the end of the week. In PSI, students may remain out of step throughout most of the semester, unless they desire the special privilege of attending a lecture or unless they are in a system that tolerates liberal time arrangements beyond the usual quarter or semester.

4. Lectures are used for motivation rather than for information. The retention of lectures in PSI is more a concession to tradition than a feature arising out of any learning theory. Lectures were used to disseminate information to groups of learners before the invention of the printing press, and custom continues to demand that the professor demonstrate his or her knowledge through the lecture. Keller (1974a) frankly admits that the lecture could be eliminated without damage, and experience is proving that when attendance at lectures is optional, students do not attend consistently or in large numbers. The research is

showing that PSI lectures are rated relatively unimportant, whether judged for their actual contribution to student learning (Calhoun, 1973) or whether valued by students for pure enjoyment or for perceived importance to learning (Nelson and Scott, 1974). Nevertheless, lectures are held to have some merit in PSI programs. They offer the opportunity to get the entire class together occasionally, and they give faculty members a chance to appear at their inspirational best before a well-prepared audience. Furthermore, the role model of the scholar presenting an articulate overview of some aspect of his or her discipline may be of considerable importance to students. Regardless of the emphasis placed by any given instructor on lectures, the role of the professor is changed substantially in PSI from that of lecturer and grader to that of organizer of materials, course manager, and confederate in learning.

5. The use of student proctors is considered one of the most important features of PSI. Proctors are usually undergraduate students (or occasionally graduate students) who serve as peer tutors. This emphasis on the personal-social aspects of learning distinguishes PSI from most other systems of individualized instruction. In one sense, it is ironic that the method of individualized instruction that is most firmly grounded in behavioristic reinforcement theory should be the one to stress the necessity for the human touch. In behavioristic terms, personal attention is a basic human reward, but the heavy reliance on peer tutors also seems a sophisticated admission that there is much that is not known about the learning process, and that the "intuition" and "sensitivities" of the proctors are a necessary adjunct to a scientific approach to teaching and learning. PSI makes a point of a "personalized" rather than an "individualized" approach to learning. While components such as self-pacing and mastery learning provide for individual differences and are in that sense individualized approaches to learning, it takes interpersonal interactions to *personalize* education.

The Keller Plan or PSI has grown rapidly in the last five years, especially in psychology, physics, and engineering. By 1972, there were reputedly 877 PSI courses in psychology alone (see Kulik, Kulik, and Carmichael, 1974), and most observers concede that the greatest growth for PSI has occurred since 1972. Nevertheless, it has not yet been introduced extensively into community colleges; only 22 percent of the colleges responding to the 1974 survey used it in one or more fields of study (Appendix A). It appears to have a rather unusual potential for further growth for several reasons. In the first place, it has a center that serves as a clearinghouse to disseminate and synthesize information about PSI. Three recent publications from the center (Keller and Sherman, 1974b; Ruskin, 1974; Sherman, 1974c) tell you almost everything you ever wanted to know about PSI. In addition, the center conducts workshops and keeps people in touch with each other and with developments in PSI through a newsletter. Second, the reliance of PSI on the traditional resources of education, books, and people makes it easier to implement than systems requiring computers or extensive revision of texts and other materials. Third, PSI seems to have broad applicability across disciplines. The booklet containing forty-one germinal papers on PSI (Sherman, 1974c), for example, boasts authors from departments of psychology, physics, engineering, mathematics, philosophy, education, human development, library science, chemistry, statistics, and foreign languages. While most of the writing has been done by faculty from four-year institutions, Sherman (1974f) reports a broad spectrum of types and levels of educational institutions represented at PSI workshops. Finally, and perhaps most important, PSI has generated the research that is essential for growth and improvement. There are over three hundred papers, articles, and research reports on PSI (Sherman, 1974f), and more are on the way. The origin of PSI in psychology, whose business it is to study the learning process, is no doubt responsible for its enviable record of research.

Research. It is rare, in educational research, to find such clear findings as those reported in the PSI literature. There is substantial agreement in the research that students learn more under PSI approaches than they do in conventional classes, and they like it better. In reviewing PSI research, I started to take careful notes on the design and findings of various research studies, so that agreements and conflicts could be reported and conclusions, if any, teased from this analysis. I soon discovered that if PSI is working in the class at all—that is, if students continue to move toward completion of the units—PSI students do perform better than students in conventional classes on typical content-oriented final examinations, and they are quite unequivocal in their endorsement of PSI over conventional approaches. Most of these highly favorable findings, however, have occurred in science classes, or classes with equally concise subject matter, and mostly with students who are above average in academic achievement (for instance, in university classes rather than community college classes). More will be said about these limitations later.

A few examples should suffice to demonstrate the research conclusions with respect to student achievement and enthusiasm. McMichael and Corey (1969) compared a PSI course in introductory psychology with three control groups learning through conventional fifty-minute lecture sessions meeting three times a week. The average scores out of a possible fifty points on the final examination were 35, 34, and 34 for the control groups and 40 for the PSI group. The performance of the PSI students shows a significant statistical superiority. Course ratings followed a similar pattern. Out of a possible ten points, PSI students gave their course a mean rating of 9, compared with mean ratings of 5, 6, and 7 for the control groups. Furthermore, follow-up studies conducted nineteen weeks and ten months after course completion showed significantly better retention for students learning to mastery under the conditions of PSI.

Hoberock and his associates (1974) report similar results for the use of PSI in engineering. The final examination scores for a PSI course in electrical engineering averaged 84 percent, compared with 75 percent, 74 percent, and 73 percent for the last three times the course was taught by the lecture method. Most students also liked the PSI course better, as indicated by the following percentages considering "PSI better than the lecture method": 72 percent for the PSI class in nuclear engineering, 64 percent in the mechanical engineering class, 91 percent in electrical engineering, and 59 percent in applied statistics.

Myers (1974) asked a University of Wisconsin class in statistics to compare the PSI approach used in his class with conventional lecture methods. Judgments on each of eighteen questions favored PSI by a substantial margin, with students especially laudatory about the amount of material fully understood, their confidence in solving statistical problems, and their lack of boredom in the PSI-taught class. The features that students liked most about the class were self-pacing, receipt of positive reinforcement for each unit, and having immediate knowledge of test results.

Admittedly, the evaluation of student learning is a complex matter, and all manner of uncontrolled and uncontrollable variables enter into even the best of experimental designs. Nevertheless, it seems quite safe to adopt the conservatively stated conclusion reached by Kulik and his associates (Kulik, Kulik, and Carmichael, 1974, p. 383), who reviewed some 261 papers and reports on PSI: "On the basis of present evidence it can be concluded that content learning (as measured by final examinations) is adequate in Keller courses. In published studies, content learning under the Keller Plan always equals, and most often exceeds, content learning under the lecture method." Ruskin's (1974) review of the literature also endorses the superiority of PSI courses and places the increase in student achievement at from 10 to 15 percent over traditional lecture approaches.

The summarization of student ratings of PSI is not as complex, from the standpoint of research design, as the evaluation of learning. It is quite clear and uncontroversial that students generally prefer the PSI model to the lecture model: "In every published report, students rate the Keller Plan much more favorably than teaching by lecture" (Kulik, Kulik, and Carmichael, 1974, p. 383). Similarly, according to Sherman (1974f, p. 62): "The student preference for PSI courses approaches 90 percent, and the grades in PSI courses are typically higher than those in traditional courses."

While positive results predominate in the literature, an occasional article appears that shows no significant difference between experimental and control groups. For example, Harris and Liguori (1974), in a study that appears well designed and well researched, found that counting final examination scores in the grade had a more positive influence on achievement (as measured by the final examination) than whether the course was taught by PSI or conventional means. As they observe, however, the · control groups offered some of the PSI advantages, since the classes were small, daily homework assignments were required, and weekly quizzes were given. Thus, in a sense, these classes approximated the personalized attention and frequent feedback that are the hallmarks of PSI, and the differences between PSI and conventional lecture classes were minimized.

With hundreds of reports of favorable comparisons of PSI to traditional courses, Nelson and Scott (1974, p. 37) correctly point out that "comparisons of personalized courses with other course formats has well enough demonstrated the advantages of the personalized model to make further collection of similar data redundant." To the credit of those in the PSI movement, however, they have not rested on their laurels after demonstrating some substantial advantages for their method. They are now attempting to understand the relative importance and contributions of the PSI components, a necessary first step to improvement. Since most of the research on PSI components has addressed the problems, both theoretical and practical, encountered in implementation, it is possible to incorporate research findings into a discussion of the problems of PSI.

Problems. Despite the generally favorable experiences with PSI, no one should be led to believe that the implementation of PSI is without its problems and failures. In a few instances PSI—more commonly, SLI (Something Like It) modifications—has produced spectacular failures. Szydlik (1974) describes with candor the failure of PSI in his physics course: only three students out of twenty-eight even finished the course during the semester. He paints a picture of demoralized students and proctors, and concludes, "Course results, student attitudes, the (not entirely unjustified) skepticism of colleagues, and the contrast of self-paced physics with a similarly conducted psychology course which is progressing swimmingly have damaged significantly the psyche of this instructor" (p. 127). Sherman (1974d), a cofounder of PSI, admits that he cannot see what Szydlik did wrong, but it does indicate that success in PSI is not automatic.

Another heart-wrenching failure is reported by Goldman, Wade, and Zegar (1974), who launched a self-paced learning experiment that departed in some ways from PSI. Their problem with self-pacing, however, is so vivid that it lends credence to the advice offered by most PSI advocates—namely, that instructors should not depart from the standard PSI formula the first time PSI is offered (Sherman, 1974e). The greatest departure in the Goldman, Wade, Zegar course was probably in the size of the learning unit offered; they used three units instead of the fifteen to twenty recommended. Whether that seemingly small departure played the significant role in their failure may never be known, but failure it surely was: *"Most students never came even close to completing the three units of the course"* (p. 199, emphasis in the original); and half of the students who did complete any of the units were either somewhat or very dissatisfied; less than one fourth of the relatively successful students expressed satisfaction.

Failures, however, are rare in the PSI literature. While not everyone possesses the candor and courage to write his failures in journals for the world to see, we can still assume that total course failures are not a common experience. The total collapse depicted in these two articles should warn PSI first-timers that a good deal of work and understanding of the method are necessary for successful implementation. There is, however, considerable discussion in the literature of less all-encompassing problems with the implementation of PSI courses.

One of the most disturbing problems with PSI has to do with its greatest advantage—the self-pacing feature. Students have both the privilege and the burden of assuming major responsibility for their own learning, and some students are apparently not ready for or comfortable with that responsibility. While students give self-pacing top ranking among course features contributing to their enjoyment of learning (Nelson and Scott, 1974) and the majority claim that they do not find the burdens of self-pacing frustrating (Hoberock and others, 1974), 71 percent of the faculty respondents to a recent survey reported difficulty with student procrastination (*PSI Newsletter,* June 1974, p. 3). Perhaps, however, as Keller and Sherman (1974a) point out, our own ingrained notion that students should finish a course in a given time period has *created* the procrastination problem. That is, if we did not have predetermined ideas about how long learning should take, we would not be labeling those who take longer "procrastinators." In addition, perhaps our traditional courses encourage procrastination and its inevitable partner, cramming the week or night before the examination. For a conventional course, with a midterm and a final examination, it may actually be good grade-getting strategy to study intensively just before the examination so that forgetting does not have an opportunity to occur until *after* the test period. The concept of mastery learning requires a totally different approach on the part of students, and they may have to unlearn some of the strategies that they have learned in the traditional system. Finally, when a self-paced course exists among traditional courses, students are tempted to meet the time demands of the other courses by neglecting the course that makes no rigid external demands.

The literature is full of suggestions for dealing with student procrastination. Gallup (1971) suggests that we avoid the "doomsday contingency," which requires students to finish by a certain date or else. Keller and Sherman (1974a) suggest that the first learning units be made short, interesting, and relatively easy, so that the student gets a good start in the course. Roth (1973) requires students to come to class to study during the first learning units; this positive start, he says, produces the momentum necessary to keep the student progressing. Dessler (1974) advocates setting an early deadline for the completion of the first unit, so that everyone gets started. The notion behind all of these approaches is that "nothing succeeds like success." The student who experiences success in the early units will continue to work for success in the later units.

The importance of getting New Students (low achievers) off to a good start through experiencing early success can hardly be overemphasized. (See Chapter Two in Cross, 1971.) Students who have not experienced success in school-related tasks are especially likely candidates for problems with procrastination and subsequent withdrawal. Protopapas (1974, p. 103) quotes an insightful statement made by one of his students: "I think this type of course is good for a smart student, but not so good for a slow or, at times, lazy student like myself, because it is very easy to fall behind." The orientation of students to PSI, the careful preparation of the study guide, the personal attention provided by the instructor and proctors should all be geared to special attention in the *early* units for New Students. The momentum gained through initial success should sustain the student until at least the midterm, when Dessler suggests another gentle prod consisting of a one-hour open-book midterm examination covering the first few units but not counting toward the final grade. A partial compromise between reward and punishment used by Gallup (1971) is to place an upper limit on the number of units that can be earned in the later weeks of the semester—or one could give greater rewards for work earned early in the semester. Either of these schemes probably has to compromise the grading system to some extent, since grades serve as the standard rewards and punishments of education. These examples serve to illustrate the interrelatedness of the PSI system; as soon as modifications are made in one component, other components are necessarily affected.

The problem of student withdrawals is closely related to that of procrastination, since it is frequently those with poor study habits who withdraw. Of great concern to open-door colleges, already struggling with the problem of keeping New Students in college, is the charge that the withdrawal rates are higher for PSI courses than for courses with greater external controls (Born, 1971; Keller, 1968; McMichael and Corey, 1969; Sheppard and MacDermot, 1970). Specifically, poor to mediocre students withdraw in greater numbers from PSI courses than good students (Born, Gledhill, and Davis, 1974; Sheppard and MacDermot, 1970)—but that should come as no surprise to anyone working with New Students. There has not been enough study of whether New Students are more likely to withdraw from a well-managed PSI course (with its built-in personal attention and tutoring help) than from a well-run traditional course (with its greater emphasis on external control). Nevertheless, faculty working with New Students need to be especially alert to lagging students in the very early phases of a PSI course—even if it means compromising to some extent the ideals of PSI in granting the freedom to fail in the management of one's own learning. Perhaps during the early stages extra administrative and tutoring help should be engaged to call students, write postcards, and in general be rather aggressive in trying to determine what problems the student is having with the course. One highly successful physics course at Harvard is "loaded" with extra checkpoints—small-unit tests and periodic review tests—on the grounds that "the only serious learning is done right before tests" (Papke, 1973, p. 19). While students in a Harvard physics course are markedly different from typical community college students, lack of self-discipline may be a common problem for many students.

One problem in the implementation of PSI courses has to do with grades. An instructor who submits grades that depart significantly from the bell-shaped normal curve will have some explaining to do. Theoretically, any student who "masters" the course content should be given an A, and everyone else should get an incomplete until such time as mastery is demonstrated. In actual practice, PSI gears the grade to the number of units completed; and most, including the original Keller (1968) formula, permit 25 percent of the grade to be determined by the final examination. Most students in PSI courses make A grades, and most PSI teachers are careful to "prove" to their colleagues that A students in PSI courses know as much content as A students in conventional courses. In fact, Sherman (1974b) suggests that the inevitable challenge to the grading distribution is one dandy reason for keeping a final examination. If a final exists in PSI courses, even though it may be considered not totally consistent with PSI philosophy, student performance can be demonstrated and the number of A's defended. There will still be those, however, who feel that education is not providing future employers and graduate schools with adequate evaluations of the *relative* potential of students if the normal curve is not adhered to. To put it even stronger, there are those who will not tolerate "too many" A's. One administration flatly rejected the PSI grading scheme that had been explained to students and insisted that something closer to the normal curve be submitted (Sherman, 1974e).

Closely related to the grading distribution of PSI is the problem of defining "mastery." Sherman (1974e) argues that a 70 percent criterion is unacceptable. When students are not punished for errors, it becomes reasonable to demand excellence, and to most PSI instructors that means 90 percent correct. Where performance standards are set is an important issue in working with New Students. Young people who have a record of poor school performance have never, after the first few years of elementary school, been expected to do as well as others in the class, and the situation rapidly deteriorates to a self-fulfilling prophecy, robbing students of self-respect and compromising educational standards. Block (1972) has conducted an extremely interesting investigation of the cognitive and affective effects of setting the criterion at 65, 75, 85, or 95 percent. He found that the 95 percent criterion resulted in the greatest cognitive advantages in terms of achievement, retention, transfer of knowledge, and learning efficiency but at some cost in student attitudes and interests. The 85 percent criterion seemed to best maximize the affective impact of mastery learning, while the 95 percent criterion maximized the cognitive component. Thus, the 90 percent criterion advocated by PSI seems to be a mastery criterion that enables students to achieve high levels of cognitive learning while enjoying their accomplishments.

An administrative problem in implementing PSI is one of finding and training undergraduate proctors. (The Center for Research on Learning and Teaching at the University of Michigan is developing a course for undergraduate proctors in PSI courses. It is in the PSI format, with eight learning modules covering the proctors' roles as instructional assistant, tutor, and quiz evaluator.) It is the proctors who "personalize" PSI; without them, the system cannot operate. Green (1974, p. 118) goes so far as to write that if "you can't get undergraduate tutors for love, credit, or money," you may as well forget about PSI unless the class is very small.

The essential function of the proctor is to provide the personal attention that makes a "teaching method something more than a device for inculcating knowledge or imparting skills, however important these may be" (Keller, 1974b, p. 54). Occasionally, graduate students have been used as proctors; but Keller, as well as PSI instructors to follow later, found them unsatisfactory because of their tendency to lecture to students and to appear as knowledgeable young professionals rather than to provide simple feedback and human concern. Thus, the typical proctor today is an undergraduate student who completed the course in a previous semester. Later research has validated the decision to use undergraduate students (Born and Herbert, 1971).

While Green (1974) testifies that finding proctors for lower-division courses is no problem in four-year colleges, the situation may be very different in two-year colleges. The literature is silent on proctoring problems in two-year colleges, probably because PSI is just getting started there and experience is limited. We would anticipate more problems in two-year institutions because the pool of students who have completed the course is not great, and the work schedules of many community college students may leave little time or flexibility to engage in proctoring activities. There are, however, several promising variations that might be suggested.

One such variation was initially suggested as a way of solving the problem of compensating proctors for their work. A survey of PSI instructors shows that most proctors are given course credit for their work—on the grounds that proctoring is a legitimate learning experience. But 43 percent of the proctors are paid (*PSI Newsletter,* June 1974, p. 5). Sherman (1974b) admits that money is an attractive reward to proctors, but he advises against it on the grounds that PSI courses, once introduced into a department, have a way of spreading. If pay gets established as the proper reward, it can have a serious impact on department budgets. He suggests the use of "internal proctors,".

students in the PSI class who are one or two units ahead of the students they proctor. Since the same students do not always remain out in front, "rotating proctors" is the result. This variation seems an ideal solution for community colleges for several reasons. It solves the problem of recruiting and compensating external proctors, who may be in short supply in commuter community colleges. More than that, proctoring can be an important experience for community college students. It helps them to learn more and to review and integrate their learning; most important, it permits them to serve in a role where they are looked up to—a not very common experience for many New Students. The experience of helping others to learn may be one of the most important experiences of the student's entire college career in both cognitive and affective respects. Most community colleges are working hard to provide their students with experiences that will generate feelings of self-respect and that will help students to feel that their contributions are valuable. Peer tutoring has been adopted with enthusiasm by the majority of community colleges—65 percent, according to the 1974 survey (Appendix A). Experienced faculty and staff claim that the tutoring experience does as much for the tutor as for the tutee. (For an exception to this rule, see Harris and Liguori, 1974.) Colleges serving first-generation New Students should look to the use of internal proctors as an idea well worth trying. (See Sherman, 1971, for further discussion.)

Just how much proctoring is necessary or desirable is a question that has received some research attention. Farmer and his associates (1972) found that the 100 percent reinforcement advocated in PSI may not be necessary. While proctoring was found clearly superior to nonproctoring (providing test results but no personal attention), proctoring every test did not seem to provide significantly better performance than proctoring only one fourth of the tests. While research suggests that some savings in personnel time could be realized through the use of intermittent rather than continuous proctoring, further research is needed on the subject. The use of easy examinations in the study may have been responsible for their findings.

Another variation on the theme of proctoring has been

introduced by Ferster (1974). He incorporates an interview into the proctoring function. Students take turns presenting or listening to a summary of ten to fifteen pages of text. Ferster describes the interview as follows:

> The interview is a formal arrangement in which the listener, who has already read that part of the text, uses a timer and listens to the speaker without interruptions. Both students refer to text or notes as they speak. After the speaker finishes talking, the listener comments on how the speaker covered the topic of the text, mentions important omissions, corrects inaccuracies of concept or language, or converses on some aspect of the subject matter. If both students are satisfied that the interview shows mastery of the text, they record the results on a class chart and the speaker finds another student to whom he speaks; if not, the speaker restudies the part and repeats the interview. Each student is required to listen once for each time he speaks. At the end of three to five sections (a chapter), the student takes a brief quiz to demonstrate his mastery of the course.... The written exercises are graded by the section assistant, and if the essay is satisfactory, the student goes on to do interviews on the next chapter. If it is not, a remedial procedure is discussed with the instructor or section assistant [p. 189].

This variation, too, appears to have promise for two-year colleges. It has the merit of forcing interviewers actively to consolidate their knowledge and understanding into an articulate summary that communicates to a listener. The experience gives practice in the art of communication—a skill quite inadequately developed in many New Students.

Still another variation that might be appropriate in community colleges is the use of the standard external proctoring system originally proposed by Keller, but with course credit granted for experience in situations calling for interpersonal skills. A thesis of this book is that we can and should educate people for careers demanding high interpersonal skills. Students who have the talent and desire to achieve excellence in human relations might use proctoring opportunities where possible as a sort of mini-internship in the domain of working with people.

The Keller Plan and other forms of individualized instruction have enough substance in terms of learning theory and research that they would make a logical second-year class subject in which students receive credit for cognitive understandings of human learning plus practical experience in working with other people through proctoring experiences. This should have the multiple advantages of providing an unusually well-motivated and well-qualified pool of proctors who are adding to their own learning.

We really have not had enough experience with New Students and PSI to know whether it will work or not. There is mixed evidence as to whether low-achieving students have difficulty with the responsibilities and self-discipline required by PSI (Connolly and Sepe, 1973; Goldman, Wade, and Zegar, 1974; Myers, 1974). But PSI appears to have many advantages for the open-admissions students whose characteristics are described in *Beyond the Open Door* (Cross, 1971). In the first place, the division of the courses into small concrete learning units with clearly specified objectives is of great help to learners who typically have difficulty selecting the important from the unimportant and concentrating their attention for more than short work spans. Second, the opportunity to succeed—the "guaranteed success" of PSI—is an essential first step to working with the "turned-off" attitudes of New Students, who have experienced mostly failure in the school system. Third, given the generally poor but spotty backgrounds of most New Students, peer tutoring is an advantage that most community college teachers already know about from personal experience. Fourth, the sometimes complicated work and commuting schedules of community college students make the self-pacing feature a huge advantage. But topping all of these considerable advantages is the self-confidence that is engendered in students who succeed through their own efforts. In my opinion, the "social promotion" policies, whereby students are pushed along in the school system because no one thinks they can learn anyway, have rendered a huge disservice to New Students. Some college instructors are perpetuating the evil by their misguided efforts to see that "disadvantaged" students receive some of the advantages of their more fortunate peers—even if those advantages are simply credentials rather than educational competence. Where *mastery of subject matter* is the goal, it would be hard to find a more promising approach on the scene now than PSI.

This brings us to one of the most serious challenges to PSI. Mastery of subject matter is *not* the ultimate goal of all education. In fact, most educators do not accept a mission of turning out "walking encyclopedias"—even if they *could* stimulate that much factual learning. While most teachers are trapped by tradition into teaching content and measuring achievement in terms of content, few believe that knowledge of the content of their discipline is an adequate measure of the student's education. Green (1974) is frank to admit that the goal of some courses is to provide an *experience* rather than to master a subject matter. For such courses, he sees "no possibility of or motive for using the Keller Plan to teach them" (p. 118). There is, however, an in-between ground, where the goal is neither to "provide an experience" nor to "cram facts into the student's head" but rather to teach intellectual skills such as analysis, problem solving, and creativity. The common complaint against most courses using behavioral objectives is that they are fine for facts but poor for higher-order intellectual skills. The criticism is neither new nor limited to PSI. Before we land too heavily on PSI, we should ask just what we do to teach the "higher-order intellectual skills" in traditional courses, but it is still fair to ask people who claim to have found a better way to solve old as well as new problems in education.

Until we have some better measures of creativity and problem-solving ability, we cannot say what *any* form of education does or does not do to develop these skills. While PSI researchers seem to have had as much trouble as anyone else in measuring intellectual skills as opposed to academic content, there are some data that bear on the question. Morris and Kimbrell (1972) found that PSI students outperformed students in a traditional class on the recall and application items of the final—as opposed to recognition items, which are presumably more "rote." Sheppard and MacDermot (1970) report a similar finding; PSI students outperformed others when essay rather than multiple choice questions were used as performance criteria. Sheppard and MacDermot also found that students reported more stimulation to work, more effective interactions with other students, and more interest in pursuing further study in the area—none of which sound like rote learning outcomes. Ruskin (1974, p. 25) concludes, "A considerable amount of research seems to verify that PSI is effective in courses stressing the acquisition of complex academic repertoires." He admits, however, the need for further study. There is large agreement, inside and outside the PSI movement, that no one knows the impact of various teaching methods on the learning of high-level intellectual skills. All that we can realistically say now is that PSI is no more deficient in this realm than anything else.

Nevertheless, PSI does emphasize content learning. Although its advocates claim that it has been used successfully in subjects such as philosophy, history, and art (Keller, 1974c), its greatest success and widest use has without question been in subjects having a "hard" content, such as the sciences and psychology. Interestingly enough, these are also the subjects in which factual knowledge is most quickly outdated. Critics raise just this issue when they ask whether academic content is the proper stuff of education. Some people, including most college students (Peterson, 1973), think that there is too much emphasis now on the teaching of academic knowledge in the disciplines. If PSI is simply a way to make faster progress down the wrong path, then it hardly represents progress. This is, I believe, a valid concern, and it is treated more fully in Chapter Six. Suffice it to say here that no technique and no curriculum is sufficient unto itself in higher education. We must learn to use both knowledge and talent for the jobs for which they are uniquely suited. PSI seems uniquely well suited to teaching for mastery learning.

Conclusions

Two rather complete systems of individualized instruction have been presented in this section—the audio-tutorial method and the Keller Plan or PSI. Although both systems

build heavily on the concepts of mastery learning and programmed instruction, they are different in features and points
of emphasis. The audio-tutorial is multimedia, whereas PSI
emphasizes print. Each has its advantages and disadvantages.
The audio-tutorial method has obvious advantages for labora-
tory-oriented subjects, where handling specimens, conducting
experiments, and viewing biological processes on film are important parts of the course. The multimedia approach of audio-
tutorial also has important advantages for students who have
reading difficulties and those who learn more easily with a large
amount of variety and physical activity. The emphasis on the
written word of PSI has advantages too, however, especially for
nonlaboratory courses. No special equipment is required, and
students can do their studying at home, in their dormitories, or
even on the subway. Furthermore, since most education is still
conducted via the written word, familiarity with the medium is
conducive to lifelong learning.

Another important difference between audio-tutorial and
PSI lies in the form of the provision for interpersonal experiences. The audio-tutorial method capitalizes on the advantages
of the small discussion group, whereas PSI offers the advantages
of the personal attention provided by student proctors. The
integrated quiz session of audio-tutorial requires students to
integrate their learning and to gain practice in communicating
their knowledge to others. In addition, certain aspects of small-
group interactions cannot be duplicated in one-to-one relationships. Whereas the variety and breadth of human interaction
may be greater in the group sessions of audio-tutorial, the depth
and personal support may be stronger in the tutorials of PSI. We
should not forget either about the considerable advantages that
accrue to the proctors in the PSI system. These students almost
always have a rich and rewarding experience.

Finally, the self-pacing functions of PSI are considerably
more flexible than those of audio-tutorial. The PSI student may
pace himself or herself through the semester, or two or three
semesters, whereas the audio-tutorial student must keep up with
the class week by week in order to take advantage of the integrated quiz sessions at the end of each week. Which approach an
instructor chooses appears to be largely a matter of subject field

and personal preference. It must be noted, however, that the research evidence and the theory base are considerably stronger for PSI than for A-T. But this is more the result of the *positive* evidence in favor of PSI than of any *negative* results for A-T.

The disadvantage of all the approaches to individualized instruction reviewed in Chapters Three and Four is what I perceive to be an overemphasis on the teaching of content. Admittedly, the individualized systems are highly effective ways to teach the traditional academic disciplines. Admittedly also, students must have a solid base of knowledge before they can engage their minds in the higher intellectual processes. I am concerned, however, about the strength and the potential power of the individualized systems. If we get rid of the many "inefficiencies" of the classroom, we may inadvertently be discarding the unidentifiable "something" in the academic environment that stimulates great and even lesser minds to unusual accomplishments and cognitive satisfactions. While we are a long way from adopting *universal* individualization of instruction, there can be too much of even a very good thing. Diversity is a to-be-prized value in education, especially with our inadequate knowledge about the learning process.

✳✳✳ 5 ✳✳✳

Cognitive Styles

✳✳✳✳✳✳✳✳✳✳✳✳✳✳✳✳✳✳✳✳✳✳✳✳✳✳✳✳✳✳✳✳✳✳✳✳✳

Most of the creative energy that has gone into the instructional revolution so far has been directed toward the seemingly modest goal of breaking the lockstep of education with respect to time requirements. And as we saw in Chapters Three and Four, the simple expedient of giving students control over the *rate* of presentation results in improved learning for many students. But the problem of individual differences is more complicated than dividing people into "fast" and "slow" learners. People are fast learners in one subject perhaps and slow in another, or they learn rapidly by one method and more slowly when a different approach is used. I may learn rapidly by being shown, for example, but slowly if I must read a manual of instructions. Cronbach (1967) urges attention to the *interaction* of learning rate with other learning variables.

It now seems clear that we are not going to improve instruction by finding *the* method or methods that are good for all people. The research on teaching effectiveness has been inconclusive and disappointing because, I suspect, we were asking the wrong questions. When we ask whether discussion is

111

better than lecture, whether television is as good as a live teacher, whether programmed instruction is an improvement over more traditional methods, we find that for that mythical statistical *average* student it seems to make little difference how we teach. But when we look at the data student by student, it is clear that some students improve, some remain unaffected, and a few actually regress under various teaching conditions. The very process of averaging the pluses, the minuses, and the non-changers wipes out the message that different methods work for different students. Psychologists are now asking the more sophisticated interaction questions about learning styles—which methods work for which students?

It takes no special knowledge of research to recognize that we all have characteristic "styles" for collecting and organizing information into useful knowledge. Some people do their best learning in interaction with others, some in lone study and contemplation. Some people prefer to learn a skill by manipulating concrete objects, some by watching, some by listening, some by reading the manual of instructions. Some people approach learning tasks systematically and methodically; others are more intuitive and global. In brief, people have characteristic ways of using their minds. Psychologists label these mental characteristics *cognitive styles,* and their importance to education is fundamental and pervasive: "Cognitive style is a potent variable in students' academic choices and vocational preferences; in students' academic development through their school career; in how students learn and teachers teach; and in how students and teachers interact in the classroom" (Witkin, 1973, p. 1).

Unfortunately, not one teacher or counselor in a hundred knows anything at all about cognitive styles despite the fact that research on cognitive styles has been going on for some twenty-five years in psychology laboratories. For some reason, the research has not been widely applied to educational problems. Kogan (1971, p. 243) politely understates the case when he observes that until recently there was an "almost total lack of articulation . . . between the psychological study of cognition, on the one hand, and educational research and practice, on the other. Cognition, after all, refers to the process by which knowledge is acquired: perception, memory, thinking, and imagery—and one might have anticipated a long-term and fruitful association between psychological research and the world of education." It is perhaps not too much to hope that a long and fruitful association lies in our future.

There is some attempt now to bridge the gap between research and practice. Researchers are writing about implications (Witkin, Moore, and others, 1975), and practitioners are studying the research. Project Priority, a project of the Two-Year College Development Center at the State University of New York at Albany and twenty-three cooperating community colleges, has taken some leadership in bringing together researchers and practitioners to see how knowledge about cognitive styles can be utilized in the improvement of teaching and counseling (Hodge, 1974; Martens, 1975). Furthermore, a number of people have created *applied* models that purport to use the concept of learning styles. The "cognitive mapping" technique devised by Joseph Hill, a community college president, is familiar to some practitioners (for further information see DeLoach, Dworkin, and Wyett, 1971; Hampton, 1972; Hill, 1971; Martens, 1975). The McKenney Model, devised at the Harvard Business School, is also receiving some attention from educators (for further information see Keen, 1974; McKenney and Keen, 1974; Nelson, 1973). And there are a panoply of scales and instruments designed to measure individual differences in learning styles (see, for example, Canfield and Lafferty, 1973; Riechmann and Grasha, 1974). Indeed, the concept has become so popular that England's Open University has issued a learning module on learning styles (Cashdan and Lee, 1971).

While all of this interest in the *process* of learning is to be applauded, the great variety of approaches lends some confusion to a general discussion about cognitive styles. Usually, the term *cognitive style* is reserved for those dimensions that have their roots in the study of cognitive functioning in experimental research. Most people using other schemes for arriving at dimensions of difference refer to "learning styles," "cognitive maps," "learning modalities," and other variations on the theme. I shall observe these customary distinctions in the vocabulary of this chapter.

Because this book is oriented toward the synthesis of published research, I shall give major attention to the cognitive style dimensions that are treated in the literature of research psychology. This excludes some of the applied models being used today, but it is not necessarily a judgment about their possible usefulness. In most cases, not enough information is available to make an evaluation. Perhaps by 1980 we will have some good research evaluations of the applied models and some good field trials of the research models.

Dimensions of cognitive styles. At least a dozen separate cognitive dimensions have been the subject of systematic research study, and perhaps half a dozen more have been identified but not extensively studied. A definition of each of nine cognitive styles has been provided by Messick (1970), pp. 188-189):

> 1. *Field independence versus field dependence*—"an analytical, in contrast to a global, way of perceiving [which] entails a tendency to experience items as discrete from their backgrounds and reflects ability to overcome the influence of an embedding context" (Witkin, Dyk, others, 1962).
>
> 2. *Scanning*—a dimension of individual differences in the extensiveness and intensity of attention deployment, leading to individual variations in vividness of experience and the span of awareness (Holzman, 1966; Schlesinger, 1954; Gardner and Long, 1962).
>
> 3. *Breadth of categorizing*—consistent preferences for broad inclusiveness, as opposed to narrow exclusiveness, in establishing the acceptable range for specified categories (Pettigrew, 1958; Bruner and Tajfel, 1961; Kogan and Wallach, 1964).
>
> 4. *Conceptualizing styles*—individual differences in the tendency to categorize perceived similarities and differences among stimuli in terms of many differentiated concepts, which is a dimension called *conceptual differentiation* (Gardner and Schoen, 1962; Messick and Kogan, 1963), as well as consistencies in the utilization of particular conceptualizing approaches as bases for forming concepts—such as the routine use in concept formation of

thematic or functional relations among stimuli as opposed to the analysis of descriptive attributes or the inference of class membership (Kagan, Moss, and Sigel, 1960, 1963).

5. *Cognitive complexity versus simplicity*—individual differences in the tendency to construe the world, and particularly the world of social behavior, in a multidimensional and discriminating way (Kelly, 1955; Bieri, 1961; Bieri and others, 1966; Scott, 1963; Harvey, Hunt, and Schroder, 1961).

6. *Reflectiveness versus impulsivity*—individual consistencies in the speed with which hypotheses are selected and information processed, with impulsive subjects tending to offer the first answer that occurs to them, even though it is frequently incorrect, and reflective subjects tending to ponder various possibilities before deciding (Kagan, Rosman, and others, 1964; Kagan, 1965).

7. *Leveling versus sharpening*—reliable individual variations in assimilation in memory. Subjects at the leveling extreme tend to blur similar memories and to merge perceived objects or events with similar but not identical events recalled from previous experience. Sharpeners, at the other extreme, are less prone to confuse similar objects and, by contrast, may even judge the present to be less similar to the past than is actually the case (Holzman, 1954; Holzman and Klein, 1954; Gardner, Holzman, and others, 1959).

8. *Constricted versus flexible control*—individual differences in susceptibility to distraction and cognitive interference (Klein, 1954; Gardner, Holzman, and others, 1959).

9. *Tolerance for incongruous or unrealistic experiences*—a dimension of differential willingness to accept perceptions at variance with conventional experience (Klein, Gardner, and Schlesinger, 1962).

Kagan (1971) provides an excellent and very readable discussion of each of these dimensions and adds a tenth style, described as risk-taking versus cautiousness.

A brief study of Messick's descriptions reveals the variety of cognitive style dimensions. People see and make sense of the world in different ways. They give their attention to different aspects of the environment; they approach problems with different methods for solution; they construct relationships in distinctive patterns; they process information in different but personally consistent ways. The study of cognitive styles is fascinating because people tend to be consistent across a wide variety of tasks; they tend to remain strikingly stable in their cognitive style over many years, and their style has a broad influence on many aspects of personality and behavior: perception, memory, problem solving, interests, and even social behaviors and self-concepts.

The purpose of this chapter is not to provide encyclopedic information about the varieties of cognitive style dimensions, but rather to provide practitioners with some illustrations of how the carefully researched concept of cognitive style might be applied to the design of educational programs. Thus, I have analyzed *one* dimension in depth but have also provided references to other dimensions that may hold particular attractions for some readers. (References to other cognitive style dimensions may be found in Kogan, 1971; Martens, 1975; Nelson, 1973; Sperry, 1972.)

The dimension selected for illustration here is field dependence versus field independence. This is not an arbitrary choice. Field dependence-independence is the primary focus of this chapter for two reasons: (1) It holds a substantial lead over any other dimension in the extent and quality of research; some two thousand studies are referenced in two major bibliographical searches of the literature on field dependence-independence (Witkin, Cox, and others, 1974; Witkin, Oltman, and others, 1973). (2) It is significantly related to interpersonal competencies; therefore, it sets the stage for Chapters Seven and Eight of this book, and it provides important research background for the viability of the pluralistic model outlined in Chapter One.

Field Dependence Versus Field Independence

The field-dependence-independence dimension of cognitive styles was introduced in 1954 by Witkin and his associates (Witkin, Lewis, and others, 1954). Their interest at the time was in the psychology of perception—specifically, in the distinction between global and analytical ways of perceiving objects and situations. As the name implies, the field-independent person is likely to deal with elements independent of their background, whereas the field-dependent person deals with the total field or situation. The field-independent person consistently approaches a wide variety of tasks and situations in an *analytical* way, separating elements from background. The field-dependent individual approaches situations in a *global* way, seeing the whole instead of the parts.

The field-dependence-independence dimension is dramatically illustrated by some experiments conducted in the psychology laboratory. In Witkin's earliest experiments, a subject was seated on a chair in a tilted room and was asked to adjust the chair and his body to the true upright. Some people consistently aligned themselves to the tilt of the room, leaning perhaps as much as thirty degrees but perceiving themselves to be sitting upright. Others, however, ignored their immediate surroundings, using internal cues to adjust their bodies to an upright position. In another type of test, the subject was seated in a darkened room with a luminous rod in a luminous picture frame which was set aslant. The task was to set the rod to the true vertical position. Again, people were found to perform the task with remarkable consistency; some aligned the rod to the slant of the frame, while others ignored the frame and set the rod upright. Furthermore, there was substantial correlation between the two tests. People who ignored the tilt of the room also ignored the slant of the frame; these people were described as field independent. Field-dependent people, on the other hand, relied consistently on the surroundings, the room or the frame, for their orientation. Later experiments with an embedded-figures test extended the concept of field-dependence-independence and also enabled diagnosis without complicated equipment. People at the field-dependent extreme of the continuum were unable to locate simple line figures embedded in a complex design in the three minutes allowed for the test, whereas field-independent people quickly separated the figures from the background.

The common element in all of these experiments is the extent to which people are influenced by a surrounding visual field. But the influence is not limited to visual perception. Similar phenomena occur when people are asked to identify a simple tune located in a complex melody or to close their eyes and locate by touch a simple figure embedded in a complex figure with raised contours. Indeed, field dependents are not likely to differentiate even themselves sharply from the surrounding field. They, more than field independents, are sensitive to what other people are doing and thinking and are dependent upon others for their own orientation.

How people get their cognitive style is unknown, but numerous cross-cultural studies have been conducted in an effort to determine the role of socialization in cognitive styles. Witkin and Berry (1975) have recently reviewed 179 cross-cultural reports; their review can be summarized by the following conclusions:

1. In other cultures as well as American culture, there is movement toward field independence up to early adolescence, followed by a plateau and some move toward field dependence around the age of fifty. These age patterns seem to hold regardless of culture, but individuals show remarkable stability throughout life with respect to their *relative* position on the continuum.

2. Cultures that emphasize conformity, "tight" role definitions, and social control seem to encourage field-dependent perceptual modes; "loose" cultures, with more emphasis on self-control and independence, encourage field independence.

3. Strict child-rearing practices, emphasizing obedience and parental authority, are associated with field dependence; practices that encourage autonomy and are tolerant of violation of parental authority are associated with field independence.

4. Although women in Western culture show small but persistent differences in the direction of greater field dependence than men, these differences are not universal in non-Western data. This finding supports the general conclusion that, although there may be a genetic component to cognitive style, cognitive styles are largely determined through socialization. American culture, with its definitions of dependence and nurturance for women and achievement and independence for men, could well account for the quite consistent finding that on the average men are more field independent, more analytical, than women.

In general, then, people probably learn habitual ways of responding to their environment early in life. These habits, spontaneously applied without conscious choice, determine one's cognitive style. Psychologists believe, however, that people can be taught to make conscious choices about which cognitive process to use in given situations. Such deliberate choices are termed *cognitive strategies*. If cognitive strategies can be taught, field independents might learn, for example, to be more sensitive to other people, and field dependents might learn to be more analytical. The educational correlates of cognitive styles have been of particular concern in recent years to Witkin and his colleagues at Educational Testing Service (Witkin, 1973; Witkin and Moore, 1974; Witkin, Moore, and others, 1975).

Educational correlates. Ever since Binet and his work on intelligence testing, the educability of a child has been associated with IQ or intelligence. A child with "more" IQ is more easily taught than one with "less." But it may not be that simple. The concept of cognitive style introduces the notion that the subject to be learned and the manner in which it is presented interact with abilities to influence learning. For example, it may be possible to teach mathematics to people who "have always had trouble with math" in a way that makes the subject easily understood. One of the advantages of working with cognitive styles in the education of New Students is that cognitive styles are free of the value connotations associated with IQ. Whereas a high IQ is "good" and a low IQ is "bad," value judgments cannot be readily assigned to cognitive styles. Look, for example, at two contrasting descriptions of field-dependence-independence. "Field-dependent . . . individuals . . . lack a well-developed sense of their own identity and separateness from others. During their development these individuals have failed to internalize a stable set of standards with which they can interpret and react to the world. . . . Field-independent . . . [individuals have] a highly developed sense of their own self-identity. They tend to be regarded by others as socially more independent than their field-dependent counterparts and evidence a ready capacity to function with little environmental support" (Spotts and Mackler, 1967, pp. 241-242). After reading that description, most of us would probably prefer to be considered field independent. On the other hand, we might prefer to be field dependent if we were given the following definition: "The field-independent individual appears cold and distant to others, and tends to be individualistic, while the field-dependent individual makes a favorable first impression, is gregarious, affectionate, considerate, and tactful" (Osipow, 1969, p. 535).

Although these descriptions favor a particular style, they are obviously in disagreement over which style is better. And the more sophisticated approach today is to place no value judgments on field dependence or field independence but rather to look at interaction between style, learning methods, and tasks or situations. Learning tasks requiring the separation of elements from background will favor field independents, whereas tasks requiring a more global approach will favor field dependents. Broadly speaking, field dependents are "other-directed" rather than "inner-directed." They take their cues from their environment. In social situations, they tend to be conforming and sensitive to what others think of them. Their tendency is to try to blend in with the crowd, rather than to stand out as distinctive. Not surprisingly, this interest in what other people are thinking and feeling results in the greater social sensitivity of the field dependent: "Field-dependent persons are particularly sensitive and attuned to the social environment. The result, overall, is a picture of highly developed social skills" (Witkin, 1973, p. 9).

Research documentation for the social interest and sensitivity of field dependents is substantial and varied (see reviews by Witkin and Moore, 1974; Witkin, Moore, and others, 1975). Laboratory experiments show that field dependents like to be physically close to others; they spend more time looking at the faces of those with whom they interact; they are especially able to recall words in verbal communications that have social implications; they are likely to adjust their own rate of speech to those with whom they interact; they are alert to words with emotional content; they are sensitive to external social referents in defining their own position; they are more popular, and they know and are known by more people than field independents.

The social orientation of field dependents carries over into their choice of a college major. Field dependents tend to choose fields of study that involve people and human relations—social services, counseling, teaching, business. In contrast, field independents favor the sciences—mathematics, physics, biology, engineering. Furthermore, field dependents who initially choose a science major are especially likely to change their major—from the sciences to a more people-oriented field (Witkin, 1973). The relationship between cognitive styles and career interests is sufficiently strong to operate within professions as well as across them. Nagle (1968) found that graduate students entering the people-oriented profession of clinical psychology were significantly more field dependent than those entering the more scientifically oriented specialty of experimental psychology. Likewise, high-achieving students in psychiatric nursing were found significantly more field dependent than high-achieving students in surgical nursing (Quinlan and Blatt, 1972).

Field-dependence-independence seems not to be correlated in any meaningful way with general intelligence in the sense that tests of cognitive style measure the same things as IQ tests. Field independence, however, has been shown consistently and positively correlated with one aspect of intelligence: analytical intelligence, which requires the separation of elements from background. It is not significantly related to intelligence factors of verbal comprehension and attention/concentration (Goodenough and Karp, 1961; Witkin, Dyk, and others, 1962). Correlations of cognitive styles with school achievement, however, present a mixed picture. Recent research on the college grade point averages of extremely field-dependent and field-independent students showed no differences (Witkin and Moore, 1974), but there was a predictable difference in the mix of courses in which similar grades were obtained. Field independents tended to include more courses in mathematics and science whereas the grades of field dependents included a heavier proportion of courses from the social sciences and humanities. As might be expected, field independents make better grades in the sciences than do field dependents. At the lower levels of education, where students are not permitted to specialize in subjects in which they do well, there is some evidence that field dependents have more learning problems in school than do field independents (Keogh and Donlon, 1972; Stuart, 1967; Wineman, 1971). It is possible, however, that the learning difficulties of field dependents may be more a function of the way learning is structured in the schools than of the intelligence of the learner. School learning may favor field-independent children, who tend to be task and achievement oriented and to be self-sufficient and independent; field dependents may be easily distracted because they find the people around them more interesting than the mathematics problem in front of them.

Although it is speculative at this time, I am struck by the similarities between the characteristics of field dependents and New Students. While it is clearly inappropriate to assume that *individual* New Students are field dependent, I suspect that field dependents are overrepresented among New Students now entering college under open-admissions policies. I also suggest that traditional education has been geared more to the style of field independents than to the style of field dependents, giving field independents the advantage in school situations.

New students and field dependence. Table 1 shows some similarities between New Students and field dependents. The characteristics of New Students are those documented in *Beyond the Open Door* (Cross, 1971); the characteristics of field dependents are those described in the research and extensive reviews conducted by Witkin and his colleagues. (The best and most recent summaries, along with citations of the original research documents, are to be found in Witkin, 1973; Witkin and Berry, 1975; Witkin and Moore, 1974; Witkin, Moore, and others, 1975.)

Despite the interesting similarities between the profiles of New Students and field dependents, there is no consistent or compelling research evidence that academic achievement is related to cognitive style. The characteristic shared by the New Students described in *Beyond the Open Door* is, of course, their relative failure to do well on traditional tests of academic achievement. Unfortunately, data on the cognitive styles of the New Students were not available. But certain conditions of the

Table 1
Some Characteristics of Field Dependents and New Students

Field Dependents	New Students
Like being with and relating to people. Well-developed social sensitivity.	Spend leisure time with people. Report most important college learning experiences relate to getting along with others.
Attracted to careers and college majors emphasizing interpersonal relations.	Attracted to careers working with people.
Sensitive to the judgments of others. Tend to be guided by authority figures. Dependent on others for self-definition. Lack independence and autonomy.	Low scores on tests of autonomy, measuring independence of thought and judgment. Compliant to wishes and ideas of those in authority.
Extrinsically motivated; responsive to social reinforcement.	Motivation for education is extrinsic; high interest in grades, better jobs, higher salaries.
Poor at *analytical* problem solving.	Low scores on Theoretical Orientation (TO) scale of OPI (Omnibus Personality Inventory), a scale measuring preference for analytical and critical thinking.
Favor a "spectator approach" to concept attainment. Tend to accept problems as defined by others rather than impose their own structure.	Score low (are more passive) than traditional students on the OPI Active-Passive scale. Tend to accept situations as defined by others.
Field-dependent women favor traditional women's roles.	Career choices are strongly sex stereotyped.
Come from social and cultural backgrounds stressing obedience to authority and "tight" role definitions.	Come from blue-collar families. Favor traditional social values and respect for authority.

data would tend to place field dependents in the New Student group. In the first place, the tests used to define New Students had components calling for *analytical* abilities—quantitative tests, for example. Other things being equal, field dependents would tend to make somewhat lower scores because of the manner in which academic achievement is defined by test batteries that include significant amounts of analytical tasks. Second, students from blue-collar backgrounds were overrepresented among the New Student group. Since the cultural patterns of blue-collar families tend to stress "tighter" and more conforming behaviors, we would expect more field dependents than field independents in the New Student group. While it seems probable that field-dependent students are overrepresented in the New Student group, more study is needed on the relationship between cognitive style and academic success under various conditions. It seems appropriate, however, to take a speculative look at how our educational approaches might affect students of different cognitive styles. My hypothesis is that traditional education favors the field independent and that it is no accident or mere coincidence that students who do not do well in school have some important characteristics in common with field dependents. It is possible that field dependents find themselves in less hospitable learning environments than field independents.

Cognitive styles and educational environment. When schools took their present form, self-sufficiency and independence were virtues that had survival value in a pioneer society. Today, survival may be related more to one's ability to cooperate with others than to go it alone. More people lose their jobs because of failure in interpersonal relations than because of lack of job skills. Divorce, alienation, and people-related problems are major maladies of our times. Yet the educational system is still geared to the reward of independence, not often balanced by equal rewards for interpersonal cooperation. Thus, despite the known fact that social situations are often highly effective learning experiences, the traditional classroom is not a very social place. Beginning with their earliest school experiences, children are cautioned to do their own work, to keep their eyes on their own paper, and not to talk to their neighbors. Rarely do we permit, let alone encourage, social problem solving.

Learning to be responsive to people is rarely perceived as a learning task in schools; hence, it is not often taken into account or rewarded. People who learn something other than the defined learning task often appear deficient on standard measures of learning. There is some evidence that New Students may be learning something other than the defined curriculum.

In my data (Cross, 1971), New Students, more than others, were likely to say that their most important experience in college was learning to get along with different kinds of people—despite the fact that New Students were more likely to attend commuter colleges without dormitories, extensive student activities, and the other opportunities for social interaction that characterize residential campuses.

I found that, at the college level, New Students are twice as likely as traditional students to say they prefer having a problem explained to them to figuring it out themselves. Most teachers are convinced that the "independent" learner who figures out the problem for himself is considerably ahead of the "dependent" learner. But the research on the social orientation of field dependents raises a question. Is the student who says he prefers an explanation to an independent solution being dependent and mentally lazy, as most task-oriented educators assume; or is he instead actively seeking social interaction with the explainer in the learning process? Suppose that students were permitted to work with others toward the solution of the problem. (This is "cheating" in many schools.) Might the social stimulation activate a formerly unmotivated learner? Or, to carry the analysis further, suppose that social interaction, rather than independence, were highly valued in the schools and that all students were *required* to work with others in problem solving. Would the person who prefers to figure things out for himself then become passive, unchallenged, and uncooperative? If, in fact, New Students do lean toward the field-dependent end of the continuum, might the cool and detached social atmosphere of most schools be in part responsible for the passivity, lack of motivation, and occasional hostility shown in the research on New Students?

There is research evidence that students with a high desire for close, friendly interpersonal relations develop problem-solving skills better when they are assigned to work on the problems in pairs, whereas those low in affiliation needs achieve better alone (Sutter, 1967). Similarly, we have some research support for the notion that weak students are especially likely to profit from peer tutoring (Reed, 1974; Wallace, 1965).

Although we cannot say with certainty that field dependents are disadvantaged by traditional educational approaches, it is clear that different students prefer different amounts of human warmth and support. Certainly, then, we have much to gain and nothing to lose by offering alternatives.

Implications of Cognitive Styles for Educational Practice

There is a great deal of interest today in applying knowledge about student learning styles to educational practice. Suggestions vary from elaborate and quite specific schemes for "matching" the cognitive style of learners to the teaching resources of the institution to the more conservative and scarcely controversial recommendation that students be allowed to choose the approach that seems most effective for them. The notion of matching the student's "cognitive map" to the learning resources of the institution is the fundamental principle at work in the Hill (1971) strategy of cognitive mapping. The student takes a three-hour battery of tests designed to reveal a cognitive map—that is, a profile of some 84 traits describing a student's learning style. The test results are processed by computer, and each student's cognitive map then provides a basis for building a "personalized educational prescription (PEP)." This procedure can produce up to 2304 combinations of student learning patterns and nineteen ways of teaching the same course material (Hampton, 1972).

While the complexity of the system has bothered some practitioners, the simplicity of the "matching" concept is more likely to trouble research psychologists. In the first place, they may question the assumption that it is desirable to place students in learning environments geared to their predilections. In the second place, they may question the assumption that the student's profile remains constant and that the institution's resources are infinitely flexible. For example, if we know that a field independent learns best and most pleasantly in independent study, are we necessarily serving him well if we offer him a steady diet of independent work? Maybe he needs to learn to work cooperatively with others. "Matching" him to his own style or preference may push him toward further field independence, and that may be maladaptive in certain social situations. Maybe we should expose him to a "challenge match"*— that is, place him in an uncongenial or conflict setting, so that he is forced to develop an area of weakness or at least some flexibility in dealing with uncomfortable situations. Or perhaps we should try to correct his weakness—for instance, his inability to relate to people—through a "remedial match." Then again, we may wish to consider the use of a "compensatory" match, in which the student can compensate for deficiencies in one skill area by using skills that are more adequately developed. For example, if the student is a whiz with a hand calculator, perhaps we should permit her to study algebra without insisting that she also be good at computation. To make our dilemma even greater, if the field dependent shows leanings toward being especially talented in interpersonal relations, or if the field independent is on his way to becoming a brilliant mathematician, perhaps we should design "capitalization matches" to develop these unique strengths. There are a number of matching strategies that can be used. Which one is selected should depend on the situation and on the purpose of the instruction.

The assumption of the constancy of student learning style is also troublesome at this stage of knowledge. There is some evidence that cognitive styles remain rather stubbornly with people throughout life. So far at least, short-term training efforts to change them have not been especially successful (Elliott and McMichael, 1963). But researchers are becoming more optimistic about the possibility of teaching students to diversify their learning *strategies*. Perhaps students with a distinctive cognitive style can be taught to adopt a learning strategy that is effective in a particular situation. Herein lies a danger of any automatic matching approach. A consistent match of teaching strategy to student cognitive style may leave the college graduate unprepared to cope with nonpreferred strategies

*I am indebted to Samuel Messick for his presentation of the four kinds of matches mentioned here to a conference on cognitive styles held at Educational Testing Service, Princeton, New Jersey, July 25-26, 1974.

that will inevitably face him or her in the real world. One of the truly important achievements that we can hope students might learn in college is the flexibility to adapt to changing conditions, whether worldwide or personal.

As long as we are aware of the dangers of oversimplifying, however, there is merit in attempting to place students in comfortable and productive learning situations for *them*. If we are going to arrange a "challenge" or "conflict" match, we should do so deliberately and with the understanding of the student— not unconsciously as we do at present by placing students with certain cognitive styles in a hostile environment and then wondering why they seem uncooperative and poorly motivated. We do know something about hospitable learning environments for field dependents and field independents. We know, for instance, that field-dependent students generally are more easily reinforced by external evaluation (grades, praise, criticism), whereas field independents are less influenced by the rewards of their social surroundings (Witkin, 1973). We also know that relatively dependent students prefer clear directions and instructor responsibility, whereas more internally directed students like to take responsibility for their own learning; similarly, field dependents are less likely than field independents to do well in organizing their own learning materials (Witkin and Moore, 1974, p. 10).

Teachers, too, of course, have cognitive styles, and they tend to teach by the methods most comfortable for them unless they are consciously attempting to use a teaching strategy to accommodate student learning styles. A major dimension of faculty teaching styles is the didactic versus the evocative style: "A didactic teacher takes for granted his greater knowledge and authority, and invites students into the materials in terms set by him. The class is a production in which the instructor is the producer, the director, and the writer, while the students are the actors under his direction and also the ultimate audience. At the very least, what is asked of them is that they 'get the material,' but the effort also may be to help them become active and go off on their own. In the classes we came to call evocative, the instructor was less concerned with covering ground or conveying ideas than with getting the students to connect what they were reading with their own experience, even at the cost of a certain fuzziness of outline. The invitation to learning was put in their own hands; they were allowed to help write the script or even rewrite it" (Riesman, Gusfield, and Gamson, 1970, p. 22).

The research of Wilson and his associates (1975) showed that community college teachers tend to be evocative whereas university professors tend to be didactic. If New Students tend toward field dependence, then, it appears that community college faculty—perhaps without knowing why—have devised teaching strategies that would be predicted effective for field dependents. (There is research evidence that people adapt rather easily to the cognitive styles of other people without knowing anything about cognitive styles and without knowing the styles of those with whom they are interacting; see Witkin, Moore, and others, 1975.) Whereas community college teachers emphasize individual attention, student participation in class, and the personal development of students, university faculty emphasize subject matter, lectures, and task-oriented classes (Wilson and others, 1975). Especially interesting is the finding that the more informal personally oriented approach of the community college faculty is accompanied by *greater* structure and control than in university teaching. Community college teachers are significantly more likely than university faculty to describe objectives at the beginning of each class session, to follow the textbook closely, to require class attendance, and to give unannounced quizzes to check on learning progress. The combination of well-defined structure within a warm interpersonal environment appears to be a very appropriate strategy for working with field-dependent students.

Just as certain cognitive styles seem especially suited to certain academic disciplines (for example, field independents, whether teachers or students, probably tend to choose specialties in mathematics and science), perhaps certain teaching methods are especially suited to certain disciplines. Perhaps, for example, the subject materials of mathematics and science are better suited to didactic methods of teaching. As a matter of fact, Rennels (1970) found that when the subject to be taught was spatial relations, both field-dependent and field-independent children did better when taught by the analytic methods that had been designed to complement the styles of the field independents. Thus, we have to consider not only teacher-student interactions but subject-matter-teaching-method interactions as well.

As knowledge about cognitive styles accumulates, it is easy to be Pollyanaish about the way things are. If structure-minded teachers teach structured subjects to students who prefer independent learning situations, things seem to be working out well even without educational strategies. To make this happy scene even happier, we have the research finding that students and teachers with similar cognitive styles like each other better and find people with styles similar to their own more competent (DiStefano, 1969; James, 1973). While the implication of these findings could be "leave well enough alone and people will find their own salvation," the more enlightened conclusions might be these:

1. Teachers and students should be helped to gain some insight into teaching and learning styles.

2. In general, people will probably be happier and more productive if they are studying or teaching via a method compatible with their style. But any system of automatic matching seems counterproductive. The type of match or mismatch should be flexibly determined, depending on the circumstances and goals of a particular learning situation.

3. No one method should be regarded as a panacea for all students in all subjects. The structured self-paced approaches discussed in Chapters Three and Four, for example, may be most useful for those who need structure and organization to guide their learning efforts. According to Witkin and Moore (1974), these would be the field-dependent students. On the other hand, self-paced learning modules call for independence, and they frequently stimulate interpersonally "cool" learning environments, which are difficult for field dependents. Perhaps, then, the peer tutors and the mentors of PSI and the discussion groups of the audio-tutorial methods discussed in Chapter Four

are especially important to field dependents and probably to many, if not most, New Students. The research to date indicates that a promising approach to working with New Students would be to design clear, strongly structured learning tasks that can be pursued jointly by several students or by groups of students working together toward common learning goals. The clear delineation of the task plus the social support of other people seems to be a potentially powerful combination of forces for field dependents.

There is also some evidence that field independents are able to deal with larger modules and with less frequent feedback than field dependents (Renzi, 1974; Schwen, 1970). In the preparation of learning modules, attention should be given to the type of student served. Small-step programs (but not all the way back to the boring "frames" of programmed instruction) are probably better for field dependents, whereas larger modules may serve the needs of students who are relatively field independent in their approach to academic learning. The best guess that I can provide with the research knowledge at hand is that the self-pacing methods discussed in Chapters Three and Four have considerable merit for use with New Students but that module size must be designed for the New Students, and the use of learning modules should be supplemented with considerable personal attention from peers and teachers.

4. There are some subjects and some skills that all students need to learn, and we need to be knowledgeable in devising cognitive strategies to teach them. A mathematician may have to devise a more personally interactive approach in order to help a field dependent learn mathematics. Likewise, a group-oriented social scientist may have to devise some tasks that will help field independents gain emotional insight and social sensitivities into human behavior—not all of which is as logical as some field independents might hope.

5. Educators need to be aware of the cognitive styles of students in order to provide the appropriate kinds of reinforcement. There is now evidence that field independents learn better than field dependents when motivation is intrinsic but that the differences disappear when external rewards are introduced

(Steinfeld, 1973). If New Students do tend to be field dependent, then present moves to abolish grading may be ill-advised.
It is clear that the New Students themselves are more interested
than traditional students in grades and other extrinsic rewards
(Cross, 1971). Since field dependents are also more sensitive to
criticism than field independents (Witkin, Moore, and others,
1975), it has seemed reasonable to attempt to avoid the fear-of-
failure syndrome by eliminating failing or poor grades for New
Students. But the research on cognitive styles indicates to me
that extrinsic reward is desirable for New Students, hence my
recommendation in Chapter One that we attempt to have the
best of two worlds by giving grades in the areas of excellence
(where New Students will work toward success) and abolishing
grades in the areas of adequacy (where New Students can avoid
the stigma of failure and where graduated judgments are not
necessary anyway).

6. Any single school or institution should make certain
that the learning program is not systematically biased in favor
of a particular cognitive style. Alternatives should be freely
available, and, if at all possible, required subjects should be
taught by several strategies. The availability of pluralistic cognitive alternatives is especially important for remedial classes.

7. More attention needs to be given to the potential of
cognitive style for educational and vocational guidance. The
value-free connotation of cognitive styles makes their use less
threatening than IQ, and they do not align themselves along so-
called "status" lines. For example, field independents are likely
to show interest in practical career fields such as farming, car-
pentry, and mechanics as well as in professional fields such as
architecture and engineering (Witkin and Cox, 1975). Another
advantage of the use of cognitive style in guidance has to do
with the pervasiveness of cognitive style dimensions. Information is provided simultaneously about cognitive and personality
characteristics. Finally, the stability of cognitive styles over long
periods of time makes them useful for long-range planning.

8. Relatively greater attention should be given to the
"capitalization" match, which builds on the strengths of individuals—at the expense, if necessary, of our obsessive concern
with the "remediation" match that has characterized education

for New Students so far. Specifically, a curriculum oriented toward helping people to work with people would capitalize on the social sensitivity and interest of field-dependent students (see Chapters Seven and Eight).

9. Since knowledge about cognitive styles is tentative and incomplete, educators should remain flexible and experimental in their use of the concept. One campus I visited recently was using cognitive mapping with unusual effectiveness—largely because one counselor had stimulated a great deal of interest on the part of both students and faculty in attending to individual differences. Her secret seemed to lie in the flexibility with which she used the system to promote interest in learning rather than to assign or prescribe specific educational treatments. In discussing a cognitive map with a student or faculty member, she used the "scores" only as a point of departure for discussing the self-awareness of learning preferences. She pointed out that, as with all tests, there is room for error in the application of results to individuals. If the diagnosis or prescription did not seem right, the individual should try something else. The three-member mathematics faculty adapted the ideas behind cognitive mapping to their organizational structure and to their individual teaching. They discovered that one of them preferred to play the individual mentor role in the learning laboratory, one preferred small-group discussions, and one did his best work in more formal presentations. All three options were offered, and many students with special learning difficulties in mathematics were trying all three with some enthusiasm. Morale was high because to a large extent faculty were doing what they felt they did best.

At this stage in the development of knowledge about cognitive styles, there is no formula that can be applied automatically to bring about more effective learning for an individual. The application of research about cognitive styles will need to be filtered through the well-informed judgment of faculty members and counselors for some years to come. But knowledge about cognitive styles should make educators more sensitive and alert to some dimensions of difference in the learning styles of their students.

PART III

THE CURRICULAR EVOLUTION

*** 6 ***

Education for
Personal Development

<hr>

Student development is a little like the weather. Everyone talks about it and is interested in it, but no one does much about it. Just as we are pleased when a nice day comes along, so we are happy when a student graduates from college with social and intellectual maturity and a sense of personal direction. Like weather forecasters, we enjoy modest success in predicting what will happen when certain elements are present in the environment, but we rarely know how to take the action that will increase the probability for bringing about desired ends. We know, for example, that most students become more tolerant and open-minded as they proceed through college, but we do not know what is responsible for this rather consistent research finding, or why some students grow more than others, or how to structure learning opportunities to maximize such growth. Yet, almost every college catalog promises students and parents that the education provided by its institution is con-

137

cerned with more than intellectual development, and virtually all teachers consider themselves something more than conduits for the dissemination of academic subject matter.

But what is that "something more than subject matter" that all educators aspire to but few know how to accomplish? It has been said that education is what remains after course content has been forgotten. Throughout history, inspirational and analytical writers have tried to define what it is that we hope remains in the lives of educated people. Cardinal Newman ([1852] 1941, p. 196) expresses it this way: "Education . . . gives a man a clear conscious view of his own opinions and judgments, a truth in developing them, an eloquence in expressing them, and a force in urging them. It shows him how to accommodate himself to others, how to throw himself into their state of mind, how to bring before them his own, how to influence them, how to come to an understanding with them, how to bear with them." Except for the use of a language that needs to be brought up to date with respect to a specific awareness of the needs of women for the same sorts of goals, that sounds fine. Few would disagree. But how do we go about teaching a student how to "accommodate himself [or herself] to others" or "how to throw himself [or herself] into their state of mind" or indeed "how to bear with" his or her fellow human beings? For the most part, these enduring values of education are the result of a combination of fortunate accidents and exposure to people and events that make a difference. The major advantage of college may simply be that the probability of bumping into growth-inducing experiences is somewhat greater than in the everyday work world. It is not at all clear that personal development, or even the more narrowly conceived intellectual development, is the natural result of studying the subject matter that most students and some faculty members equate with college education. Perhaps, then, as Sanford (1969, pp. 8, 9) maintains, "The time has come for us to control our zeal for imparting knowledge and skills, and to concentrate our efforts on developing the individual student. . . . By education for individual development, I mean a program *consciously undertaken* to promote an identity based on such qualities as flexibility, creativity, openness to experience, and responsibility" (emphasis added).

Few colleges in the country have consciously undertaken to offer such a program. To be sure, most colleges offer a program of extracurricular activities, which they hope will help students develop leadership abilities. Most colleges offer concerts and art exhibits, which they hope will stimulate esthetic appreciations. Most colleges offer counseling services, which are designed to help students make considered decisions about their education, careers, and personal lives. And indeed, many professors consciously attempt to cultivate the qualities espoused by Cardinal Newman through using subject matter as a *means* to intellectual development rather than as an *end*. Such resources, however, although desirable and even necessary, are hardly sufficient for maximizing educational impact. People can presumably learn to work with people through trial and error and experience. No doubt, people can formulate values and achieve a sense of identity through meeting life's challenges as they occur. But trial-and-error learning is almost always inefficient, and while experience is often a good teacher, it is not necessarily the best teacher. Human beings have the unique capacity for symbolic and vicarious learning. If we value characteristics such as tolerance, autonomy, interpersonal sensitivity, and personal integrity, can we not begin to be deliberate in our efforts to develop some of the behaviors and attitudes of the educated person rather than leaving them to chance? Some people contend that we cannot—that for classroom education to attempt to deal with more than the mind of the student is to ask for trouble.

After all the years spent in academe analyzing the fallacy of various forms of dualism, it is ironic that we should find ourselves practicing cognitive-affective dualism in education. We have created separate (and not quite equal) structures to handle a dualistic conception of education. The vice-president for student affairs is generally assigned responsibility for the out-of-class education of students while the vice-president for academic affairs deals with in-class education. Student personnel staff presumably have more expertise in affective education, whereas academic personnel are experts in cognitive education.

At best, this division of labor represents an administrative convenience; at worst, it depicts an erroneous and even dangerous conception of education in which values and attitudes are considered affective education—as though human values were devoid of intellectual analysis—while the study of physics is considered cognitive education—as though the development of humane and compassionate use of scientific knowledge were irrelevant to its possessor.

Although the history of education is full of criticism of the failure to homogenize affective and cognitive learning, the feat has rarely been attempted. John Dewey's plea to teach the "whole child" foundered when overenthusiastic reformers became pitted against sober-sided debunkers; but the ideal of the educated person has always included intellectual, emotional, social, and moral maturity. This perspective is apparent in the rhetoric of academic leaders. *Time* Magazine (October 2, 1964) gave this summary of some renowned academics addressing college freshmen:

> Brainy college freshmen under the impression that their next four years would be spent as assembly-line workers in ivy-covered fact factories got a sharp jolt last week. "You demand facts, facts, facts," guest speaker A. L. Sachar, president of Brandeis, told the entering class at the University of Illinois. What they need just as much, he insisted, is values to serve "in a world where the harsh voice of unreason cries down the generous passions," and "the elasticity of your minds will be a shield." On campuses across the U.S., college presidents were playing up the value of values.
>
> Yale President Kingman Brewster, Jr. said that although freshmen were picked for their intellectual ability, their "moral capacity" had also been taken into account. Success at Kenyon, said Dean Bruce Haywood, ultimately depends on a student's "individual taste and moral judgment." "The collection of knowledge is only the starting point," echoed Curtis Tarr, president of Lawrence University of Appleton, Wis. At Pomona College, one of the six associated Claremont Colleges of California, President E. Wilson Lyons also greeted freshmen with a call to use knowledge for moral ends.

> The most fervent plea for a "moral quest" came from Princeton's Robert F. Goheen. He told bright Tiger cubs that if they expected "only to accumulate knowledge, I would advise you to begin negotiations with another institution where you can attach yourself to a pipeline of inanimate learning and become full, like a storage tank, sealed by a diploma and otherwise useless."

The idealism expressed by these leaders is shared by professional educators and laymen alike. In fact, there is research evidence that most people want broad-based goals for colleges, goals that go beyond subject-matter mastery. Peterson (1973) conducted a study of the goals of 116 public and private colleges in California. Respondents consisting of students, faculty, administrators, and community residents were asked to rate their institution as it really is and as they thought it should be with respect to the implementation of twenty goals. Three scales—academic development, intellectual orientation, and personal development—showed especially large discrepancies between the *is* and *should be* rankings. The three scales were each defined by four goals statements (Peterson, 1973, Appendix B). The goals for *academic development* are (1) to help students acquire depth of knowledge in at least one academic discipline; (2) to ensure that students acquire a basic knowledge in the humanities, social sciences, and natural sciences; (3) to prepare students for advanced academic work (for example, at a four-year college or graduate or professional school); (4) to hold students throughout the institution to high standards of intellectual performance. The goals for *intellectual orientation* are (1) to train students in methods of scholarly inquiry, scientific research, and/or problem definition and solution; (2) to increase the desire and ability of students to undertake self-directed learning; (3) to develop students' ability to synthesize knowledge from a variety of sources; (4) to instill in students a lifelong commitment to learning. The goals for *individual personal development* are (1) to help students identify their own personal goals and develop means of achieving them; (2) to help students develop a sense of self-worth, self-confidence, and a capacity to have an impact on events; (3) to help students achieve deeper levels of self-understanding; (4) to help students be open, honest, and trusting in their relationships with others.

As Table 2 shows, the greatest discrepancies between education as it *is* and as it *should be* (that is, the greatest dissatisfaction) occurs with respect to the priority presently given to the personal development of students. Students and the general public agree that this goal should receive a much higher priority than it presently receives, moving from seventeenth or eighteenth priority to fourth in the university and from tenth to second place in the community colleges. While community college faculty and administrators think that student development should receive a quite high third-place priority, university faculty are more reluctant; they would grant it only tenth-place priority. Nevertheless, all groups would like to see more attention given to helping students to understand themselves and to achieve a sense of direction.

At the same time, all constituent groups of the campuses feel that academic development (the accumulation of knowledge in the academic disciplines) is overemphasized. The complaint should not be regarded as antiintellectualism, since all groups believe that *more* attention should be given to intellectual orientation (the cultivation of intellectual skills and attitudes and interests that characterize the educated person). Apparently, however, the desire of faculty to give more emphasis to intellectual orientation falls far short of their accomplishments. Chickering (1969) found that even in small colleges where classes number less than thirty and where teaching is emphasized over research, a majority of the students said that they spent *most* of their time listening and taking notes and that, in preparing for classes, they spent much more time memorizing than they did analyzing, synthesizing, applying, or evaluating. Thus, the research as well as the rhetoric gives a picture of present institutions of higher education placing too much emphasis on the student as a "storage tank" filled with "facts, facts, facts" and giving too little attention to the education of the student as a fully functioning human being capable of using knowledge to moral and social ends.

Table 2
Is and *Should Be* Rank Orders[a] for Three Goal Areas

		Faculty		Under-graduates		Administrators		Community People	
		UC[b]	CC[b]	UC	CC	UC	CC	UC	CC
Academic Development	SB[c]	7	12	14	9	6	12	7	6
	IS[c]	4	4	3	1	3	4	2	1
Intellectual Orientation	SB	1	4	3	4	2	6	2	4
	IS	7	11	7	8	5	10	6	8
Personal Development	SB	10	3	4	2	8	3	4	2
	IS	14	8	18	10	13	8	17	10

[a]Ranks range from 1 (top priority) to 20 (lowest priority).
[b]UC = University of California; CC = 69 community colleges.
[c]IS = Rating of school "as is"; SB = rating of school as it "should be."

Source: Adapted from Peterson (1973).

Research on Student Development

Despite the rather obvious fact that we do not do much deliberately and consciously to help students develop all or even a major portion of their human potential, higher education as a whole is more successful than many people think in helping students grow toward personal maturity. The literature on the personal development of students as they proceed through college is voluminous—Feldman and Newcomb (1969) cite more than 1200 studies; it is amazingly consistent across research studies and across varying types of colleges; and there have been numerous and quite adequate efforts to synthesize the knowledge (Chickering, 1969; Feldman and Newcomb, 1969; Withey, 1971). I will present a brief synopsis of the research for those not familiar with this huge body of literature in higher education. At the outset, however, several caveats should be entered.

In the first place, most of the research took place in the span of a single decade—from 1960 to 1970. This was a decade in which an unusual amount of attention was given to college students and their age group. They were large in numbers and as such demanded, and for the most part got, the attention of merchants, legislators, and educators. Adolescents and post-adolescents of the 1960s were characterized by an activist orientation and a feeling that they were a generation that could change society. The fact that almost all research shows increasingly liberal political attitudes among young people in college may thus be more a result of the times than an inevitable result of a college education. The point is that most of our present research on the impact of college on student attitudes should be viewed in the context of the times in which the data were collected.

The second weakness of our present knowledge base is related to the first but concerns the *place* of the data collection. Most data have been collected on residential campuses. There is very little information about what happens to community college students, for example. Furthermore, most of the longitudinal research has been conducted in selective or moderately selective colleges with quite different students from those now coming from the lower socioeconomic classes and from blue-collar backgrounds. In other words, most of the data on student development are derived from the study of rather traditional students studying on traditional campuses. Since we are rapidly moving to a generation of nonresidential, commuting, and external-degree students, the findings may not be generalizable to even a majority of today's students. (One sign of the times is a whole new literature on *adult* development: Chickering, 1974b; Hodgkinson, 1974; Levinson and others, 1974.) Despite these reservations, we do know a lot about what happened to the attitudes and values of several generations of students as they proceeded through college.

There is clear documentation that the students in the 1960s became more relativistic and less moralistic in ethical judgments, less supportive of traditional religion and other traditional values, more liberal with respect to political and social issues, and more open-minded as measured by scales on authoritarianism, dogmatism, ethnocentrism, and prejudice (Chickering, 1969; Feldman and Newcomb, 1969). This constellation of changes seems to add up to an increasing awareness of the complexities of life. As students proceed through college, they become more cautious about accepting simple stereotypes or pat answers to complex questions. One can postulate that the curriculum, with its growing emphasis on examining issues instead of providing definitive answers, is partly responsible for this change. Indeed, Perry (1970) cites some interesting research showing that professors at Harvard College became increasingly relativistic in their final examination questions over the years from 1900 to 1960. They tend now to ask more questions requiring analysis and multiple frames of reference and fewer questions with single-frame answers. But society, too, has moved steadily toward complexity, and students may simply reflect that social trend, heightened and perhaps exaggerated on college campuses.

Two other major clusters of changes have been found in college students. There is an increase in esthetic, cultural, and

intellectual interests, as well as a decrease in concern about
material possessions.* And there is evidence of personal integration, as well as a growing sense of autonomy and personal identity. Although the "cause" of these changes remains to be
demonstrated, most educators would be eager to claim that the
increase in intellectual and cultural interests is a direct out-
growth of the intellectually enriched environment of the
campus with its concerts, exhibits, lectures, and community of
scholars. What specific experiences there are in college to enhance the growth of autonomy and personal integration is more
problematical. This growth could be the result of simple maturation; or it could reflect trends in the broader society or the
experience of establishing independence away from home or the
diversity of challenges from people and events in the college
community. Rarely does anyone claim that the universally
observed growth in autonomy has much to do with the academic curriculum. In any event, the time seems ripe for experimentation with a variety of programs and courses in personal
development (Kohlberg and Mayer, 1972; Mosher and Sprinthall, 1971; Perry, 1970). We shall look at some of these programs later.

   While individuals, of course, show the usual human diver-
sities, the consistency with which groups of students demonstrate the general movement toward liberal values, open-mindedness, flexibility, and autonomy is puzzling in some of its
aspects. The college and its programs, for example, seem not to
make much difference. The entering classes seem to move in the
same directions at strict traditional colleges as they do at per-
missive innovative colleges. In fact, in a study of student change
at thirteen very diverse small colleges, the investigators concluded, "Not one of the thirteen [colleges] musters sufficient
force to retard, accelerate, or deflect the general developmental
trends shared by their diverse entering students" (Chickering,
McDowell, and Campagna, 1969, p. 324). Such findings might

   *Since entering college students of the mid-1970s are presumably
reverting to materialism (Stickgold, 1975), it will be interesting to see
whether *these* students become less materialistic as they move through college.

lead us to conclude that the observed changes are the result of maturation rather than education; that is, perhaps young people become more flexible and open-minded just as surely as they become taller. Research has demonstrated, however, that, generally speaking, the greater the contact of students with colleges, the greater the change. Students living on campus, for example, change more than students living in off-campus housing, who change more than students living with parents at home (Chickering, 1974a). In similar vein, Trent and Medsker (1968) found that students who persisted in college showed more change than those who withdrew, who, in turn, showed more change than those who never entered college.

College probably does have an impact, then, on student values and attitudes; but we still do not know how particular students react to particular environments. When Chickering refined his analyses to study only students who were similar as freshmen but who went to diverse types of colleges, he found that the characteristics of the college did indeed have the expected impact (Chickering and McCormick, 1973). Perhaps some of the in-depth case studies (Heath, 1964; Perry, 1970) and analyses of carefully selected subgroups of students will provide some understandings not possible through the larger cross-sectional studies.

Another way to learn more about the impact of education on student development is to create stronger environmental influences for students. From what we know now, it seems reasonable to hypothesize that maturational elements probably do contribute to the growth of autonomy, for instance, since few college environmental influences are deliberately designed to foster autonomy. Were we to design educational experiences with the deliberate intention of helping students to move toward greater autonomy, we might see more rapid and/or stronger trends. Fortunately, there are people working on environmental modifications and direct intervention, which should lead to increased knowledge about the process of personal development.

Three general approaches to student development are discernible in the 1970s. For convenience in discussion, I shall label them *humanistic, developmental,* and *multidimensional.* There is overlap among the three approaches and probably more agreement than disagreement among their adherents, but they grow out of different backgrounds and they make somewhat different assumptions. None of the models in existence today can be considered complete models of human development. Some concentrate on constructing an in-depth approach to a relatively narrow area of human development, whereas others cover a broader spectrum while sacrificing analytical depth.

Humanistic Approaches

Humanistic approaches to student development grow out of the theories of G. Stanley Hall, Abraham Maslow, and Carl Rogers, who believe that man is basically good and, given the right conditions, will move in positive directions. These theorists liken human development to the growth of a plant, which follows a predetermined pattern of growth. If nourished properly, the organism or plant will reach its maximum potential. A poor environment, on the other hand, will stunt or arrest growth. Humanists would assist each student to grow and develop in unique individualistic ways through providing a warm and accepting environment that encourages self-examination and self-actualization. They would not impose their own ideas on the direction that growth should take, any more than a gardener would try to make a tulip into a rose. Since the ideas and programs of the humanists are given extensive treatment in Chapter Seven, I will give their program only brief attention here, emphasizing those aspects that relate specifically to student development programs in colleges.

Goals. Humanists in the student development areas do not spend much time defining their terms, and they probably run into more trouble over the vagueness of their goals statements than over the more complex issues of theory and research. Today's humanistic leaders fall heir to a legacy of language that has been roundly criticized in the past. Goals for student programs are likely to be couched in typical humanistic language: to help each student "become what he can be, to realize his potential for perfection, to develop a repertoire of behavior that enables him to meet any challenge his environment provides" (Grant, 1972, p. 195) or to "provide a learning climate in which the greatest possible development of potential and fulfillment can take place" (O'Banion, Thurston, and Gulden, 1972, p. 200). Humanists who talk about creating an environment in which all people may realize their "full potential" are especially frustrating to scientists interested in the orderly study of human behavior. How, ask these critics, does anyone know what an individual's "full potential" is and how close he or she is to achieving it? Humanists respond to the complaint by reiterating their confidence that students, given freedom and responsibility for their learning, will choose healthy alternatives if the environment is right—warm, caring, supporting, challenging, stimulating. Some of the new humanists are calling for "behavioral objectives," which may lead some people to think that they are becoming "tough-minded" after all; however, the behavioral objectives endorsed by the true humanist are highly individualistic, typically arrived at through discussion between student and counselor.

When humanists are specific about common goals, they are likely to talk about helping students develop qualities such as openness, honesty, and self-awareness. These goals bring forth criticism from the developmentalists, who charge that such traits are a "bag of virtues" that are culture-bound, vague, and arbitrary. Sprinthall (1972a, p. 352) expresses the developmentalist's scorn: "The virtues are topical and current but are still an arbitrary list of static traits, time-limited and situational. In this sense it is no different to talk about openness, spontaneity, etc., than it would have been to talk about being brave, clean, and reverent in a previous era. The traits are more up to date, but we are still dealing with a bag of virtues as educational objectives." Furthermore, say the developmentalists, that honesty is a virtue that can be taught was pretty well discredited in the character education era of the 1930s, when the Hartshorne and May studies showed that there is no such thing as a stable trait of honesty. Honesty depends on the situation. So, too, goes the reasoning, does openness and spontaneity.

Despite such harsh criticism (which today's humanists seem disinclined to answer), the humanists do have a rather well-developed theory (discussed in detail in Chapter Seven) and a plan for action.

Implementation. Humanists propose developing a total campus environment that is "accepting" and "loving" and "caring." Although these words are criticized by cognitively oriented faculty members, they represent a program for action to the dedicated humanist. Humanists stress the dignity and worth of the individual, holding that if people and cultures would not thwart and misdirect development, people would grow in healthy and self-actualizing ways. They emphasize self-discovery, emotional feeling, spontaneity, and freedom. Since no "outsider" knows the innate capabilities and dispositions of another individual, they suggest that the thing to do is to develop a warm and accepting climate in which the individual can find his true nature without threat or embarrassment. Humanists believe that there is, in each person, a self-actualizing person waiting to emerge under the right conditions.

A 1970s' humanistic approach to student development is presented by O'Banion, Thurston, and Gulden (1972). They advocate that the "old" profession of student personnel work should reorient itself to a "new" profession of student development facilitation: "*Facilitate* is an encountering verb which means to free, to make way for, to open the door to" (p. 204). Student development facilitators are described in typical humanistic terms: "They tolerate ambiguity; their decisions come from within rather than from without; they have a zest for life, for experiencing, for touching, tasting, feeling, knowing. They risk involvement; they reach out for experiences; they are not afraid to encounter others or themselves. They believe that man is basically good and, given the right conditions, will move in positive directions. They believe that every student is a gifted person, that every student has untapped potentialities, that every human being can live a much fuller life than he is currently experiencing" (p. 204). In addition to these personal qualities, the student development facilitator must have the set of professional skills required for guiding the creation of a total environment which "facilitates the release of human potential" for everyone—students, faculty, staff, even citizens of the community. Courses in student development would be taught in basic encounter groups similar to those described in Chapter Seven. They would be "courses in introspection: the experience of the student is the subject matter."

For some thirty years, educational institutions have flirted off and on with group methods for self-exploration, and the techniques have met with considerable resistance each time they have surfaced. Nevertheless, the humanistic approach to student development has made considerable impact on a few institutions and a modest impact on a substantial portion of community colleges. My 1974 survey of institutional practices showed that one fourth of the community colleges offered T-groups or sensitivity training (see Appendix A), and Ludwig (1973) found that the humanistic philosophy has made substantial impact on the teaching of human development courses in community colleges. Among the eighty-nine colleges in his survey that offered credit for personal development courses that utilized some form of basic encounter group, over 90 percent endorsed such humanistic concepts as the use of student experience as course content, the use of basic encounter processes, the provision of a supportive environment, and the provision of a reference group where students can openly express concerns. In a few colleges, the humanistic influence has been extensive, with administrators, faculty, and students working to create a total humanistic environment.

Developmental Approaches

Developmental approaches to student development grow out of the work of personality theorists such as Erik Erikson (1950) and Jane Loevinger (1970) and cognitive theorists such as Jean Piaget and Jerome Bruner. John Dewey also had a potent influence on their thinking. Developmental theorists are interactionists, holding that the individual and the environment interact in a continuing dialogue that leads to new organizations of knowledge and new perceptions of experience within the individual. Unlike the humanists, developmental theorists are perfectly comfortable taking a position that certain directions of development are universally desirable. Theirs is a hierarchical model in which there is an invariable order for increasingly advanced stages of development. Every human being passes through the same stages; no stage can be skipped; each stage is more complex than the preceding one; and each stage is based on the preceding one and prepares the individual for the succeeding one. The desirable goal is the highest level attainable, which not many people achieve.

Goals. The developmentalists are distinguished by their precise and explicit description of the stages of human development. There are a number of theorists that could be used to illustrate the developmental approach to personal development. Among the better known are Erik Erikson (1950) and Jane Loevinger (1970) who posit life-cycle stages of ego development. Since they give more attention to child and early adolescent years than to the college years, their work although important, is not reviewed here. Developmental theories are here illustrated by the work of Perry and Kohlberg, who have concentrated on high school and college students. Perry's nine developmental positions (1970, pp. 9-10) were derived through close observation and measurement of Harvard undergraduates as they proceeded through college in the 1950s and 1960s:

> *Position 1:* The student sees the world in polar terms of we-right-good vs. other-wrong-bad. Right Answers for everything exist in the Absolute, known to Authority, whose role is to mediate (teach) them. Knowledge and goodness are perceived as quantitative accretions of discrete rightnesses to be collected by hard work and obedience (paradigm: a spelling test).
> *Position 2:* The student perceives diversity of opinion, and uncertainty, and accounts for them as unwarranted confusion in poorly qualified Authorities or as mere exercises set by Authority "so we can learn to find The Answer for ourselves."
> *Position 3:* The student accepts diversity and uncertainty as legitimate but still *temporary* in areas where Authority "hasn't found The Answer yet." He supposes

Authority grades him in these areas on "good expression" but remains puzzled as to standards.

Position 4: (a) The student perceives legitimate uncertainty (and therefore diversity of opinion) to be extensive and raises it to the status of an unstructured epistemological realm of its own in which "anyone has a right to his own opinion," a realm which he sets over against Authority's realm where right-wrong still prevails, or (b) the student discovers qualitative contextual relativistic reasoning as a special case of "what They want" within Authority's realm.

Position 5: The student perceives all knowledge and values (including Authority's) as contextual and relativistic and subordinates dualistic right-wrong functions to the status of a special case, in context.

Position 6: The student apprehends the necessity of orienting himself in a relativistic world through some form of personal Commitment (as distinct from unquestioned or unconsidered commitment to simple belief in certainty).

Position 7: The student makes an initial Commitment in some area.

Position 8: The student experiences the implications of Commitment, and explores the subjective and stylistic issues of responsibility.

Position 9: The student experiences the affirmation of identity among multiple responsibilities and realizes Commitment as an ongoing, unfolding activity through which he expresses his life style.

Perry's model moves from perceiving the world in absolutist terms (positions 1, 2, 3) to making more room for diversity and recognizing the problematic nature of life (positions 4, 5, 6) to finding one's own place through personal commitment in a relativistic world (positions 7, 8, 9). In brief, development moves through sequences—from simplicity to complexity and from differentiation to integration. In Perry's scheme, the immature person perceives the world in either-or, good-bad, permitted-not permitted terms. A child or an immature student looks to an outside authority—parent or teacher—for the "right" answer. Gradually he begins to discover that authorities disagree and that the values of fellow students differ from his own. In an effort to resolve the differences between equally credible people, he adopts the "everyone has a right to his own opinion" stance or the "I'll do what *they* want even though I don't see why" attitude. The individual attaining more advanced levels of development begins to see that he must find integrity for himself in a relativistic world, identifying the things that are important and central to his sense of self.

In his research, Perry found that most Harvard freshmen enter college at stages 3, 4, and 5 and graduate in positions 6, 7, and 8. Position 9 was rarely observed in college students. It, like position 1 at the other extreme, is a logical extrapolation of the limits of the definition. Although Perry's method differs considerably from that used by survey researchers in studying student development, his definitions of the stages of development conform rather closely to the changes in college students documented by survey researchers. Seniors are less likely than freshmen to make simple and moralistic judgments; they are more flexible and able to cope with complexity and ambiguity; and they are more autonomous and integrated, with a clearer perception of identity.

Another model, also arising from study at Harvard, is the one developed by Lawrence Kohlberg. Kohlberg's model for "moral development" has much in common with Perry's scheme. He, like Perry, arrived at his model through extensive interviews and careful study of a small group of people. Both men, incidentally, studied primarily males. Perry used eighty-two men from Harvard and two women from Radcliffe, and Kohlberg worked with seventy-two teenage boys. While Perry's work leans strongly to research, Kohlberg is more concerned with conceptualization and theory. Rest (1974, p. 241) observes, "The enthusiasm that Kohlberg and his associates have recently generated in value education programs lies not so much in new curriculum materials and new teaching techniques, nor in the demonstration of spectacular results in their pilot programs, but rather in the way they discuss their general directions and purposes in terms of philosophical and psychological theory and research. . . . Educational programs with such a venerable lineage (Dewey-Piaget-Kohlberg, and so forth) have created interest because of the intellectual heft behind them and the promise of initiating something more than a superficial, piecemeal, short-lived fad."

Kohlberg is concerned with the *process* of development. He finds that the dictionary's definition of "development" makes a perfectly good starting point. To develop means "to make active; to move from the original position to one providing more opportunity for effective use; to cause to grow and differentiate along lines natural of its kind; to go through a process of natural growth, differentiation, or evolution by successive changes" (Kohlberg and Mayer, 1972, p. 483). Kohlberg, like Perry, has clearly set forth a hierarchical sequence of the stages of moral development (Kohlberg and Turiel, 1971, pp. 415-416):

I. Stage 0: Premoral Stage
Neither understands rules nor judges good or bad in terms of rules and authority. Good is what is pleasant or exciting, bad is what is painful or fearful. Has no idea of obligation, should, or have to, even in terms of external authority, but is guided only by can do and want to do.

II. Preconventional Level
At this level the child is responsive to cultural rules and labels of good and bad, right or wrong, but interprets these labels in terms of either the physical or the hedonistic consequences of action (punishment, reward, exchange of favors) or in terms of the physical power of those who enunciate the rules and labels. The level is divided into two stages:
Stage 1: The punishment and obedience orientation. The physical consequences of action determine its goodness or badness regardless of the human meaning or value of these consequences. Avoidance of punishment and unquestioning deference to power are valued in their own right, not in terms of respect for an underlying moral order supported by punishment and authority (the latter being Stage 4).
Stage 2: The instrumental relativist orientation. Right action consists of that which instrumentally satisfies one's own needs and occasionally the needs of others. Human relations are viewed in terms like those of the marketplace. Elements of fairness, reciprocity, and equal shar-

ing are present, but they are always interpreted in a physical or pragmatic way. Reciprocity is a matter of "you scratch my back and I'll scratch yours," not of loyalty, gratitude, or justice.

III. Conventional Level

At this level, maintaining the expectations of the individual's family, group, or nation is perceived as valuable in its own right, regardless of immediate and obvious consequences. The attitude is not only one of conformity to personal expectations and social order, but of loyalty to it, of actively maintaining, supporting, and justifying the order and of identifying with the persons or group involved in it. At this level, there are two stages:

Stage 3: The interpersonal concordance or "good boy-nice girl" orientation. Good behavior is that which pleases or helps others and is approved by them. There is much conformity to stereotypical images of what is majority or "natural" behavior. Behavior is frequently judged by intention: "He means well" becomes important for the first time. One earns approval by being "nice."

Stage 4: The law and order orientation. There is orientation toward authority, fixed rules, and the maintenance of the social order. Right behavior consists of doing one's duty, showing respect for authority, and maintaining the given social order for its own sake.

IV. Postconventional, Autonomous, or Principled Level

At this level, there is a clear effort to define moral values and principles which have validity and application apart from the authority of the groups or persons holding these principles and apart from the individual's own identification with these groups. This level has two stages:

Stage 5: The social-contract legalistic orientation. Generally with utilitarian overtones. Right action tends to be defined in terms of general individual rights and in terms of standards which have been critically examined and agreed upon by the whole society. There is a clear awareness of the relativism of personal values and opinions and a corresponding emphasis upon procedural rules for reaching consensus. Aside from what is constitutionally and democratically agreed upon, the right is a matter of personal values and opinion. The result is an emphasis upon the legal point of view, but with an emphasis upon the possibility of changing law in terms of rational considerations of social utility (rather than rigidly maintaining it in terms of Stage 4 law and order). Outside the legal realm, free agreement and contract is the binding element of obligation. This is the "official" morality of the American government and Constitution.

Stage 6: *The universal ethical principle orientation.* Right is defined by the decision of conscience in accord with self-chosen ethical principles appealing to logical comprehensiveness, universality, and consistency. These principles are abstract and ethical (the Golden Rule, the categorical imperative) and are not concrete moral rules like the Ten Commandments. At heart, these are universal principles of justice, of the reciprocity and equality of the human rights, and of respect for the dignity of human beings as individual persons.

Theory and implementation. The developmentalists are stronger on theory than on implementation, but their theory is so strong that it leads to inescapable conclusions about implementation. The problem, which is a serious one, is that they have spent so little time designing programs and evaluating them that their theory remains largely untested. Kohlberg and some associates will attempt to correct this shortcoming with the launching of an extensive moral development program in Boston-area high schools in 1974-1977.

Kohlberg refers to his theory as cognitive-developmental. In the choice of the name and in the structure of the theory, he follows in the path of such illustrious and respected theorists as Dewey, Piaget, and Bruner. There are four presuppositions of cognitive-developmental theory: "(1) Each stage of moral development is an integrated whole. The concept which defines a stage is reflected in the consistency of many acts and a consistency in the individual's response in regard to those acts. (2) A particular stage is seen as being integrated into the next stage and finally replaced by it. (3) Each individual actively works out his moral synthesis; he does not merely adopt a synthesis provided by the family, society, etc. (4) The individual must pass through all the previous stages before he can move on to the next stage. Thus, the order of succession of stages is constant and universal" (Craig, 1974, p. 121).

Embodied in these presuppositions are three fundamental ideas: *structural organization, developmental sequence,* and *interactionism* (see Rest, 1974). For Kohlberg, *structure* is an internalized conceptual framework through which the individual experiences and perceives and interprets and analyzes problems. Unlike the humanists, who value transitory states such as spontaneity and joy, developmentalists emphasize that learning experiences are valuable primarily for their cumulative effect on the development and evolution of the cognitive structure. The aim of education is to "stretch" the existing structure to accommodate new ideas and to stimulate the student to search for an organizational structure that will handle increasingly complex ideas and experiences. The notion of *developmental sequence* is a kingpin of developmental theory. More complicated and differentiated structures grow out of simpler structures to form "higher" stages of development. The lower stages are prerequisites to the higher stages, and while individuals might hit periods of "no growth," or become fixated at a lower level, people do not regress to earlier stages of development. A goal of education is to stimulate the individual to move to the next stage in the sequence. Finally, the notion of *interactionism* has the most direct implications for implementation. Developmentalists specifically reject the notions that cognitive structures are either genetically predetermined or a simple result of environmental rewards and punishments. They maintain that a new experience interacts with the previously established cognitive structure, thereby modifying that structure and making it more adequate; this modified structure in turn influences the new perceptions that are incorporated into the more complex structure. And so it goes, experience modifying structure and structure modifying experience.

These theoretical positions about the process of development suggest that developmentalists wish to influence *structure,* rather than competencies or specific capabilities, and that environmental influences must be stimulating and occasionally uncomfortable if the individual is to move to the next stage of development. Kohlberg's (1973) freshman course on moral development consists primarily of small-group discussions of moral dilemmas and of principles for solving them; there are also lectures and readings designed to raise some basic issues in moral philosophy and psychology related to personal development. The course appears similar to the original pilot studies initiated by Blatt and described by Rest (1974, p. 247). "Blatt's 'curriculum' consisted of a number of dilemmas and probing questions to initiate the discussion. . . . The teacher's role was to introduce the dilemma; to encourage class members to take a stand on what ought to be done and to explain why; to encourage confrontation and mutual probing by the class members of each other's reasoning without personal assaults (encouraging the clash of ideas, not personalities); to encourage listening and paying attention to each discussant's points and evaluation of the adequacy of the arguments; to furnish occasional high-stage responses as the +1 modeling of the highest students; to interject a probe question here and there; to reflect and summarize group deliberations; and to facilitate good group-discussion process. Upon deciding that profitable discussion had been exhausted on a dilemma, the teacher would then move on to the next one." Questions have been raised about the value of the "+1 modeling" referred to above. The rationale for +1 modeling is that the student should be exposed to some examples of behavior one stage beyond his own. This is most easily accomplished through heterogeneous discussion groups, where students can learn through exposure to the thinking of students more advanced than they; presumably the teacher must serve as the +1 model for the most advanced student in the class.

A somewhat different implementation of developmentalist theories is represented in the Deliberate Psychological Education programs proposed by Mosher and Sprinthall (1971, p. 9): "a comprehensive set of educational experiences designed to affect personal, ethical, esthetic, and philosophical development in adolescents and young adults." Sprinthall's various programs (Mosher and Sprinthall, 1971; Sprinthall, 1972b; Sprinthall and Erickson, 1974) emphasize a "learning by doing" approach. A seminar combined with a practicum is the key concept. The practicum always involves working with other people on the grounds that observing, listening, and responding to the needs

and feelings of others, when combined with the cognitive understandings of the seminar, will help students understand their
own "life-cycle" developmental processes. Thus, high school
students might gain an understanding of the childhood phase of
the life cycle through studying child development while working in a nursery school or tutoring children in elementary
school. To promote their own occupational development, students would study the psychology of work and other occupational literature; they would study and talk with adults in their
work roles; and they would be placed as unpaid interns in occupations that interest them.

While Kohlberg's is primarily a classroom approach and
Sprinthall expands his to include a practicum, Perry (1970) con-
ceives of the total college environment as the arena for development. Like Kohlberg, Perry places considerable importance on
classroom teaching, but his study led him to the conviction that
the most important source of support for positive student development derives from the realization of community—from the
feeling that the student is part of a community of people, all of
whom are working out their own "Commitment," which is
Perry's highest position of development. In order to help students move up the stages of development to their highest attainable level, Perry suggests that educators should be open with
students in sharing their own "thinking, groping, doubts, and
styles of Commitment." He notes that "Most of our students
seemed to have found one or more models of this kind, and to
be appreciative of them" (p. 213). He also recommends that
educators recognize and confirm the student as a fellow member of the community. This confirmation can be bestowed in
numerous ways. One student, for example, reported as the
standout experience of four years the feeling of community
that came over him when a grader wrote "nice point" in the
margin beside a paragraph that the student considered especially
meaningful. To take another example, students in the Perry
study were very appreciative of the interest of the researchers in
their growth as people. Many observed that every student
should have an interview, such as that conducted by the researchers, in which personal and intellectual growth is discussed
with representatives of academe.

Perry also makes some observations about the teaching process. He found that the most difficult transition for students occurred when they moved from seeking "answers" to looking for relativistic understandings in subject matter. Students need support and understanding as they grope toward this higher level of cognitive development. Many community college students, especially those with few positive learning experiences in the past, may not reach this developmental stage in their two years in community college, but others will be ready to move toward it and instructors must be alert to the need for support.

The concept of different levels of student development should also help instructors understand why different students perceive individual faculty members in different ways. The student at the right-wrong answer stage of development may feel annoyed and confused with the instructor who does not spell out exactly what the student is to do and how he will be graded, whereas the student at a higher level of development may understand and appreciate ambiguity and flexibility. According to Perry, teachers must meet students where they are and help them to advance to the next stage. (For an especially good discussion of matching teaching approaches to student developmental status, see Joyce and Weil, 1972, Chap. 17. See also Chapter Five on cognitive styles.)

Much of Perry's book (1970) is a detailed analysis of his research and is intended primarily for those who are interested in the scholarship of cognitive development. One chapter, however, is an essay written for the general reader who wants to know more about how students perceive themselves and their experiences as they proceed through four years of liberal arts education. I recommend it to faculty who want to gain further insight into the developmental stages of their students.

As we have seen, there are numerous ways to implement developmental theory. The basic idea is to introduce students to problems that will *stretch* the cognitive structure, permitting it to grow to more advanced levels of development. Kohlberg does this through class discussion of moral dilemmas; Sprinthall, through cognitive and experiential analysis of life cycles as they are lived by people; Perry, through the concept of a community of scholars. Teachers and counselors planning to use developmental theory need to be thoroughly familiar with the stages of development and with the concept of cognitive organization. The theory is especially attractive to educators because it integrates very neatly what one *is* with what one *knows.* And higher education has long insisted that knowledge should have an impact on values and attitudes.

Multidimensional Approaches

Multidimensional models for student development conceive of an individual growing at different rates along separate, but not necessarily independent, dimensions. Models typically measure developmental status along eight to twelve "scales" or "vectors" or "competencies" spanning the breadth and depth of human abilities. Multidimensionalists are held together not by a common philosophy or theory about student development but rather by the pragmatism of their methods. Typically they define their dimensions, devise strategies to attain their goals, and design assessment procedures to measure attainment. Contrasted with humanists, who are holistic, and developmentalists, who emphasize a central organizing structure, the multidimensionalists are pluralistic. Developmental status of students is indicated not by a single structure or core but by a profile showing the level of attainment reached on each dimension of personal development.

Goals. The developmental goals of multidimensionalists are defined by their particular set of dimensions, and the dimensions may come from almost anywhere. They may come from a group of people sitting down together and agreeing that a particular set of competencies will constitute their definition of personal development; or they may be derived through the application of various kinds of research procedures. Panos (1968, p. 309), for example, suggests that the best way to translate the vague goals of education into useful objectives is to obtain "a clear picture of what actually happens to the students. Perhaps, after we have been able to discover and adequately document what the outcomes of college are, we can think about whether we like them or not and what we can or cannot do about them." Such a way of establishing goals is not as revolutionary as it sounds. Articulation of the goal when one knows what will happen anyway is a sure path to creating correspondence between goals and actions. In actual fact, most "theorists" do start their theory building with some research about "what will happen anyway." Perry and Kohlberg, for example, both started with research observations about developmental phenomena. Their goal, like that of Panos, is to enhance the desirable.

Finally, multidimensionalists can develop complex and comprehensive schemes for arriving at significant dimensions of personal growth. Researchers have applied the statistical methods of factor analysis or the Delphi technique to reveal dimensions. Chickering (1969) used a systematic review of theory and research on college student development to arrive at his seven vectors of student development. Whatever the origins of the particular dimensions, multidimensional models typically cover a broad range of human development, including intellectual, social, physical, and emotional aspects. An example of a multidimensional model is the "eight-competencies" model of Alverno College (1974):

1. Develop effective communication skill

2. Sharpen analytical capabilities

3. Develop workable problem-solving skill

4. Develop facility in making independent value judgments and independent decisions

5. Develop facility for social interaction

6. Achieve understanding of the relationship of the individual and the environment

7. Develop awareness and understanding of the world in which the individual lives

8. Develop knowledge, understanding, and responsiveness to the arts and humanities

Another multidimensional model is Chickering's (1969) seven vectors of student development:

1. Achieving Competence
   a. Intellectual
   b. Physical
   c. Interpersonal

2. Managing Emotions

3. Becoming Autonomous

4. Establishing Identity

5. Freeing Interpersonal Relationships

6. Developing Purpose

7. Developing Integrity

Although the particular dimensions represented in these two models differ, the models themselves are similar. Both define an explicit set of developmental tasks to be accomplished by the maturing individual. Both incorporate provisions for assessing the level of attainment on each dimension. Both assume that a goal of education is to help students make progress along each dimension through offering a diversity of growth-inducing experiences.

Theory and implementation. Multidimensional models are typically weak on theory and strong on research and implementation—a direct reversal of the priorities of the developmentalists. Fundamentally, although not usually explicitly, multidimensionalists are behaviorists. They define measurable objectives, attempt to find some relationship between cause and effect, and devise strategies to bring about the desired result. They may, however, also use theoretical concepts in explaining growth along certain dimensions. Chickering (1969), for example, uses the developmental concepts of differentiation and integration in much the same manner as Perry and Kohlberg.

Most research studies of student growth in college use multidimensional models (see, for example, Chickering, 1969; Feldman and Newcomb, 1969; Trent and Medsker, 1968; Withey, 1971). Researchers decide on the "relevant" dimensions, take measurements of student growth, and attempt to determine how students changed and why. The findings of the research then become their recipe for implementation. For example, if students attending a college with a distinctive image show significant change in the expected direction, whereas similar students attending a less distinctive college show no change, then it is assumed that the factors contributing to the distinctiveness of College A are responsible for the observed changes. If the changes are perceived as desirable, then a college would try to emulate the conditions of College A in the hope of inducing student change in the observed direction. Chickering (1969), for example, hypothesizes that colleges can accelerate or retard growth on each of his seven vectors of personal development. He turns to past research, or in the absence of relevant research, to hypothesis building to locate the major sources of influence. He has identified the following variables as those constituting "conditions for impact": (1) clarity of objectives and internal consistency; (2) institutional size; (3) curriculum, teaching, and evaluation; (4) residence hall arrangements; (5) faculty and administration; (6) friends, groups, and student culture.

Wherever possible, Chickering relates the six "conditions for impact" to his seven vectors of personal development. His major attention is directed to pulling together the various research studies in which "treatment" has some measurable effect on "outcome." As one would expect, there are not one-to-one relationships between treatments and outcomes. Rather, Chickering (1969, pp. 145-157) arrives at some fairly broad and general conclusions, which he presents as hypotheses that have been documented by research findings:

1. Impact increases as institutional objectives are clear and taken seriously, and as the diverse elements of the college and its program are internally consistent toward the objectives.

2. As "redundancy" (too many people for too few significant responsibilities) increases, development of competency, identity, and integrity and the freeing of interpersonal relationships decreases.

3. When choice and flexibility are offered, when direct experiences are called for, when teaching is by discussion, and when evaluation involves frequent communication concerning the substance of performance and behavior, the ability to analyze and synthesize is fostered, as are sense of competence, freeing of interpersonal relationships, and development of autonomy, identity, and purpose.

4. Residence hall arrangements either foster or inhibit

development of competence, purpose, and integrity and the
freeing of interpersonal relationships, depending upon the diversity of backgrounds and attitudes among the residents, the
opportunities for significant interchange, the existence of
shared interests, and the degree to which the unit becomes a
meaningful culture for its members.

5. When student-faculty interaction is frequent and
friendly and when it occurs in diverse situations calling for
varied roles, intellectual competence and sense of competence,
autonomy, and purpose are fostered.

6. The student culture either amplifies or attenuates the
impact of curriculum, teaching and evaluation, residence hall
arrangements, and student-faculty relationships.

In addition to research models, there are competency-
based programs of education that represent a multidimensional
approach to student development. Alverno College (1974) provides a good example. Not especially concerned with theory or
past research, the college has devised educational strategies that
will help students attain the competencies deemed necessary for
the well-educated person. While research as a body of literature
is not critical to them, research as a methodology involving
effective assessment and evaluation is of the utmost importance.
Their implementation hinges on assessing present levels of competency, determining goals, and evaluating attainment. The
Alverno model defines eight competencies, each with six levels
of accomplishment. Levels are sequenced in steps of increasing
complexity and conceptual difficulty, and students proceed
step by step to demonstrate competency. Demonstration of
competencies at the highest level also requires integration across
competencies.

While the multidimensionalists are a less closely knit
family than the humanists or developmentalists, they represent
another alternative to the development of deliberate education
to promote personal growth in students. Clearly, we have some
suggested models for taking the personal development of students out of the realm of the "accidental" benefits of college
and placing it in the "deliberate" educational program. The
emphasis of the multidimensionalists is on the identification of

cause-and-effect relationships. Their developmental programs consist of creating the conditions that bring about the desired effect. They would not exclude offering a course on moral development or an encounter group experience if these "treatments" could be shown relevant to goals. In one sense, the approach of the multidimensionalists to student development is more a method than a theory.

Conclusions

We have reviewed three different approaches to deliberate education for personal growth and development. They share the conviction that education for personal development is an important responsibility of colleges and that we can do a much better job of it than we are presently doing. Although their approaches and emphases differ, there is more agreement than disagreement among them, and we can make some generalizations about the present state of knowledge about student development through a synthesis of the points of agreement. All three schools of thought would probably agree with the following propositions: (1) Development is a lifelong process occurring in sequences and spurts rather than in linear or regular progression. (2) Development involves the total being, integrating cognitive and affective learning. (3) Development involves active internal direction rather than "adjustment" to culturally determined criteria. (4) Development is stimulated when the individual interacts with an appropriately challenging environment. (5) The phenomena of developmental growth can be submitted to scientific study. (6) Educational programs and interventions can be designed to make an impact on the rate, level, and direction of development.

While we have not yet reached an adequate understanding of the processes of human development, the models of student development presented in this chapter contain many helpful suggestions. There is, for example, no excuse for not giving more attention to the establishment of the type of "community" in which educators demonstrate their interest in students' personal as well as intellectual development. Likewise, there is no excuse for concentrating on the dissemination of knowledge in the academic disciplines to the exclusion of provoking students to thought and analysis through discussion and a pitting of their ideas and thoughts against those of others in the community. There is no lack of challenging intellectual problems and moral dilemmas in the subject matter of the real world. We need not retreat to the study of areas in which we know the "answers" and can therefore "teach" with confidence. Surely we owe it to ourselves and our students to think through what it is that an educated person should be able to do. Is there any evidence that would lead us to believe that helping students to attain the competencies that they and we think are important is not an improvement over the present time-serving of much of today's education? Is there any reason to think that the positive faith in people shown by the humanists is not a good thing for all of us to demonstrate? In brief, even in the absence of a completely adequate theory of student development, no educator should be without ideas about what he or she can do to help students in their quest for personal development.

In reality, most practitioners are theoretical eclectics, drawing on the ideas that fit their personal style or particular educational assignment. Teachers, for example, might find the ideas of the developmental theorists most useful in their work because of the emphasis on cognitive structure and the development of problem-solving skills. To have before them the three basic ideas of structural organization, developmental sequence, and interactionism can be extremely helpful in thinking about the kind of teaching and learning experiences that will stimulate students to a higher stage of development. Helping students to reach higher levels in a Kohlbergian model, however, does not rule out the use of encouraging the search for self in an atmosphere of trust and support that is so strongly emphasized by the humanists. Nor does acceptance of those practices preclude defining competencies and measuring attainment in a multidimensional approach. As a matter of fact, working toward carefully defined competencies may well *require* the use of teaching and counseling concepts developed by humanists, developmental theorists, or eclectics.

Certain counselors may find humanistic precepts more useful for creating an environment in which students can explore without threat where they are in their stage of development and how to get where they would like to be. Other counselors might find themselves comfortable and useful teaching a class in moral development; still others may wish to help students work toward specific competencies.

There is an infinite variety of things that can be done to enhance the personal development of students. Certainly the present state of knowledge about student development does not provide a legitimate excuse for anyone to sit around and wait for the *right* approach to student development. While research and theory provide no assurance that what we do will work, it is probably safe to assume that doing something in an informed and thoughtful way has an extremely good chance of being more helpful to students than doing nothing. The more faculty, counselors, and college administrators read and think about their role in providing the best possible education for students, the better chance we will have of making a difference.

7

Learning About People
from People

❊❊❊❊❊❊❊❊❊❊❊❊❊❊❊❊❊❊❊❊❊❊❊❊❊❊❊❊❊❊❊❊❊❊❊❊❊

The most direct approach to learning about people is through experiential learning in small groups emphasizing interpersonal interaction. So great is the interest in this type of learning that T-groups, sensitivity groups, and their offspring have swept across the country with amazing, and sometimes alarming, speed. *The New York Times* labeled 1968 "the year of the group"; and the well-known psychologist Carl Rogers (1969, p. 6) asserts, "It is probable that the most important social invention of this century is the encounter group (T-group, laboratory, sensitivity training). The demand is utterly beyond belief." The primary growth has been outside the educational establishment, among people interested in improving interpersonal relationships for personal or business reasons; but various kinds of group experiences are beginning to appear on the community college scene. Almost one fourth of the colleges responding to the 1974 survey reported some use of T-groups, sensitivity training, or similar small-group sessions (Appendix A).

Current estimates place the number of people participating in group experiences of one kind or another between three and six million people (Appley and Winder, 1973). The figures take on significance when compared with the national enrollment in community colleges (three million) or the total enrollment in all segments of higher education (ten million). The movement is interesting enough and strong enough to furnish a lively topic of conversation across many segments of American life. Its ardent supporters proclaim it a new religion while its detractors denounce it as a quack nostrum. The more detached "neutrals" label it a fad, predicting that it will soon pass from the scene. But few fads endure for thirty years, showing the steadily accelerating rate of growth of T-groups and variations on the theme. The group movement has grown in many directions, some reputable and well accepted, especially by industry, and some not so reputable.

Training groups (T-groups) and "sensitivity training" were controversial when they were introduced by a reputable group of scholars at Bethel, Maine, in the mid-1940s: "The hostility was so great in the early days that one might have placed his professional reputation in jeopardy" by according recognition to group work in interpersonal relations (Argyris, 1967, p. 153). Among some academics, the hostility persists even in the 1970s. Many faculty members who consider themselves open-minded and enlightened and eager to learn are frank to admit that they know nothing about group work in interpersonal relations but that they are adamantly opposed to it. They are embarrassed and uncomfortable in the presence of talk about "sensitivity training" or even the less emotionally charged "human relations education." Nevertheless, it is time for "respectable academics" to look at what is known about this difficult area. Some of their fears about the viability of the methods will not be removed by better information, but at least they will approach the subject from a position of knowledge rather than ignorance.

Since a number of mutations and variations all spring from the central method of people interacting with one another in small face-to-face groups, the general term *laboratory educa-*

tion has been used to connote the experimental, active learning experience typical of the movement. What is laboratory education? The most succinct and direct definition is one used by Schein and Bennis (1965, p. 4): "Laboratory training is an educational strategy which is based primarily on the experiences generated in various social encounters *by the learners themselves,* and which aims to influence attitudes and develop competencies toward learning about human interactions." Simple as that definition is, there has been enough misunderstanding about the terms used in human relations education that chapters and even entire books have been written to attempt clarification of the differences between various forms—for example, between therapy groups (for people with difficult personal problems) and T-groups (for people without emotional problems who want to learn more about themselves, other people, and group procedures) (Appley and Winder, 1973; Frank, 1964). One author (Wells, 1970) suggests that the very words *sensitivity training* and *encounter groups* have acquired an emotional load that frightens many people and thus impedes responsible progress. And Wiggins (1970) proposes that the term *sensitivity training* be eliminated from the vocabulary of educators concerned with human relations education.

Throughout this discussion, I shall use the terms *T-groups, training groups, laboratory education,* and *human relations education* to designate appropriate learning experiences for basically undisturbed people who wish to improve their skills in interpersonal relations. I will not discuss therapy groups, because their purpose is inappropriate for the development of a general college course of study; they assume the correction of personal and emotional problems rather than emphasizing the development of talents and strengths. The popular terms *encounter groups* and *sensitivity training* will be used only rarely because their use and misuse has left a residue of confusion regarding their meanings. In one book entitled *Encounter* (Burton, 1969), for example, the definitions of the various authors—who are all presumably addressing "encounter" experiences—run the gamut from "the second psychiatric revolution" (Steinzor, 1969) to "providing affective domain experience for the 'normal' college student seeking paths to productive, satisfying, and creative living" (Morris, Pflugrath, and Taylor, 1969, p. 196). The term *sensitivity training* has met much the same fate. Once used to express the broad notion of helping people to become more sensitive in human interactions, it has acquired a multitude of meanings, ranging from the rather unemotional "humanizing job relations in industry" to the highly emotional "indiscriminate tearing away of [psychological] defenses" (Edwards, 1970, p. 260).

In any case, both *sensitivity training* and *encounter group* have, rightly or wrongly, picked up questionable reputations as well as connotations of heavy emotionalism. Appley and Winder (1973, p. xvii) aver that, unlike T-groups, which "place reason and intellect on a par with affect," encounter groups offer primarily instant need gratification and heightened emotional sensitivity. Edwards (1970, p. 261) goes further: "Emotionalism is the mode of operation in almost all sensitivity training groups. Intellectualizing is strictly forbidden." Needless to say, educators are not likely to take kindly to curricular innovations that *forbid* intellectual analysis and cognitive understanding. Laboratory education encourages cognitive understandings, and the literature in the field abounds with the vocabulary of learning; *learning how to learn, analysis, diagnosis, understandings, awareness, insights, behavioral skills, interpersonal competencies,* and *transfer of training* are words that appear consistently as laboratory educators set forth their goals.

Characteristics of Laboratory Education

Although laboratory educators seem to feel it necessary to develop their own set of goals statements, the agreement among the goals developed for various purposes is high. Differences in wording arise primarily as a result of specific goals and emphases. Thus, the National Training Laboratories (NTL) tend to stress group dynamics and societal change, whereas the Esalen Institute is more concerned with individual dynamics and personal growth (see Brown, 1971). The goals of a laboratory for business executives (Strauss and Sayles, 1972) differ somewhat from those of a laboratory for college students majoring in elementary education (Marshall, 1970). Perhaps the best general statement of goals is that provided by Miles (1960, p. 301): "The usual aims of human relations training are not informational in the usual 'educational' sense—though a good deal of cognitive reorientation may be involved—nor are they 'curative' and therapeutic, strictly speaking, though a good deal of change in the social self seems to emerge. Most human relations training laboratories focus on improving the person's sensitivity to social phenomena, on increasing the sophistication with which he is able to diagnose the reasons for ineffective interpersonal and group situations, and, of course, on his ability to act effectively and satisfyingly in concert with others."

The T-group (or training group) is the fundamental unit of laboratory education. It usually consists of ten to fifteen members and one or two staff members, who serve as "trainers." Members of the group may be strangers without much in common except a desire to improve interpersonal effectiveness; they may be strangers who share occupational goals (business executives, teachers, or academic vice-presidents), or they may be colleagues who work together (for instance, in an academic unit including administrators, faculty, and students). Whatever the constituency, T-groups are typically unstructured. The trainer may offer a very brief explanation that the group will decide what to do and how to learn from the experience. There is no formal teacher and no agenda. The fundamental purpose of the group experience is to help people learn how to learn from the data provided by the behavior of other people. Appley and Winder (1973, p. 105) note: "The activities that are required for being in the group seem simple enough: participation, observation, listening, responding, analyzing, trying out some new (for them) behaviors, seeing what happens." The task of the group is to create a temporary community that is "psychologically safe," so that each person in the group can look, without fear of reprisal, at his own behavior, its effect on others, and their effect on him. The learning environment is one emphasizing openness, trust, risk taking, interdependence and collaboration, and a spirit of inquiry.

The techniques of the T-group, then, are based on the assumption that if the hindrances to personal growth can be removed, basically normal people will seek self-actualization: "Growth, self-actualization, the striving toward health ... the yearning for excellence ... must by now be accepted beyond question as a widespread and perhaps universal human tendency" (Maslow, 1970, pp. xii-xiii). Most of the methods used by laboratory education are designed to remove the barriers to healthy growth and to permit the self-actualizing person to emerge. The learning experiences offered by laboratory education are different in many ways from those used in conventional schooling. The major characteristics of laboratory education are described below.

Here-and-now focus. One of the basic characteristics of the T-group is the emphasis on "here-and-now" learning. Since the content (the material to be learned) is human interaction, what better way to learn it than to experience it (affective learning) and to analyze the experience (cognitive learning)? The "here and now" is preferred to the "there and then" because the whole point is for all members of the group to see the same demonstration, so to speak, and to bring their varying perspectives to the analysis of what is happening as people interact. This is what is meant by T-groups generating their own data. The purpose of the T-group is to watch itself in action. It cannot do this if members describe a back-home situation ("there and then") because other members are not able to experience the same situation. Furthermore, the description of "there and then" is not regarded as valid, since it is subject to filtering by the reporter. "Here-and-now learning," write Schein and Bennis (1965, p. 39), "is based on experiences which are shared, public, immediate, direct, first-hand, unconceptualized, and self-acknowledged." This is in marked contrast to conventional learning, which is vicarious, impersonal, and usually directed by an authority.

Ambiguous situation. Almost everyone has experienced the frustration of participating in a work group that was not clear about what it was to accomplish or how to go about it. The usual approach is to attempt to reduce frustration and increase productivity by structuring the group—designating a leader, defining the task as clearly as possible, preparing an agenda. The T-group, however, is deliberately leaderless and agendaless and ambiguous, because members are there to observe how people react to people—not how capable people are of doing a task or how efficiently the group can marshall its forces. Schein and Bennis (1965, p. 16) describe the emotional impact of the opening session of the usual T-group suddenly left to its own devices by the trainer, who has explicitly denied that he has leadership responsibility for the group: "Different members use different strategies. Some ask further questions of the trainer; some try to get him to be more of a leader or guide; some lapse into an anxious watchful silence; some get angry; and some attempt to organize the group with various tasks like 'introducing ourselves.' As the members fill the vacuum with their behavior, they begin to generate the raw data from which they will have the opportunity to learn about themselves, their impact on others, others' reactions to them, and how groups work."

One of the purposes of creating uncomfortable ambiguities is to promote the process known as unfreezing or unlearning or reduction of defensiveness. In the absence of familiar procedures, behavioral grooves are upset and group members are forced to search for new behaviors and thus to begin the process of new learning. Kurt Lewin, the theorist with the greatest impact on laboratory education, identified three stages of change—unfreezing, changing, and refreezing. Change begins with disequilibrium—with feeling a need for change. Thus, the ambiguity of the initial session sets the stage for individuals to seek new information about themselves.

Nonthreatening environment. Getting a group of people together to interact and study the process sounds deceptively simple—so much so that relatively inexperienced people have attempted to form experimental T-groups without the services of staff people trained in psychology and laboratory education. But the group can be tyrannical as well as supportive, and experienced trainers are careful to create a "safe environment." The theory is that if people are to learn new behaviors when interacting with other people, they must be free to try new things, free to receive honest feedback, and free to share openly their reactions without fear of reprisal. Such freedoms are given high value in the T-group. Most testimonials to the power of the T-group make reference to the supportive, collaborative atmosphere which evolves in the group: "We are always amazed at this supportive and ameliorative strength of the group in freeing its members for creative and courageous acts. . . . The main source of psychological safety for the individual delegate is his sense of support and strength earned in and somehow borrowed from his T-group" (Schein and Bennis, 1965, p. 45).

Feedback. The concept of feedback is a kingpin of most learning theory. People learn most effectively if they have immediate and continuous feedback about their performance, and learning effective human relations is no exception. After people reach a certain age, however, direct feedback about their effect on others is nonexistent or subtle. Some people who have developed sensitive antennae to the feelings of others pick up subtle feedback cues, and presumably continue to grow, whereas others are relatively immune to the reactions of others, and thus have difficulty improving. In any event, laboratory educators contend that almost everyone needs valid data in order to improve social learning skills. The T-group is devised to provide the one kind of feedback that is ordinarily missing from daily life.

The most common feedback mechanism in laboratory education is the direct and simple one of open and frank discussion within the T-group. Other feedback mechanisms include the use of scales to gather data about perceptions, dyadic interviews in which two people compare reactions to group incidents, group-process observers, and videotape recording and replaying of group sessions.

Analysis. Although the focus of T-groups is on "here-and-now" learning, laboratory education does not exclude reflection, looking back, and cognitive analysis. How much cognitive analysis is appropriate is a matter of controversy: "Some trainers favor practically no cognitive material; others desire a rather large portion. The decision about the quantity and type of theory material to be used is usually made on the basis of needs of the delegate population, the importance of conceptualizing the experience, the need for linking the material to action steps, and the inclinations of the staff" (Schein and Bennis, 1965, p. 47). When T-groups are used in the college setting as part of the curriculum, heavy emphasis on cognitive learning seems essential. Research from a comprehensive study of group experiences at Stanford University suggests that cognitive analysis is a central characteristic of productive groups (Lieberman, Yalom, and Miles, 1973). Furthermore, since humanistic educators have been critical of traditional education for overemphasizing the cognitive aspects of learning, it hardly seems like progress to go to the other extreme and overemphasize affective learning to the point of excluding the conceptual framework that provides the basis for continued learning.

There are essentially two ways in which cognitive analysis takes place: in the group, where each member becomes an observer as well as a participant; and in lectures and theory sessions, where experiences of the T-groups are tied together with information about the processes and theory of laboratory education. Especially for those planning to pursue careers in human relations, cognitive understandings are necessary.

Theory

Laboratory education shares the problems of inadequate theory development with the social sciences in general. Given enough time and enough trial and error, we stumble onto something that seems to work. But we have a very difficult time explaining why it works. That is where laboratory education is today. It seems to work for many people; but, until we have a conceptual framework, we cannot create the hypotheses that will advance understanding through research.

The laboratory group movement was initiated by theorists and researchers attempting to understand the sociology of groups; it then shifted in the early 1950s to a psychological emphasis, attracting people trained in clinical psychology or psychiatry. Today, it is a multidisciplinary, highly eclectic field of study involving people from sociology, psychology, psychiatry, business administration, education, theology, and social welfare. Unfortunately, there has been little cross fertilization among these disciplines. While we have learning theories, personality theories, and theories of group behavior, we lack knowledge about the dynamics of learning as it takes place in the individual. Since human relations education has a cognitive element, an emotional element, and a behavioral element, the search for theory is further complicated.

Laboratory education, however, has a problem that is not shared by the social sciences in general. It seems to attract many more practitioners than researchers or theorists. It is estimated that practitioners outnumber researchers by 100 to 1 (Appley and Winder, 1973). Lieberman, Yalom, and Miles (1972, p. 30) remark that the use of personal-growth groups "has mushroomed so rapidly that the gap between what is done and what is known has widened alarmingly."

Nevertheless, there is some broad theory underlying the movement, and it springs largely from two sources: Maslow's optimistic theories about human growth (1962, 1967, 1970) and the field theory and attitude-change studies of Lewin (1951, 1953). Other theories more specific to the operation of T-groups (see Bradford, Gibb, and Benne, 1964; Buchanan, 1969) are mostly "rationalizations of practices that are growing up in a rapidly expanding field of professional activity" (Gibb, 1964, pp. 184-185).

Maslow's theory is so all-encompassing that it might be termed a philosophy about human nature. His work is bright and hopeful and especially relevant to our search for better growth experiences for New Students. Psychologists, in his view, should not be obsessed with studying man's weaknesses and deficiencies but should turn their attention to the study of human strengths. In a very moving article, Maslow (1967) tells how he became interested in studying people who were unusually successful human beings; he calls them self-actualizing people. His efforts were stimulated not by academic psychology but by his attempts to understand two teachers "whom he loved, adored, and admired and who were very, very wonderful people" (p. 279). His doctoral training in psychology had provided him no basis for understanding them: "It was as if they were not quite people but something more than people" (p. 279). Through observational notes and descriptions, it dawned on him that their two patterns could be generalized. Furthermore, the pattern held constant as he added other self-actualizing people to his observations. "Self-actualizing people are, without one single exception, involved in a cause outside their own skin, in something outside of themselves. They are devoted, working at something, something which is very precious to them—some calling or vocation in the old sense, the priestly sense. They are working at something which fate has called them to somehow and which they work at and which they love, so that the work-joy dichotomy in them disappears" (pp. 280-281). Young people, in Maslow's view (p. 281), have the potential for self-actualization within them; "they are looking for values and . . . would love to have something to devote themselves to, to be patriotic about, to worship, adore, love. These youngsters are making choices from moment to moment of going forward or retrogressing, moving away from or moving toward self-actualization. As counselors . . . what can we tell them about becoming more fully themselves?"

Maslow (1967, pp. 281-284) answers his question by listing eight ways in which one becomes self-actualizing:

1. "Self-actualization means experiencing fully, vividly, selflessly, with full concentration and total absorption."

2. Life is a process of choices—choices toward safety, defensiveness, or fear; and choices toward growth. "To make the growth choice instead of the fear choice a dozen times a day is to move a dozen times a day toward self-actualization."

3. We must assume that there is a self to be actualized—that people can respond as they really are rather than as others think they should be.

4. Each assumption of responsibility for honest self-appraisal is a step toward self-actualization.

5. "One cannot choose wisely for a life unless he dares to listen to himself, *his own self,* at each moment in life." Self-actualizing people must possess the courage to make the choices that are right for them.

6. Self-actualization is a continuous process toward maximizing one's potential. "Self-actualization means working to do well the thing that one wants to do. To become a second-rate physician is not a good path to self-actualization."

7. Conditions should be established for maximizing peak experiences. "Learning what one is not good at . . . [is] part of discovering what one is in fact."

8. Repression is not a good way of solving problems. One needs to be open with oneself and to give up defenses even if the process is painful.

Maslow believes that we will learn more about human beings by studying self-actualizing people than we will by research that looks for a statistical average in a natural setting. Gibb and Gibb (1967, p. 162) present a good analogy: "It is as if, wishing to determine how well men could hit golf balls, we lined up fifty average adult males at a golf tee, had each hit two balls, measured the distances, and concluded that the average man's driving potential was 30 yards. After practice and effort, perhaps the average man could hit the ball 155 yards. However, after experiencing a refined instruction process, the average person could possibly be trained to hit the ball 225 yards." Maslow admits that his research on the characteristics of self-actualizing people is not research at all by traditional standards. He has a highly biased sample that violates all rules of statistical sampling. Nevertheless, there is support for his theory and it has generated considerable research. Maslow himself was confident of its validity: "I personally feel very confident about its major conclusions; I cannot conceive of any research that would make major changes in the pattern, though I am sure there will minor changes" (Maslow, 1967, p. 280).

Because Maslow believes firmly that there is, in each person, a self-actualizing person waiting to emerge under the right social conditions, he insists that mutual concern and respect are therapeutic tools that can be used by anyone, with or without special training: "Certainly we need not be afraid as professionals of putting into the hands of amateurs these important psychotherapeutic tools: love for other human beings and respect for other human beings. . . . Love and respect are forces almost always for good and not for harm" (1970, p. 254). At its best, a T-group does create an atmosphere of mutual respect and concern. There is virtually unanimous agreement among writers on laboratory education that, with experience, group members do show a natural and spontaneous capacity for dealing in a helpful and supportive way with other members of the group. This observational finding tends to support Maslow's theory. Likewise, testimony about the frequent "peaks" of self-actualization that group members experience under conditions of freedom from defensiveness supports the theory of Maslow.

Many other theorists in psychology, most notably Carl Rogers (1951, 1961, 1970), have supported pro-active theories of motivation. Rogers has formulated a general hypothesis growing out of his experience in therapy; but he believes that it applies equally well to healthy, well-functioning people who would like to function better. He makes his general statement (1961, pp. 37-38) in an "if-then" style:

> If I can create a relationship characterized on my part:
>> by a genuineness and transparency, in which I am my real feelings;
>> by a warm acceptance of and prizing of the other person as a separate individual;
>> by a sensitive ability to see his world and himself as he sees them;
>
> Then the other individual in the relationship:
>> will experience and understand aspects of himself which previously he has repressed;
>> will find himself becoming better integrated, more able to function effectively;
>> will become more similar to the person he would like to be;
>> will be more self-directing and self-confident;
>> will become more of a person, more unique and more self-expressive;
>> will be more understanding, more acceptant of others;
>> will be able to cope with the problems of life more adequately and more comfortably.

I believe that this statement holds whether I am speaking of my relationship with a client, with a group of students or staff members, with my family or children. It

seems to me that we have here a general hypothesis which
offers exciting possibilities for the development of creative,
adaptive, autonomous persons.

Kurt Lewin is usually credited with providing the theoretical impetus for laboratory groups. He died in 1947, just as
what were then called basic skills training (BST) groups were
being established at the Gould Academy in Bethel, Maine, but
he had participated in the planning sessions. He was a phe-
nomenologist, stressing the distinction between the objective
and the psychological environment. And his concept of field
force guides the understanding of group dynamics. He saw
social behavior as a dynamic balance of forces. If the forces
from opposite directions are balanced, then there will be no
pressure for change and the group will maintain status quo.
Before change can occur, an imbalance must exist, thereby forcing the group to seek stability once again. The imbalance can be
created by increasing the driving forces (tension) or by decreas-
ing the restraining forces. The tension induced by the ambiguity
of the T-group's task springs from Lewinian theory, as does the
notion behind marathon groups, which tend to reduce restraint.
    Lewin identified three stages of change—unfreezing,
changing, and refreezing. Schein and Bennis (1965) have used
these concepts in explaining a model for attitude change. They
observe that people, by and large, do not change as a result of
information. People ignore things they do not like to hear, or
they discount the validity of the information, or they attribute
the problem to something outside of themselves. The additional
ingredients necessary for change are heightened anxiety and
reduction of threat. These elements are not likely to be present
in most organizations. Cultural norms prevent the expression of
clear and unambiguous cues about the reactions of people to
other people. And real-world groups—especially in business
organizations—are rarely personally nonthreatening in the sense
that people are free to admit errors of behavior and experiment
with new behaviors. The T-group provides the necessary conditions for unfreezing.
    Once unfreezing has taken place and the person is ready

to change, the question of the direction or nature of the change arises. According to Schein and Bennis (1965), two options for change exist. The person can scan the environment for various cues that can be put together for their relevance to individualistic needs. Or he or she can select a model (another person) and pattern himself or herself after that person. For obvious reasons, scanning is considered preferable. Scanning for change cues is also more consistent with the theories of Maslow and Rogers, who believe that there is a unique self-actualizing and autonomous person ready to emerge. A major strength of the laboratory group is that it exposes the individual to a variety of other people and attitudes; the organizational group, in contrast, encourages emulation of a model (perhaps the boss) that reflects corporate values.

Refreezing is concerned with the stability of the change. One of the troublesome problems of T-group experience is that changes are frequently temporary; they occur in the laboratory setting but are not transferable to the back-home situation. Refreezing or stabilizing will take place to the extent that the new attitudes are consistent with the rest of the personality and to the extent that they are reinforced by important others in the environment. There is, of course, such a thing as temporary refreezing, which may take place in the supportive atmosphere of the laboratory but is dissipated when the trainee returns to the more permanent environment of the family or work situation.

How can the theory underlying laboratory education be applied to the needs of New Students? Since I view New Students as people with strengths that have not developed, due in part to our overemphasis on their academic weaknesses, the theories of Maslow and Rogers serve as crucial background for our attempts to help New Students become more effective people. If the small-group experience offers psychological support and acceptance, permitting previously suppressed strengths to emerge and develop, then it is an important educational tool for developing adequacy in interpersonal relations and in self-acceptance, an obvious first step toward developing the career-oriented interpersonal skills for working effectively with others.

Research

There is no lack of research on laboratory education. It runs the gamut from fairly abstract and theoretical analyses of group processes to concrete and pragmatic measures of the "back-home" behavior of people who have participated in laboratory education. Gibb (1971, p. 842), after reviewing 106 research articles and seven earlier reviews, concludes that "the quantity and quality of available research is surprisingly high ... [but] the results are disappointingly equivocal." A decade ago, Stock (1964, p. 435) reviewed sixteen years of research on T-groups and concluded, "Research about T-groups suggests a large checkerboard, incompletely and unevenly filled in." Sad to say, research in the intervening years has not filled in many squares. Indeed, we may have succeeded only in making a larger checkerboard. Research has raised as many questions as it has answered, and the spiral of inquiry into the complexities of human development continues to reach apparent consensus on some issues, only to raise new questions that no one thought to ask until research showed us the extent of the inadequacies of our understandings.

The research, like the theory, is eclectic and fragmented. There are so many variables in the situation that it is almost impossible to establish the controls that lead to definitive research. Groups have distinctive characteristics; leaders have varying styles; and participants bring unique personalities, motivations, and goals to the situation. To complicate the research picture further, there are numerous objectives of laboratory education, and each must be evaluated by slow, conscientious study.

T-groups, as they are used in education, have reasonably well-defined objectives. Broadly speaking, we need to know the effectiveness of laboratory education in helping students to understand themselves and to develop sensitivities to the feelings of others. We need to know whether these skills will transfer out of the mystique of the T-group into application to everyday interactions. These goals may be considered competency or adequacy goals that should be developed by all human beings regardless of their career choice. Students wishing to pursue excellence in human relations as a career, however, will also need to learn something about personal leadership and about how groups function. These goals involve complicated evaluation procedures. The variation in the competency of the evaluations is apparent, and we shall limit discussion to the most adequate designs. Let us look first at the evidence for the usefulness of laboratory education in a goal that is of special importance to New Students. Does T-group experience result in improved self-concept or self-esteem?

Effects on self-concept. There are essentially three ways of measuring changes in self-concept as a result of laboratory education. We can ask the person whether he feels better about himself. We can ask him to answer a questionnaire or inventory that is an indirect measure of how he feels about himself. Or we can ask others whether they observe changes in his behavior that would indicate increased self-confidence. All three approaches have been used in the research with varying success.

In general, most T-group participants state that they value a personal-growth group experience and that they feel better and more accepting of themselves for having participated. Gassner, Gold, and Snadowsky (1964) report that 99 percent of the students participating in a three-day human relations training program at City College of New York reported that they felt they had gained new skills and new insights. Sixty-one percent of the Stanford undergraduates participating in a variety of group experiences evaluated by Lieberman, Yalom, and Miles (1972) said that they had changed in a desirable direction as a result of their group experience, and three fourths of them expected the changes to be lasting. Over two thirds of the young people at a YMCA camp claimed that they had changed "much" or "a great deal," and almost half of the group of 420 teenagers said that increased self-identity was one of the most important things they got out of the experience (Himber, 1970). The research is sprinkled with statistics of this type, and with a large number of ecstatic testimonials: "My problem was that I could never talk around people I didn't know, so of course at the assembly I didn't say too much. But they encouraged me to participate more and feel wanted. I guess that was the most important thing that happened. Instead of always taking myself down, I'm going to try to feel just as good as everyone else." "I learned how to express my feelings and emotions a lot better. My group gave me assurance that I wouldn't be rejected and I wasn't" (cited by Himber, 1970, p. 315). "The leadership laboratory was a marvelous experience. I was in it a month ago, and I am still awestruck" (cited by Dunnette and Campbell, 1968, p. 9).

More compelling than testimonials, perhaps, is the behavioral evidence presented by Trotzer and Sease (1971). They found that the attendance and commitment of college students to their encounter groups was greater than that of comparable groups of students to more conventional discussion groups. Members in three encounter groups attended an average of 7.2 sessions out of eight, whereas the members in three discussion groups attended an average of only four sessions. Furthermore, two out of three of the encounter groups decided to continue meeting after the conclusion of the study, whereas the discussion groups did not, despite the fact that the topics discussed (Vietnam, student unrest, religion, sex, drugs, and social prejudice) were presumed to have high interest value.

With this evidence of the breadth and depth of satisfaction of participants in personal-growth groups of one kind or another, it is not especially surprising that the movement has mushroomed largely through word-of-mouth advertising. While we would be foolish to discount these testimonials and statistical summaries of customer satisfaction, they fail to provide the data needed by educators to determine the *educational* merit of the experience. While most of us would be pleased if students left our classes with the "high" of enthusiasm that seems to overtake growth-group participants, we want to know whether the changes are real, whether they are lasting, and what happens to those who do not experience satisfaction. (Just to keep things in perspective, we should also evaluate traditional educational experiences along these criteria. How lasting is the knowledge we dispense, how much difference does it make in behavior, and what happens to those who do not experience success?)

It is difficult to cope with the question of how "real" the

changes in self-concept might be. In full recognition of the fact that people can answer questionnaires or respond to interviews with the "right" answers to please the researchers, some investigators have used more subtle measures, such as discrepancies between the "real" and "ideal" self. The assumption is that the greater the correspondence between the way a person sees herself and the way she would like to be, the greater the self-acceptance. Throughout the literature of psychology, self-acceptance plays an important role. There is theoretical and research support for the notion that self-accepting people are better adjusted and more accepting of other people than those with large discrepancies between the perceived self and the way they would like to be (Berger, 1952; Carlson, 1965; Lecky, 1945; McIntyre, 1952; Rubin, 1967; Wylie, 1961).

Since the T-group directs attention to changing the real rather than the ideal self, it is assumed, not without some research evidence (Burke and Bennis, 1961; Grater, 1959), that a decrease in the real/ideal gap is due more to changes in the real self than to changes in the ideal. Research on this question is important because it relates to Lewin's theoretical predictions about the necessity for "unfreezing" old behaviors and perceptions before new growth can occur. The rationale for greater self-acceptance with group experience is summarized by King, Payne, and McIntire (1973), who point out that most people perceive more negative self-traits than do observers. In the explorations of the group, people begin to realize that their inadequacies are not unique and that even with their shortcomings they can be accepted and even admired by others in the group.

Unfortunately, the research findings about the effects of T-groups on increased self-acceptance have been equivocal. It is the old story, it seems, of research designs and measuring instruments that are questionable enough to leave considerable doubt about whether the research or the treatment is at fault in the failure to present definitive conclusions. Burke and Bennis (1961) found convergence between "real" and "ideal" self; but Gassner, Gold, and Snadowsky (1964) found that convergence occurred in their control group as well as in the experimental group. While Gibb's (1971) review of the literature is cautiously supportive of the effectiveness of T-groups in bringing about increased self-acceptance, the studies seem to run the gamut from no significant change to significant and lasting change. If one simply takes a numerical count of the studies showing positive results or no significant results, then the positive findings clearly have the edge with respect to improved self-acceptance as a result of group experience. A positive experience, however, is by no means universal. Klaw (1965) reports that about 10 percent of the graduates of one laboratory experience returned liking themselves less. A statement from one such person captures the feeling: "I seemed to have lost all the positive aspects of my self-concept. I realized that I had built up concepts about myself that were untenable. But I had not gained anything to replace them" (cited by House, 1967, p. 3). We shall return to a discussion of the dangers of small-group confrontations later.

In general, there is reason to think that with better research the findings would be more, rather than less, positive. Obviously, some situations are more conducive to positive growth than others, and if positive forces were identified and utilized, we should expect improved effectiveness. Marathon groups, for example, seem to result in greater change than groups spacing their sessions throughout the semester (King, Payne, and McIntire, 1973); groups led by "caring" leaders show more positive change than those with "charismatic" leaders (Lieberman, Yalom, and Miles, 1972); and people who have conflicts regarding self-identity change more than those with clearly defined self-concepts (Stock, 1958).

But even if carefully designed research showed people reporting, directly or indirectly, that they felt better about themselves, there would still be problems. There are those who question the validity of self-report data (Dunnette and Campbell, 1968). Some researchers have sought greater objectivity through asking others to report changes in the subject's behavior. While the concern is quite valid, one must ask in this instance whether acceptance of the person's own word regarding his feelings about himself is less valid than that of an observer, who must make inferences about how the person feels. The finding by Lieberman, Yalom, and Miles (1972) that change estimates by leaders, other group members, and the self were nearly uncorrelated complicates the picture further and raises real questions as to whose word one should accept.

Follow-up studies are helpful in this regard if we can assume that participants are more realistic after six months or a year, when the initial glow of enthusiasm that seems to overtake most people has waned. And the "peak" experience does seem to abate. Lieberman, Yalom, and Miles (1972) found that whereas the ratio of high to low evaluations stood at 4.7 to 1 immediately following the group experience, it dropped to 2.3 to 1 six months later. If change has occurred, however, it tends to persist to at least a moderate extent in follow-up studies (Guinan, Foulds, and Wright, 1973; Himber, 1970; Lieberman, Yalom, and Miles, 1972). Reddy (1973) believes that we need more *longitudinal* research to help untangle the complexities of the personal-growth experiences of laboratory education. He reports the interesting finding that YMCA administrators who made changes in self-actualization *during* a ten-day residential sensitivity workshop did not show significant growth in the year following the workshop, whereas some of the administrators who showed no change during the workshop did show change a year later. Perhaps, he suggests, the anxiety associated with the training period prevented change for some people, who moved ahead only after they returned to more familiar and supportive environments. Or perhaps there are plateaus in personal growth, as there are with cognitive learning, so that those who spurted ahead in the laboratory period had made the growth that was possible for them during the year. While they generally maintained their position, they may have needed new insights and experiences to stimulate the next stages of growth toward self-actualization.

Effects on sensitivity to others. How successful is laboratory education in helping people relate to others? Gibb (1971), in his review of the literature, made a tally of seventeen studies with data on the influence of training on interpersonal sensitivities and reported fourteen with positive results and three with no change. Furthermore, testimony and statistics can be cited to show that, in a global self-assessment, T-group participants

think they have learned something about how to relate effectively to others. For example, 86 percent of the college students
participating in a twenty-four-hour marathon group reported six
months later that they communicated with others more effectively, and two thirds of the group felt that they were more
understanding of others and had more confidence in other
people as a result of their experience (Guinan, Foulds, and
Wright, 1973). Likewise, Himber (1970) found that, at a global
level, over half of the high school and college students participating in a YMCA training program noted a "better understanding of others" as the most important outcome of their T-group
experience. These feelings of warmth and trust that are generated in the group seem to spread to people in general, so that
participants describe people and situations in more interpersonal terms (Campbell and Dunnette, 1968; Gibb, 1971; House,
1967). The fact that these descriptions are at a global verbal
level does not make the case for increased sensitivity, but
neither does it detract from the idea that someone who *believes*
that he is more understanding and empathic actually begins to
behave more humanly. Dissonance theory suggests that people
who say they are more human act more human. Carron (1964),
for example, found that managers participating in T-group training placed more emphasis on consideration and less on structure
as desirable leader behaviors. In a rational world, men who feel
that consideration of others is a characteristic of good leadership should show changed behavior; but that step is not easy to
demonstrate.

Lieberman, Yalom, and Miles (1972) concluded from
their studies that the changes that people experienced were
largely internal; they were not subject to observational verifica-
tion by friends and associates. In fact, friends were likely to
find positive changes in members of both experimental and control groups—a finding that casts suspicion on Himber's (1970)
finding that 72 percent of the parents of teenagers who had
attended T-groups at camp reported changes in attitudes and
behavior, especially in the area of tolerance for others. Himber
had no control group, so we are not sure whether the changes
parents perceived in their sons and daughters were real or

whether absence simply made the heart grow fonder. House (1967), however, did review six studies purporting to measure change based on observations of the participants back home and on the job after a T-group experience. He was struck by the "lack of contradiction among the findings" (p. 18) and concluded that T-group training resulted in observable changes, most of them positive but some negative. The positive changes were related to greater openness and concern for others; the negative changes, in at least one instance, concerned a greater show of emotion, which, the author noted, was not likely to be appreciated in the business world.

In addition to self-reports and behavioral observations, some investigators have tried to measure sensitivity by asking people to state their perceptions of the feelings and probable responses of others. In their 1968 review, Campbell and Dunnette concluded that the results of this approach have been largely negative. With or without T-group training, people do not seem to be able to predict the answers of others very well. I have found no body of research since 1968 that would change that general conclusion. One must, I think, question whether knowing how a friend would answer a questionnaire item on even such personal items as values is an adequate measure of sensitivity to the feelings of others. The largely nonanalytical ability to respond to a pattern of cues, some of them nonverbal, does not appear to call for the same skills that are used in analyzing the attitudes, opinions, and values of another.

Myers and her colleagues (1969) used a different approach to the predictions of the responses of others. They provided for regular instrumental feedback during training, in order to determine whether participants would increase their sensitivity to interpersonal phenomena occurring in the group. And, indeed, they found that people who knew how others were reacting to their behavior showed less discrepancy between the ratings they actually received and those they expected from others. As Myers and her colleagues point out, however, the results could be interpreted as simple conformity to group norms rather than as enlightened understanding of group interaction. Nevertheless, increased sensitivity as a result of T-groups is predicated upon the assumption that honest feedback in a nonthreatening environment will compensate for the social façade that prevents people from knowing how others react to them and how others feel about situations that become the common experience of the group. Therefore, procedures that result in constructive feedback (as opposed to destructive feedback, which is also possible in the T-group situation) should be a desirable procedure to incorporate into the training session.

In summary, the evidence for the effectiveness of T-groups in increasing interpersonal sensitivities looks very much like that for demonstrating increased self-acceptance. People generally *feel* that they have gained new insights, but it is difficult to prove one way or the other. We could take the position at this point that since the data on customer satisfaction are consistently positive, and other areas are positive at least as often as not, why not recommend the T-group as a viable alternative to more conventional teaching about human behaviors in a psychology course? That question brings us into direct confrontation with research pertaining to the possible dangers of T-groups. This is a critical question, of course, to responsible educators, and we wish the research and reporting were better. But let us look at the information that does exist.

Dangers and How to Minimize Them

A careful study of the literature regarding the possible negative effects of group laboratories leads to the inescapable conclusion that the topic is emotionally controversial and the data are pitifully inadequate to resolve the conflict. Two comprehensive reviews of the literature on T-groups conclude that the dangers to individuals are not so great as critics have charged. According to Gibb (1971, p. 856), "The evidence is clear that the reputed dangers are greatly exaggerated." House (1967, p. 29) generally agrees: "Instances of reported emotional collapse as a result of participation in T-group training are rare and completely undocumented." He acknowledges, however, that "the fact that they are alluded to, and a few instances reported, raises serious ethical questions for the persons responsible for instituting such a method." Indeed, because of the concern expressed among professionals, the American Psychiatric Association, the American Psychological Association, and the American College Personnel Association have all established special committees to look into the possible dangers and the ethical considerations involved in T-groups and sensitivity training. Lakin (1969, p. 928) summarizes the problem quite well: "Sensitivity training is one of the most compelling and significant psychological experiences and vehicles for learning as well as a promising laboratory for the study of human relationships, dyadic and group. It may be a superior device for personal and social change, even for amelioration or resolution of social conflict. However, it may also be abused or subverted into an instrument of unwarranted influence and ill-considered, even harmful, practices." The most appropriate professional statement regarding the use of group experiences in colleges and universities is that prepared by the American College Personnel Association (ACPA) Task Force on Group Procedures. Because of its importance, an abbreviated statement of the ACPA position is presented in Appendix B. Educators planning curricula in interpersonal relations, however, are encouraged to read the task force report in its entirety (ACPA, 1972, 1974, 1975).

While some authors fail to address the question of dangers involved, no one claims that there is no risk for the participants in the sometimes intense experiences of the typical group. No one concludes, however, that the risks are so great that the technique should be abandoned. The almost universal approach is to call for more research and to offer recommendations about how to minimize the risk. We shall attempt to look at what is known about the incidence and types of negative experience and at the recommendations for handling T-groups in a manner consistent with professional responsibility.

The figures on the incidence of negative reactions vary. Back (1972) cites official National Training Laboratories (NTL) figures: twenty-four serious psychiatric incidents out of eleven thousand participants in twenty-two years of summer programs; eight incidents out of three thousand participants in thirteen years of industrial laboratory programs. Those figures (less than

1 percent harmed) are the lowest reported, and it is a reasonable assumption that they are the lowest that any laboratory administrator could expect. The statistic obviously presents the most favorable case. The definition of damage specified "serious psychiatric incidents," and the professional training of the NTL trainers is widely reputed to be the best available. Furthermore, the NTL T-groups tend to emphasize group process more than emotional expression or therapy. Poorer supervision, a more moderate definition of "damage," or a more emotionally oriented approach would presumably raise the percentage of participants with negative experiences.

At the other extreme of the damage continuum are the figures reported by Klaw (1965), who found that 10 percent of the participants returned from a laboratory session sponsored by Western Training Laboratories liking themselves less and not knowing what to do about it. Falling somewhere between the less than 1 percent and the 10 percent is the 7.8 percent of the students from the Stanford experiment who showed negative reactions attributable to the group experience eight months after the end of their sessions (Lieberman, Yalom, and Miles, 1973). The Stanford figures can be considered conservative or inflated depending on the criteria for supervision, participation, group goals, and trainer competency. On the negative side, there was no screening of the student participants in the Stanford experiments to weed out those with preexisting personality disturbances. In addition, the groups studied ranged all the way from the rather traditional and conservative T-groups to the radical and aggressive Synanon group. The Stanford groups were selected to be representative of the types of personal-growth groups enjoying great popularity in California in the late 1960s. The researchers found that casualties were greater in groups with leaders who were charismatic and aggressive and who placed considerable emphasis on individual problems. Because the purposes and goals of some of the high-risk Stanford groups were rather different from those suggested in this chapter, colleges developing curricular T-group experience could realistically expect a considerably lower rate of casualties than the Stanford 8 percent.

On the other hand, the leaders of the Stanford groups were all carefully selected professionals with years of experience in leading groups. Furthermore, the presence of research observers at every session could be expected to have a moderating effect. Thus, the 8 percent risk factor found in the Stanford groups probably underestimates the damage from the proliferation of poorly managed group experiences available today to the general public. Indeed, the Stanford study group suggests that one of the reasons why colleges and universities should consider offering group experiences is that since students seem determined to participate in this type of experience, they might better do it under the supervision of responsible educators.

Obviously, so many variables are involved that we cannot make a realistic estimate of the potential risk; but we do know some precautions that can be taken to minimize the risks. The two most common recommendations are the obvious ones: use well-trained, competent leaders and screen the participants. The implementation of those recommendations is not as easy as it appears on the surface. How does one identify a competent leader, and how do we know which students might be hurt by the group encounter? Schein and Bennis (1965) suggest using as leaders only Fellows and Associates of NTL, and NTL has attempted to establish standards for qualified leaders. NTL requires advanced training in behavioral science, productive work in one's field, completion of a specialized training program on group participation and leading, and examination and review by an NTL board (Back, 1972). While careful screening and training of leaders undoubtedly help, the Stanford experiment shows that even with careful selection of leaders there are problems.

The work of Seldman, McBrearty, and Seldman (1974) adds to the worry about the ability of leaders to interpret the reactions of group members. They found that students with high dependency needs tended to deify the group leader, failing to distinguish between a leader who had been rated highly effective and one rated only mediocre by coworkers and supervisors. Furthermore, the less effective leader was gratified by the compliments that he received from the dependent group; he observed that they had greatly boosted his confidence in his ability as a leader. Many New Students have characteristics that would classify them as "dependent" (Cross, 1971); hence, proper selection and evaluation of group leaders are especially critical in community colleges.

The question of which students are potential candidates for harm is a complicated one, but there is some relevant research. Almost all authorities agree that participation on the part of students should be voluntary. Clearly, no one should be required or coerced into participation; but there are problems with volunteers, too. For example, there is considerable controversy over whether poorly adjusted people or well-adjusted people are more likely to volunteer for group experiences. Olch and Snow (1970) found that college students volunteering for training were less socially and emotionally adjusted than nonvolunteers. But Gilligan (1973) found that when weekend sensitivity groups were offered to a broad spectrum of students, volunteers were more self-actualized, less conservative and authoritarian, and more inner-directed than those who chose not to participate.

Screening of candidates is recommended by many authorities, primarily to eliminate students who might be hurt or damaged by the experience. Studies suggest that the screening procedure should eliminate those who are deficient in social skills (D'Augelli and Chinsky, 1974) or overdependent on others (Seldman, McBrearty, and Seldman, 1974) or those with low self-esteem, poor self-perceived mental health, and psychological distance from others (Lieberman, Yalom, and Miles, 1972). Stock (1964) found that responsive, outgoing people are most likely to profit from T-group experience, and D'Augelli and Chinsky (1974) found that those with the greatest interpersonal skills contribute most to effective group functioning. These findings suggest that T-group methods may be more appropriate for those seeking careers in human services (that is, for those wishing to develop *excellence* in working with people) than for those concentrating on the development of interpersonal *adequacies* (see Chapter One). Students electing people-oriented careers are likely to enjoy other people and respond comfortably to them and are also likely to contribute more to the group-growth experiences.

There has been a disturbing trend in community colleges in recent years to use sensitivity sessions with so-called "remedial" students in the hope that such sessions will build the self-concept presumed necessary for improved academic performance. I know of no evidence to indicate that such group-growth experiences result in improved academic performance. In view of the evidence we now have, it appears that offering unstructured, emotionally intensive group experiences to remedial students is a risky and undesirable practice. There are, however, some new variations on the growth-group theme that carry almost no risk for harm, and they may prove useful in helping some students cope with their feelings of inadequacy. The human potential movement, for example, is being used in almost one quarter of the community colleges in their work with New Students (Appendix A). Although the research is not yet adequate to evaluate the promise of Human Potential Seminars (HPS), the experience to date is sufficiently positive to warrant its consideration for use in the adequacy minor. (See Chapter Eight for discussion.)

Conclusions

One of the ways to help people improve interpersonal functioning is to offer actual experience in relating to people. There is every reason to think that experience accompanied by analysis is a more powerful learning tool than cognitive analysis alone. Despite the cool logic of that proposition, the implementation of it has been a subject of hot controversy for some thirty years. Admittedly, the methods of laboratory educators stand in marked contrast to conventional education. The wisdom of the best minds of the past presented by an acknowledged authority is replaced by "here-and-now" learning that uses immediate data generated by the group. Furthermore, the goals of the two forms of education are quite different: one purports to teach *about* human behavior; the other, to present direct experience *with* human behavior.

Nothing in the reported experience with group work or in the research evaluations of it to date would lead us to deny the proposition that the *combination* of direct experience with academic analysis is a better pedagogical approach than either one alone. There are three critical questions to be answered by the research on group work: Does participation in T-groups improve self-concept? Does it result in improved interpersonal relationships? Can it harm anyone? The answer to all three questions is a qualified yes.

The question of self-understanding is an important one for students planning careers in human services because there is evidence that people who understand and accept themselves are more understanding and accepting of others. While the research is not unanimous—it rarely is when dealing with the unpredictability of human subjects—there is reasonable consensus across a wide spectrum of studies that the majority of group participants feel that they gain self-insight and that this self-perception continues for periods of a year or more following the experience. The evidence is not as conclusive regarding the improvement of interpersonal sensitivities. Nevertheless, there are more positive than negative findings for behavioral changes that are observable by friends and associates of the participants. And once again, it is fairly clear that participants feel that they are more aware of and concerned about the feelings of others. There is also evidence that following group experiences participants describe other people in more accepting ways.

Although there are some hazards in T-groups and their less reputable cousins, encounter groups and sensitivity sessions, it is probably reasonable to suggest that a carefully designed program with competent leadership and screened participants should not run a significant risk. In any event, even conventional education is not without risk. Learning, if it has the potential for *changing* an individual, always involves risk. Only when we can be sure that learning will make no impact on students can we be assured that we are running no risk in exposing them to the new ideas that constitute learning. Finally, we might well ask ourselves whether the 10, 20, or 30 percent of the young people who are labeled "dumb" by the school system may not suffer as much damage to self-concept and to effective functioning as group participants who feel themselves labeled "unpopular" or "obnoxious" by the group. There are ways to reduce the potential damage in both situations. This chapter has set forth some suggestions for the care and handling of T-groups; this book sets forth some suggestions for reducing the deleterious effects of traditional schooling on New Students. We do not have any answer yet to the exceptionally complex learning task of improving interpersonal functioning. The group methods under discussion here represent young (less than thirty years old) and rather primitive first attempts. If we are to find better methods, scholars, practitioners, and educators need to join in responsible and constructive experimentation. It is time for critics to replace blind prejudice with informed evaluation and for supporters to replace emotional advocacy with sound analysis.

8

Interpersonal Skills

****

In contrast to the unstructured, holistic group methods for improving interpersonal relationships (the methods discussed in Chapter Seven), this chapter concentrates on structured approaches to skill development. Advocates of the structured approach contend that interpersonal skills do not differ in concept from typing skills or reading skills and that people planning careers in human services—or indeed planning to live with people in this mutually dependent society—need to learn interpersonal skills that can be defined and measured. Methods discussed in this chapter can be used in excellence majors and adequacy minors (see Chapter One). While my emphasis will be on the development of excellence for students planning careers in the human services, some of the people most interested in skill development have been involved in designing programs for lay helpers, paraprofessionals, and the ordinary man and woman in the street who will function in a more facilitative way with parents, children, coworkers, and friends with improved interpersonal skills.

Identifying Skills

Two approaches to the identification of human relations skills are prominent now. One arises from the work on job classification conducted by the United States Department of Labor; the other, from clinical and counseling psychology. One looks at *jobs* and the skills needed to perform them; the other looks at *people* and the impact of their characteristics on one another. These two perspectives result in somewhat different lists of interpersonal skills. Those approaching the identification of needed skills from a job analysis perspective are likely to use a vocabulary stressing specific behavioral descriptions. Action verbs such as *asks, listens, persuades,* and *counsels* predominate. Those working with the counseling or "helper" model are more likely to use descriptive nouns such as *empathy, warmth,* and *sensitivity.* One looks at what the worker *does*; the other looks at *how* he does it.

The two approaches also have somewhat different purposes. One is attempting to specify the tasks of the job as clearly and unambiguously as possible, so that the qualifications of people can be matched to the requirements of the job. The other is more interested in determining those qualities of a "helper" that will have a constructive impact on the "helpee." For the more complex professions, the helping model is probably a more complete model. It asks not only whether the individual possesses the necessary job skills as determined through job analysis, but whether the possession of such skills results in growth or self-reliance or learning of some sort in the individual being helped. A teacher, for example, might meet the job requirements of being able to present a good lecture, but the helping model would want to know how much difference that made to students.

On the surface, it might seem easier to devise a training program and evaluation procedures for the specific behavioral objectives of the job skills approach—easier to help teachers present good lectures, for example, than to help them motivate students. But both schools of thought claim that their particular sets of skills can be specified, developed through training, and evaluated. We will look later at two examples of training programs exemplifying the two models.

The cataloging of interpersonal skills is a young science—less than thirty years old. Sidney Fine, the primary architect of the United States Employment Service classification, developed the Functional Job Analysis (FJA) scheme in the 1950s. His task was to specify the job skills needed for occupations in the United States. Almost all jobs, he found, have components requiring interpersonal activities. Furthermore, it is possible to specify the *level* of interpersonal skills required for each job. In the same decade, Carl Rogers was trying to discover what skills were needed by therapists to bring about growth in clients. His answer was the beginning of the "helping model." Both approaches have a great deal to offer to the design of a curriculum in interpersonal skills, but both should be regarded as mere starting points for further developments. Knowledge and sophistication in the field of interpersonal skills are nowhere near as great as in the programs discussed in Chapters Three, Four, and Five. After all, colleges have presumably been working for hundreds of years on the improvement of teaching and learning in the traditional academic disciplines. We are just beginning our work on the development of human relations skills. There is, however, a great deal of interest now and some concentrated study and experimentation in progress.* Perhaps these new efforts will move us significantly ahead in the design of educational programs that will help people in their relationships with

*Educational Testing Service and a consortium of colleges were brought together in 1974 through funding from the Carnegie Corporation to work on the Cooperative Assessment of Experiential Learning (CAEL). They selected the *assessment of interpersonal skills* as one of their four priority areas. Their goal is to develop a taxonomy of assessment needs, to build a collection of assessment materials and methods, and to develop guidelines for the use of the assessment tools. They have issued some reports and working papers, and their materials will be subject to field trials in colleges across the nation in 1975-76 (Breen, Donlon, and Whitaker, 1975a, 1975b; Knapp and Sharon, 1975). In addition, Paul Breen and Urban Whitaker have developed two helpful slide shows entitled *Interpersonal Skills: An Analytical Framework* and *Interpersonal Literacy*. They are available through the CAEL Project at Educational Testing Service, Princeton, New Jersey.

other people, whether for personal or career purposes. Let us turn now to a closer look at two existing models for identifying interpersonal skills.

Interpersonal skills for jobs: United States Department of Labor. According to the Department of Labor, there are three families of skills, and all jobs can be classified according to the amount and level of skill required in working with data, people, or things. The *Dictionary of Occupational Titles (DOT)* contains 35,550 job titles, each one classified with respect to the skill levels required for working with each of the three categories. Table 3 shows the skills listed under each heading. The skills are listed in order of complexity. For example, *serving* other people by carrying out their requests is a lower-level skill (code number 7) than *mentoring* (code number 0), which involves decisions about how to provide guidance for other people.

Table 3
Occupational Codes

Data	People	Things
0 Synthesizing	0 Mentoring	0 Setting Up
1 Coordinating	1 Negotiating	1 Precision Working
2 Analyzing	2 Instructing	2 Operating-Controlling
3 Compiling	3 Supervising	3 Driving-Operating
4 Computing	4 Diverting	4 Manipulating
5 Copying	5 Persuading	5 Tending
6 Comparing	6 Speaking-Signaling	6 Feeding-Offbearing
7｝No significant	7 Serving	7 Handling
8｝ relationship	8 No significant	8 No significant
	relationship	relationship

Source: U.S. Department of Labor (1965, Vol. 2, p. 649).

Using the codes in Table 3, the *DOT* assigns a three-digit number to each job title. The code for an assembly line inspector, for example, is 6-8-4, indicating the need for low-level skills in working with data and people and middle-level skills in working with things. A college faculty member is coded 2-2-8, indicating the need for high-level skills in working with data and people and low-level skills for working with things.

It will be of interest to faculty members to observe that the DOT takes a rather conservative position with respect to the level of interpersonal skills required for college teaching. In 1965, at least, they considered the relationship to students to be one of "instructing" which according to the definition, involves "teaching subject matter to others." Many faculty, however, especially those working with the new "mentoring" roles, would insist on a reclassification to a higher level of interpersonal skill requirements—a classification of 0 (mentoring) rather than 2 (instructing). Mentoring involves "dealing with individuals in terms of their total personality in order to advise, counsel, and/or guide them," and this seems a necessary interpersonal skill for many college faculty members today.

The differences between the roles of instructing and mentoring become clearer when the roles are analyzed by behavioral components. The following modification of the *DOT* classification of interpersonal skills was devised by Breen, Donlon, and Whitaker (1975a, pp. 101-103) to assist colleges in assessing interpersonal skills development for students:

Mentoring
    listens
    asks questions
    reflects back feeling and informational responses
    guides conversation
    diagnoses and evaluates feelings and information
    feeds back diagnoses
    makes suggestions
    prescribes treatments and approaches to solving problems
    instructs: presents information, explains, gives examples
    forecasts possible outcomes, predicts consequences of alternative courses of action
    gives assurances and support
    motivates
    persuades and influences in favor of a point of view
    provides feedback and evaluation of progress
    makes new suggestions based on new information or circumstances

Managing
    sets goals and performance standards

establishes communication channels
promotes the free flow of two-way communication
formulates policies and directs their implementation
coordinates tasks, activities, and programs
plans conferences
makes decisions on personnel matters
provides evaluation of progress
prescribes alternative approaches to solving problems
administers and implements the policies of supervisors
allows others to lead
takes responsibility for duties and tasks under jurisdiction

Leading
establishes and implements performance standards
sets group priorities
persuades and influences in favor of a point of view
promotes group trust and cohesion
motivates
employs authority to accomplish goals through cooperation of group
maintains group harmony
controls group behavior through use of sanctions and punishments
determines the direction of the group
makes decisions on policy and procedures
solves problems by invoking symbols of his authority

Negotiating
states and argues position
bargains over terms
instructs: presents information, explains, gives examples
advances proposals
defends position with clear and coherent rationale
answers objections
presents alternative courses of action
gives and takes in a tradeoff of benefits
argues against counterproposals
discusses possible solutions
defines goals and objectives.
offers counterproposals when original proposals are rejected
reconciles opposing viewpoints
confronts opposing demands to clarify positions

Supervising
assigns tasks

discusses subordinates' use of discretion

explains operating procedure

implements performance standards

examines task outcome against stated criteria

directs studies

evaluates performance

interprets results of task performance

judges content and consequences of discretionary decisions

sets task objectives

assesses individual competence to perform a given task

ensures performance standards necessary to achieve objectives

Instructing

listens to opinions and ideas

presents lectures

elicits and discusses theories and practices

trains others in effective and cognitive principles

uses demonstration and role-playing techniques to teach
subject matter

conducts seminars and workshops

illustrates theories and principles through explanation
and example

tests and assesses knowledge and understanding of the
problem-solving process

answers questions

points out similarities and differences of viewpoints

makes inferences about the cognitive behaviors of others

Consulting

gives information and ideas based on experience and
training

recommends content and methods of training

provides sources of technical information

gives ideas to define and clarify procedures and product
specifications

informs on details of working out objectives

gives advice

explains content of programs

assists in working out of plans

guides implementation of plans

meets with, listens, discusses and answers questions to
resolve problems and promote cooperation

makes suggestions to reduce resistance and sharpen
understanding of program goals

recommends alternative courses of action

Entertaining
    tells stories and anecdotes
    selects and narrates jokes
    plays games
    gives support and assurances
    expresses sympathy
    sings songs
    acts in dramatic roles
    acts out a mime part using only gestures and actions

Persuading
    describes and explains advantages and benefits of a pro-
        gram
    converses with clients
    influences in favor of a service, product, or point of view
    demonstrates the advantages of programs, procedures,
        products, ideas, and services
    speaks and converses with individuals, groups, and or-
        ganizations
    coaxes individuals to elaborate on thoughts and feelings
    gives instruction, advice, and personal assistance

Obviously there is some overlap between categories, but it is clear that the mentoring role requires more interaction and more personal guidance than the role of instructing. Thus, mentoring is classified as a higher-level skill in the interpersonal domain because it is more responsive and reactive to the learner. This does not imply that mentoring is a more complex activity than instructing in any domain *except* the interpersonal. Preparing a well-organized lecture, for example, calls for very high levels of academic skill development. But such a skill would be indicated by high competency requirements on the Data scale rather than on the People scale.

The preparation of learning modules is a good example of a teaching skill that makes high-level demands on both Data and People scales. Initially, it requires a thorough grasp of the structure of the academic discipline; but, as we saw in Chapter Four, the first-generation module is never completely adequate because it lacks feedback from learners. In addition to having an understanding of subject matter, the sophisticated module builder needs to be a careful observer of student reactions, an astute questioner, and a careful diagnostician. Then, when it comes to using the modules, whether constructed by themselves or others, teachers need high-level interpersonal skills, enabling them to work with individual students in such matters as diagnosis, prescription, motivation, and stimulation.

The Functional Job Analysis, introduced by Fine and improved and expanded over the years, represents a carefully developed analytical approach to identifying the interpersonal skills required for careers demanding work with people (see Fine and Wiley, 1971). Unfortunately, although the methods of Functional Job Analysis appear to have great potential for clarifying curricular objectives in career specialties, it has not yet been used much to specify goals for skills training. Some work has been done on specifying the interpersonal skills required for teaching, however, and we shall look at an example of such a training program later in this chapter.

The helping skills: From counseling psychology. The "helping model" represents a somewhat different approach to the identification of important interpersonal skills from that used in the job analysis model. Its origin lies in the counseling profession, where the ultimate goal is to help the client. Thus, the behaviors of the counselor are important only insofar as they make some impact on another person. On the surface, this seems a narrow and rather unique requirement that would limit the applicability of the model. But on further reflection, it appears that the very essence of *interpersonal* skills lies in the impact of one person on another. Even in jobs not requiring complex training, the question of personal impact is an important one. The job of a receptionist, for example, calls for, among other things, "answering questions," but the *skill* needed by a receptionist might more appropriately include "answers questions to the satisfaction of the inquirer." The helping model, then, starts the search for relevant interpersonal skills by looking at the "helpee" rather than at the job. There is now an impressive array of evidence that certain helping skills result in positive growth for the helpee; the lack of such skills, on the other hand, results in no change or in actual deterioration (Carkhuff, 1969; Gazda and others, 1973; Truax and Carkhuff, 1967).

Carl Rogers (1957) was the first to write about the existence of a "therapeutic triad"—*empathic understanding, unconditional positive regard,* and *congruence or genuineness*—as the "necessary and sufficient" conditions for client growth. A decade later, Truax and Carkhuff (1967)—after reviewing the major theories of psychology, looking for elements labeled essential for effective therapy—came up with essentially the same triad identified by Rogers. They labeled the ingredients *accurate empathy, nonpossessive warmth,* and *genuineness* but concluded that this triad is necessary but not sufficient for healthy growth in clients. Carkhuff (1969) later identified eight core dimensions of successful helping: *empathy, respect, warmth, concreteness, genuineness, self-disclosure, confrontation,* and *immediacy.* Carkhuff's model can be applied to a range of careers, including teaching, counseling, social work, health services, and business management. It can also be applied to relationships with family, friends, and coworkers to create healthier human environments.

Carkhuff, who is not altogether uncontroversial in the profession of psychology, believes that everyone can and should be taught the core helping skills. He and his followers have suggested that the mystique of psychology has been overdone and that psychology can be "given away"—that it can be demonstrated effectively to the lay public. He claims that everyone can be taught to become a "helper" in society, promoting the growth of others and eventually creating an entire society that is functioning healthfully with respect to human relationships (Carkhuff, 1971, 1972; Sprinthall, 1972b). It is certainly an appealing idea; and Carkhuff has been called "a consummate genius" (Aspy, 1972) and "one of the most creative and original thinkers in current American psychology" (Ivey, 1971b). His critics, however, claim that his ideas represent at worst a dangerous oversimplification and at best an idealism that cannot be implemented.

It is too early to tell whether the proposed expansion of psychology to include everyone who serves in a "helping" relationship—all of us at one time or another—represents revolutionary change or a fad that will soon pass from the scene. Some ideas highlighted by Carkhuff's work, however, are bound to make a difference. If health-promoting conditions can be identified, and if these conditions are related to the skills of helpers, and if these skills can be developed through education, then indeed we do have a useful tool for creating some models for both excellence and adequacy in human relationships. Carkhuff's identification of important interpersonal skills, his specificity in defining and measuring them, his irreverent puncturing of the "mystique" of psychology at least give people a place to start in designing skill development programs.

Carkhuff, a pragmatic revolutionary who is interested in application and results, believes that most counselor training programs fail to produce helpers who make a positive difference in the lives of their helpees. He cites considerable research to support his contention that helpers who possess the eight core interpersonal skills can bring about constructive growth in helpees. Furthermore, he maintains that these helper attributes are *more* important than any technique or type of treatment. An abbreviated and oversimplified explanation of his training program would go something like this: The prospective helper is first taught (through such media as written descriptions, audiotapes, or videotapes or through modeling) to *discriminate* between low levels and high levels of empathy. Once the trainee can identify various levels of empathic behavior, he or she is taught how to *communicate* empathy—through responding to taped material, through role playing, or through practice with a helpee. Carkhuff emphasizes again and again the importance of the *trainer*'s "level of interpersonal functioning." The trainer must himself operate at a high level of empathy if he expects the trainee to understand the nature of the skill.

Skills Training Programs

The newest activity in teaching interpersonal skills leans heavily toward the use of structure. Skills are defined, didactic and experiential exercises are devised, and evaluation carried out to see if the program is effective in meeting its goals. The growth of the new structured programs in interpersonal skills is strikingly parallel to the highly structured programs discussed in Chapters Three and Four for the development of academic skills. There are those who claim that an academic education is more than the sum of its parts—more than the accumulation of academic skills—just as there are those who claim that a fully functioning helper is more than a bundle of interpersonal skills. Of course, they are right. But academic and interpersonal development are probably enhanced, not in any way hindered, by attention to both the whole person approach and the skill development techniques. The skills programs discussed in this section represent an illustrative rather than an exhaustive presentation.

Microteaching provides a good illustration of the job-analysis approach, and Gazda and his associates (1973) have provided an interesting application of the Carkhuff model. Because these two programs are designed for one important human relations career—teaching—they illustrate nicely the difference between a training model based on the job-analysis approach and one derived from the helping skills.

Microteaching. Microteaching was developed at Stanford University in 1963 as a technique to improve teaching skills. In the decade since its introduction, it has enjoyed widespread acceptance by teacher education programs, but it has been slow to seep into other professions requiring human relations skills. Since the technique appears to have considerable potential for analyzing and improving interpersonal skills, it is presented here as a promising component of the curriculum for excellence in human relations. It could also be adapted for use in helping people to achieve adequacy in interpersonal relations where specific skills need to be developed—for instance, in interviewing for a job (see Barbee and Keil, 1973).

Unfortunately, both the name and the developmental history of microteaching identify it so closely with teaching that faculty concerned with other human relations professions are not often exposed to discussions of the technique in journals or at professional meetings. Ivey (1971a) has applied the technique to the training of counselors and has coined the word *micro-counseling*; similarly, there is no reason why we should not talk about micronursing or microcommunity relations or microsales.

Perhaps we should coin the word *micropractice* to indicate the generic applications of the technique. I shall try, in this discussion, to describe the technique in general terms, so that its applicability to any human relations career may be discerned. But since most of the experimentation and almost all of the research have been done in teacher education, the reader will have to develop the appropriate parallels to his or her own field of study.

In a little book of 150 pages, Allen and Ryan (1969) tell all you ever wanted to know about microteaching—up until 1969 at least. And the literature reveals no major changes in emphasis between 1969 and 1974. The technique is simple and straightforward and, as developed in the Stanford Microteaching Clinic, consists of the following stages:

1. The trainee reviews a live or tape demonstration of a particular teaching skill, such as "lecturing" or "asking probing questions" or "using examples." (Notice that these skills are job-specific; that is, they are *acts* carried out by the worker.)

2. The trainee then designs a brief (five-minute) lesson emphasizing the use of the skill.

3. The trainee teaches this lesson to three or four students. The supervisor is present, and, if possible, the lesson is videotaped.

4. The students and the supervisor fill out rating forms.

5. A critique session is held by the trainee and supervisor. When a videotape is available, it is used in the critique. The objective is to help the trainee analyze his performance and to offer suggestions and alternatives for improvement. At the Stanford Clinic, the critique sessions last only ten minutes.

6. The trainee rethinks the lesson and teaches it to a new group of three or four students.

7. The procedure is repeated, focusing on different lessons involving the same teaching skill.

Fundamental to microteaching are the learning principles of *identifying objectives, modeling, feedback,* and *practice.* Microteaching is thus a technique in which the trainee is shown how to perform a specific task, is then helped to analyze his or her own performance, and then provided an opportunity to practice new behaviors in the light of the learning. There is nothing terribly new about that. What is new about microteaching, and the other approaches to skills training discussed in this chapter, is that human relations skills have not often been broken into components and deliberately taught as skills that can be learned through analysis, practice, and critique.

Until microteaching was introduced, the generally accepted assumption was that practice teaching, usually with quite minimal and frequently inexpert supervision, would help the novice teacher become a good teacher. As anyone who has observed some professors with thirty years of "practice" knows, practice does not necessarily make perfect. The same observations might be made with respect to any of the human relations careers. While internships, providing trainees an opportunity to apply classroom knowledge to actual situations, represent a giant step ahead of classroom knowledge alone, micropractice techniques may enrich internships as much as internships enrich academic knowledge.

The significant feature of microteaching is, as its name implies, the emphasis upon scaled-down encounters—scaled down in terms of class size, lesson length, and teaching complexity. Using a single skill to teach three or four students for five minutes is certainly a capsule version of the "real" teaching situation. The scaling-down feature permits focus and concentration as well as control of environmental parameters.

In their description of microteaching, Allen and Ryan (1969) first of all list and discuss the fourteen component skills that make up the complete act of teaching. These skills are defined as "general teaching skills that can be applied at many levels for teaching many different subjects" (p. 15), and they are listed as follows: stimulus variation, set induction, closure, silence and nonverbal cues, reinforcement of student participation, fluency in asking questions, probing questions, higher-order questions, divergent questions, recognizing attending behavior, illustrating and use of examples, lecturing, planned repetition, completeness of communication.

Training through microteaching involves four steps—definition, modeling, feedback, and evaluation. Let us use stimulus variation, the first skill listed to illustrate the role of *definition* in the microteaching model. Stimulus variation is a teaching skill designed to relieve the boredom of students who sit for hours watching teachers who drone on monotonously in voice and physical movement. A trainee trying to develop the component skill of stimulus variation would be helped to move about the classroom, to use nonverbal cues or gestures, and to focus attention on particular points with verbal instructions such as "Listen carefully to this" or with gestures such as pointing to objects or banging on the blackboard. Teachers can also vary the stimulus by using different interactional styles—by asking some questions of the total group, by directing questions to specific students, or by creating student-to-student interactions. Still another way to vary the stimulus is to shift the sensory channels required of students. That is, although students can learn from activities such as watching, talking, and manipulating objects, as well as by listening, teaching frequently reverts to the lecture style, in which students use only the modality of listening.

The first step in the microteaching model, then, is to help the trainee get a clear understanding of the nature of the skill. Since no interpersonal skill is so simple that there is only one way to do it, it is important to present a range of alternative behaviors. Indeed, the selection of the appropriate alternative to fit the circumstance is part of skill development.

After the component skills have been identified, they must be demonstrated; that is, the trainee must be shown how the skill looks when it is done well. The age-old technique of showing the learner how to do something has recently acquired the more sophisticated name *modeling,* and there is now considerable research on the role of modeling in learning interpersonal skills (Bandura and Walters, 1963). Modeling has assumed importance in the recent literature, probably in part as a result of the increasing complexity of skills demanded by society. Older learning theories emphasized the importance of reinforcement, but recent research points up the additional importance of making sure that the trainee has a clear idea of the behaviors considered desirable. Bandura and McDonald (1963) found that modeling had significantly more impact on behavioral change than reinforcement alone, and Wagner (1973) concludes that trainees can best learn to become student-centered rather than teacher-centered if they are *shown* the difference between the two styles. Specifically, verbal concepts should be clearly linked to demonstrated or modeled behavior. Along similar lines, Legge and Asper (1972) found that students with microteaching experience were better able to identify and evaluate teaching skills than those without such experience. The research suggests that the most effective modeling approach would be to combine verbal description with behavioral demonstration—to explain what is being done and why at the same time that the trainee is being shown what to do. Obvious as that sounds, it has not often been done in teacher training courses or any other human relations courses. And, of course, the very idea of showing an individual how to teach instead of letting him develop his own individualistic style is anathema to some (St. John-Brooks and Spelman, 1973).

Other aspects of the modeling procedure have also been researched. McKnight's review of research (1971) concludes that filmed models are as effective as live models and offer greater control over the behavior being demonstrated. One can select expert demonstrators and can edit tapes to show the desired behaviors, whereas live demonstrations are less subject to such quality control. The use of videotape also permits an accompanying commentary that points out the desired behaviors.

The preparation of modeling tapes and accompanying commentary would appear to be a valuable service that could be performed by a central agency for the use of colleges throughout the country. Indeed, the Far West Laboratory for Educational Research and Development has followed up the microteaching efforts of Stanford with the production of "minicourses," which, in addition to printed materials and evaluation forms, include instructional films describing and illustrating desired teaching behaviors plus films in which the trainee sees a model teacher demonstrating the skills in the classroom (Borg, 1972).

A third attribute of micropractice is its emphasis on *feed-back*. There are a number of possible feedback mechanisms, and perhaps no aspect of microteaching has been subjected to more research than the effectiveness of critique and feedback procedure. As if to play it safe, the Stanford Microteaching Clinic uses three different feedback techniques. The "students," young people from surrounding elementary and high schools paid to participate in the microlessons, fill out special feedback forms on their reactions to the lesson presented by the trainee. The supervisor also observes, and his or her comments are given to the trainee in a ten-minute critique session held immediately after the performance; this session between trainee and supervisor emphasizes constructive evaluation and suggestions for alternative approaches. In addition, a videotape is made of the performance, and the trainee can use this self-confrontation of the tape as further information about her performance. It is frequently, but wrongly, assumed that videotaping is a necessary element of microteaching. It is not; but the development of the technology of videotaping is an advantage in helping the novice see her performance more objectively. The videotaping component of microteaching is especially popular in community college programs. In my 1974 survey, 27 percent of the community colleges reported the use of "microteaching or similar use of videotape feedback" of student performance (Appendix A).

The research generally supports the efficacy of a combination of methods of feedback (Gibb, 1970; McKnight, 1971; Wragg, 1971). An analysis and commentary on the behavior observed, whether that of the model in the initial phase or of oneself in the feedback phase, seems to have greater impact than verbal analysis alone or than film viewing alone.

At the Stanford Clinic, performance is evaluated against the Stanford Teacher Competency Appraisal Guide (STCAG). Unless one accepts the components of the STCAG as valid indicators of teaching effectiveness, however, improved teaching competency cannot be claimed for those participating in microteaching exercises. But in the case of stimulus variation, for example, it is hard to argue that a teacher who has only one string to his bow or who uses only one technique would not be a better teacher if he used a variety of stimuli. Likewise, it is hard to deny the importance of a teacher's leading students to higher levels of thought by asking "probing questions." Nevertheless, some people are offended by the concept of micropractice. They do not question *whether* people can be taught certain skills but whether people *should* be taught to perform in ways that those running the program think desirable. It is an age-old question, and one that becomes more serious when packaged minicourses cover the nation. What if everyone met the minicourse requirements for "good teaching" in the same way? Might we not lose some of the rich diversity that is offered to students now? My own guess is that the development of specific skills does not saturate the desire for excellence, but rather lays the foundation for further individual and *individualistic* improvement. Nevertheless, it is undeniably important to urge institutions and individuals adopting micropractice units to critically evaluate the goals and criteria of any prepackaged program. We will have a healthier educational system if educators at the local level use nationally distributed materials as a starting point rather than a finishing point.

Most of the research on microteaching has concentrated on improving the technique rather than questioning the method as a whole. Perhaps that is understandable, since most of the research has been done at the Stanford Laboratory or by proponents of the method elsewhere. Furthermore, one important characteristic of microteaching is its ability to exert control over the complex variables of the teaching act. Such control should render microteaching a valuable research tool for the study of teaching, but it should also make research on the technique itself a natural. Indeed, its advocates proclaim that it is "one of the few experimental techniques which by its very structure encourages the combination of theory and practice, research and training, innovation and implementation. It is by this capacity for self-regulation that microteaching can perhaps revolutionize education" (Allen and Ryan, 1969, p. 122).

Whether it will revolutionize education or not remains to be seen, but it appears to have a good start on making teacher training more efficient and effective. Allen and Fortune (1966) found that teacher interns spending ten hours per week in the microteaching clinic were rated higher on teacher effectiveness than student teachers in a twenty-five-hour-per-week program of regular instruction plus practice as teacher aides. Similarly, Kallenbach and Gall (1969) found that microteaching interns were noted equal in effectiveness to a group of regular student teachers, although one fifth as much time was devoted to the microteaching treatment. While the time saved may be considerable for the trainee, Davis (1971) warns that the teacher trying to handle microteaching sessions without the benefit of a Stanford Clinic must be willing to devote additional time to the course just to give each student a chance at an individual microteaching session.

Research by Borg (1972) indicates that the skills learned in microteaching tend to be lasting ones. Performance ratings four months and thirty-nine months after completing training revealed retention of most of the ten behaviors taught in a minicourse related to the discussion method of teaching. The big limitation of the Borg study, however, is that teachers knew when they were being videotaped. Because of expense, it was not possible to obtain random time sample videotapes. Thus, the subject could play to the camera, doing what he knew he should be doing only when the cameras were on. Nevertheless, it is encouraging to know that teachers could, when motivated, demonstrate that they knew how to use the discussion techniques they had been taught three years earlier. It is hardly fair to demand that the training method assume total responsibility for seeing to it that, day in and day out, teachers teach as well as they know how.

The micropractice format can be applied across a wide spectrum of activities—from the simple but very important task of helping young people present themselves well in a job interview to the highly complex skills involved in psychiatric interviewing. We might well conclude with Flanders (1969, p. xv) that "microteaching [may] in the future be combined with other procedures in a 'behavioral analysis clinic.' To educators seeking a more potent curriculum for self-development, much remains to be investigated. The opportunities seem almost endless, and the future offers an attractive challenge."

The Gazda-Carkhuff model. Microteaching, as we have

Figure 1. Empathy Scale in the Gazda program (Gazda and others, 1973, p. 71).

1.0	1.5	2.0	2.5	3.0	3.5	4.0

An irrelevant or hurtful response that does not appropriately attend to the surface feelings of the helpee. However, in instances where content is communicated accurately, it may raise the level of the response.

A response that only partially communicates an awareness of the surface feelings of the helpee. When content is communicated accurately, it may raise the level of the response; conversely, it may lower the level of the response when content is communicated inaccurately.

A response that conveys the helpee is understood at the level he is expressing himself; surface feelings are accurately reflected. Content is not essential, but when included it must be accurate. If it is inaccurate, the level of the response may be lowered.

A response that conveys the helpee is understood beyond his level of immediate awareness; underlying feelings are identified. Content is used to complement affect in adding deeper meaning. If content is inaccurate, the level of the response may be lowered.

KEY WORDS—Empathy Scale

Level 4—underlying feelings; additive
Level 3—surface feelings reflected
Level 2—subtractive
Level 1—irrelevant; hurtful

just seen, defines teaching skills in terms of task-oriented job competencies similar to those found in the *DOT* classification. In contrast, Gazda and his associates (1973) look at teaching as a "helping" profession, and the skills to be developed through Gazda's program are similar to those identified by Rogers and by Carkhuff and Truax. Specifically, Gazda's program directs attention to the development of Carkhuff's eight core dimensions of effective interpersonal functioning: *empathy, respect, warmth, concreteness, genuineness, self-disclosure, confrontation,* and *immediacy of relationship.* Gazda believes, and cites research to support his position, that the students of teachers who demonstrate high-level functioning on Carkhuff's core dimensions show higher levels of learning and personal development than the students of low-scoring teachers.

The Gazda program follows the Carkhuff model. It consists of a series of exercises directed toward helping the trainee understand the nature of the skill—to know it when she sees it—and to respond to helpees by using the skill. These are the steps labeled by Carkhuff (1969) as training in *discrimination* and *communication.* Since the skill of *empathy* is widely conceded central to any kind of helping relationship (Carkhuff, 1969; Combs, Avila, and Purkey, 1971; Rogers, 1975), I will use it here to illustrate the Gazda exercises.

The first step consists of providing the trainee with clear definitions of the levels of empathy. This is accomplished in the Gazda program by means of scale definitions such as those shown in Figure 1. The empathy scale serves as a general definition which is applicable across a broad range of interpersonal situations. The definition is then made more specific by a presentation in which the helpee situation is described and a variety of possible helper responses are presented and analyzed:

Helpee Situation
    Male: "I'm so fat—I know that's why I don't have many dates."

Helper Responses
1.   *Level 1:* "Since you know what it is, why don't you do something about it?"

Discussion: This response is rated level 1 because it does not respond to surface feelings; it is judgmental or criticizing, and although it may be true that this helpee could do something about his appearance, it is too early to present this idea. Remember that there is no base between the helper and helpee at this point.

2.   *Level 1:* "Say, whatever happened to that girl you were dating so much last summer?"

Discussion: This response is rated level 1 because it ignores present feelings and shifts the topic away from the concern the helpee has expressed, thereby ignoring his present feelings.

3.   *Level 2:* "Oh, that's nothing to worry about for a guy that's been as popular as you. The right girl is going to come along."

Discussion: This response denies the helpee the right to feel the way he feels. Remember that sometimes a situation that would seem insignificant to you may be ego-shattering to someone else.

4.   *Level 3:* "I guess you feel kind of left out—you figure your weight is keeping you from being more successful with the girls."

Discussion: This response is rated level 3 because (a) it includes completely the content of the helpee statement; (b) a major surface feeling (alone) has been perceived from the helpee statement; and (c) it neither adds to nor subtracts from the helpee statement. This kind of response communicates to the helpee that you heard what he said and you are attempting to understand how he feels. Remember that your *present* task is not to solve the problem for the helpee but to respond in such a way that the helpee is able to self-explore. The helpee will probably continue to feel comfortable in disclosing further details of his situation. During this process the helper is also establishing a base with the helpee. The helper must *earn* the right to be judgmental.

5.   *Level 4:* "It's depressing to see everyone around you having fun and not being part of it. *You don't know what will happen to you if you don't improve your appearance.*"

Discussion: This response is rated level 4 because (a) it contains all the elements of a level-3 response, such as

number 4 above; and (b) it *adds* underlying feeling. It is
additive because it communicates underlying feelings that
have been perceived in this case—the idea that the helpee is
concerned with the future as well as with the present. The
part of response 5 that is additive has been italicized.
Remember that an additive response must be accurate in
order to achieve a level-4 rating. For example, if the helpee
had then responded to the helper by saying, "Yeah, if
things keep on like this, I'm *really* going to be out of it,"
our perception of the underlying feeling would have been
validated. The helpee reaction to the helper's statement
must confirm the accuracy of the statement if that statement is to be rated a level 4. [Gazda and others, 1973, pp.
70-73.]

After exposure to these skill definitions, students are presented with a number of helpee situations, each with a set of
possible responses, similar to those shown above but without
the "answers." The task is to rate the level of empathy shown
by each response. The student may then compare her ratings
with a key to see whether she is *perceiving* empathy correctly.
When the trainee has demonstrated the ability to *discriminate*
levels of empathic responses at a predetermined level of mastery, she is given practice in *communicating* empathy by formu-
lating her own responses to various helpee situations. Each of
the core conditions is treated in a similar manner. This is far
from a complete description of the model, but it serves to illustrate the method.

Although heavily structured, the Gazda-Carkhuff program is humanistic in philosophy. The goal is to provide a warm
and understanding environment in which helpees are free to
solve their own problems, albeit with guidance and support
from helpers. True to the Carkhuff theoretical position, Gazda
emphasizes that the structured exercises and discussion con-
tained in the manual are *aids*. He suggests (1973, p. vi) that
"Inevitably, the personnel who function as trainers hold the key
to the success or failure of this or any other training model. We
wish, therefore, to underscore the importance of selecting
healthy, high-functioning persons as trainers or educators."

The Carkhuff model has generated a great deal of research. There is evidence that people can be taught to make appropriate responses on the Carkhuff core dimensions and that those who score high on these scales are more facilitative with respect to a variety of measures of growth in helpees (Aspy, 1975; Carkhuff, 1969; Truax and Carkhuff, 1967). If further independent research should bear out the hypothesis that these types of interpersonal skills can be directly taught to a cross section of the American public, then the enthusiasm generated by the followers of Carkhuff may be warranted (see *Counseling Psychologist,* Vol. 3, No. 3, 1972.)

Some common elements. Microteaching and the Carkhuff-Gazda programs are probably the most completely formulated models for teaching career-relevant interpersonal skills in use today. They have a system for identifying important skills, a training program to develop the skills, and measures of skill attainment. Although the two programs are contrasted here because the skills in which they express interest are rather different, the most significant point to be made by the contrast is that once the premise is accepted that interpersonal competency can be broken into components that can be defined and measured and taught, the programs for skill development look very similar. Both stress the necessity for *discrimination* training. The trainee must know the difference between good and poor performance. Both incorporate active *practice* sessions. The trainee must have adequate experience in communicating or using the skill. Both have extensive provisions for *feedback* on the quality of performance. Not only do these two models feature similar processes, but they use similar tools and techniques. The technique of *modeling* is commonly used in the discrimination training for both programs. *Role playing* is used in practicing skills. *Videotaping* and ratings are used or could be used in the feedback process. By analyzing two apparently different programs, we have arrived at common ingredients for skills development programs. The conclusion seems to be that if we can define the skill, we can help people develop it.

Developing Adequacy in Interpersonal Relations

As we have seen, skills development for human services careers can be approached through programs as structured as microteaching and as unstructured as T-groups. Much the same phenomenon exists in helping people develop interpersonal *adequacy* for personal satisfaction. The unstructured encounter groups that have been so popular with the general public in recent years are finding new competitors in the structured experiences of assertiveness training, Human Potential Seminars, and the like. The new structured exercises have also proved popular with educators because they accomplish specific purposes and because their structure offers greater control and correspondingly low risk for damage to participants. It may prove useful here to illustrate briefly two programs that could be considered for components in an adequacy-minor curriculum (see Chapter One). There is not much solid evaluation of these programs and a panoply of similar programs springing up across the nation. But it is important now to understand the general nature of such programs and to think about their potential for college courses in interpersonal adequacy.

Human Potential Seminars (HPS). The human potential movement is increasingly popular in community colleges; 23 percent of the colleges reported the use of Human Potential Seminars in 1974 (Appendix A). The design of Human Potential Seminars (HPS) is credited to J. D. McHolland who introduced the program at Kendall College in 1967. Basically, the seminars consist of a series of structured group experiences that focus on the *positive* characteristics of participants. Kleemann (1974, p. 89) gives a useful definition: "The HPS is a time-limited, supervised, and positively oriented human development course composed of a series of specific activities designed to help persons toward greater self-regard and regard for others." The seminars have two features that make them especially appealing to community colleges. First, the emphasis on personal *strengths* is specifically designed to help New Students, who are prone to enter college with feelings of self-doubt and low self-esteem. Second, the greater structure of HPS gives more control and involves less risk than the encounter groups from which HPS grew.

Human potential groups generally consist of a series of exercises such as the "depth unfoldment experience," where each member of the group talks briefly about the experiences that have had an impact on his or her life. Following this exercise, "achievement listing" sessions may be introduced. In these meetings participants are asked to list their personal achievements from as early as they can remember to the present. The group then summarizes in a sentence what success means for each individual. This leads to a goal-setting phase. Other techniques or exercises that follow are value clarification; handling value conflict; goal setting; and "strength bombardment," in which group members stress the talents and strengths of each member as they have observed them throughout the group meetings. (For further descriptions of human potential techniques, see Kleeman, 1974; Smith and Walz, undated; Trueblood and McHolland, 1970.)

The research that has been done shows generally positive results, but it has usually been conducted by advocates of the movement and it has not yet asked the difficult questions. In the research to date it appears that Human Potential Seminars are enthusiastically received by students and that positive attitudes obtain for as long as a year regarding such things as goal setting, self-concept, willingness to try new things, self-determination, regard for others, and self-actualization (Kleeman, 1974; McHolland, 1968; Trueblood and McHolland, 1970; White, 1974). While it seems possible that students could emerge from HPS with unrealistic aspirations subject to later disillusionment, that seems not to have happened yet. Neither researchers nor practitioners have reported any harmful effects, and students seem to be electing courses in human potential in ever increasing numbers.

Skills for group membership. Johnson and Johnson (1975, p. 2) point out that everyone is a member of several groups and that the very quality of life depends on one's ability to work with other people in groups and to help groups become effective within the society: "The history of mankind is the history of organized groups created to obtain mutual benefits and to find ways of improving the quality of life and satisfying the needs of members. It is the productivity resulting from effective groups that makes the development of group skills one of the most essential aspects of our education." Their book attempts to join theory and practice through the combined presentation of cognitive understandings from the field of social psychology, skill-building exercises, and diagnostic procedures to assess skill levels. Chapters, which range through a variety of topics such as leadership, decision making, conflicts of interest, and problem solving, follow a general format in which academic information from psychology and sociology is presented first, followed by self-assessment, followed by exercises, followed by group discussion, and concluding with self-assessment. A specific example from the chapter on group goals will illustrate the use of this type of structured program to help students learn to work effectively as members of groups—surely an important skill for all of us.

A brief, typically academic discussion about group goals is followed by a quiz on cognitive understanding. Then comes a self-quiz, in which readers are asked to rate themselves on their own behavior in groups. This is followed by some group exercises. One, designed to illustrate what happens when people come to the group with hidden agendas, assigns people roles that they are to play out without revealing their role assignments to the group. This is followed by a group discussion of what occurred and a written assignment for each participant on the effect of hidden agendas on group goals. The chapter continues in this vein, interspersing cognitive understandings, self-assessment, exercises, and group discussions. It concludes with a self-checklist of skills.

The exercises are frequently simulated games incorporating some use of role playing. The use of these techniques appears to have the research-documented advantages of role playing and gaming—high student interest and active involvement. For readers not familiar with the use of gaming for educational purposes, the following example should prove helpful.

The Million-Dollar-Gift Exercise

This exercise focuses on cooperation and competition among three subgroups within a group. The exercise usually takes less than one hour, and the procedure for the coordinator is as follows:

1. Introduce the exercise as an experience concerning decision making, coordination, and group representation.

2. Divide a group into three smaller subgroups of five or more members. Members of each subgroup are told they have fifteen minutes to meet one another and get acquainted and to appoint a representative. They are also told that they will be given a common task to work on with the other subgroups.

3. Seat the three representatives in the center of the room. Members of each subgroup sit together in a position where they can see their representative clearly. The following role-playing situation is then explained. A national foundation wishes to award a million dollars to the school system that is made up of the three subgroups—on condition that the entire school system agrees on a project on which the million dollars will be spent. The representatives are then told to go back to their respective subgroups and within fifteen minutes develop a million-dollar school-project proposal to be presented to the other two subgroups. The representatives will present the proposals.

4. After fifteen minutes have the three representatives again meet in the center of the room. Tell them that they are to present their proposals and that they must come to an agreement on one that will be acceptable to all three subgroups for presentation to the foundation. After all three proposals have been presented, the representatives should reconfer with their subgroups for five minutes before continuing their meeting.

5. After the five-minute meeting with subgroups, have the representatives continue their discussion. They are to meet for five minutes and then break for another five-minute meeting with their subgroup. During the representatives' meeting the subgroups may communicate with their representative through notes. This sequence is repeated three times or until agreement is reached.

6. Ask the representatives to state what they are feeling, and the members of the three subgroups how they feel. Hold a summary discussion, paying particular attention to such issues as:

a. Did the group reach agreement on a common proposal? Were they too locked into their own position to compromise even when the prize was a million dollars?

b. Did the three subgroups tend to compete rather than cooperate? Did the degree of cooperation within each subgroup differ from one subgroup to another? If so, why?

c. What sorts of group pressures were felt by the representatives? How much power and freedom were given to each representative?

d. What were the goals of the subgroups in the negotiations? How did they affect the behavior of the subgroup and its representatives?

e. How were the decisions made within each subgroup? How were they made among the representatives?

f. Was the participation and leadership behavior distributed among subgroup members? What task and maintenance functions were present and absent? [Johnson and Johnson, 1975, pp. 95-96.]

I know of no research that has studied the effectiveness of this type of program for helping students develop the skills needed to become constructive members of groups. Frankly, it is hard for me to see why it should not have considerable advantage over the typical lecture and textbook assignments on the psychology of groups. It makes a serious attempt to incorporate what we know about pedagogical principles into the learning situation. It motivates by demonstrating the relevance to everyday life; it provides plenty of stimulus variation—reading, writing, discussion, physical activity. It calls for careful observation of people and their actions, for analysis of the written and spoken word, for integration from different sources of information, for participation and communication, and for self-assessment. This program model, whether designed by the instructor or ready-made by others, seems so sound educationally that it is worth a try even in the absence of evaluative studies. But let us hope that such imaginative program planning will stimulate some equally imaginative evaluation programs.

Conclusions

The very idea that complex human responses can be directly taught as *skills* is suspect to some people and anathema to others. At this time in history, it may be easier to convert those who think that such skills *cannot* be taught than those who think they *should not* be taught at the college level. But surely a sensitivity to and understanding of the viewpoints and concerns of other people, individually and collectively, is as much a mark of the well-educated person as is sensitivity to and understanding of ideas. If we *can* teach interpersonal skills in some useful and valid way to college students to increase their personal and career effectiveness, by all means let us do so.

The use of structured programs to teach interpersonal skills is in an infant stage of development. While it is a lusty and energetic infant, it may never reach maturity without more substantive nourishment from scholars and researchers. I suspect that one of the reasons for the great energy, as well as the simplistic nature of some of the approaches that are springing up all over the country, is that the need is so great that people at the grass roots level have grown impatient with discursive academic discussions and irrelevant research and have taken steps to provide some action. Some of the action has been good, and some has been shallow; but all efforts await substantive evaluation. And scholars and researchers have been slow to provide the necessary conceptual schemas and evaluation procedures to advance knowledge in the field.

There is an urgent need for *outside* evaluations of some of the models that are receiving increasing use today. Faculty workshops, campus consultants, special training seminars abound. Some of the entrepreneurs who are attracted to this field have made efforts to evaluate and improve their own programs, but their evaluations are suspect, regardless of how well intentioned. Funding agents may have been reluctant to allocate resources to the evaluation of "commercial" enterprises (which many of the structured exercises are, despite the fact that most are designed and promoted by college professors), and individual researchers are not likely to feel that such research will enhance their professional reputations.

It will be difficult to capture the talent and skills needed to advance knowledge on the subject of interpersonal skill development as long as the topic remains on the fringes of academic respectability. Students, the general public, industry, and to a considerable extent faculty in community colleges have been much more open to new ideas on the subject than have "establishment" educators and researchers. There should be nothing intellectually degrading about studying a major social phenomenon of our times. The social need for the development of interpersonal skills is unarguable; the demand on the part of people has been demonstrated; the major deterrent to progress is our lack of substantive knowledge. Let us hope that this will be remedied in the decades ahead.

Questionnaire on Remedial or Developmental Services

❋❋❋❋❋❋❋❋❋❋❋❋❋❋❋❋❋❋❋❋❋❋❋❋❋❋❋❋❋❋❋❋❋❋❋❋❋❋❋

The questionnaire was mailed in October 1974 to a 20 percent random sample of two-year colleges listed in the *1973 Community and Junior College Directory*. Responses were received from 184 colleges for an 84 percent return. This questionnaire was, for the most part, a repeat of a questionnaire mailed to a 20 percent random sample of two-year colleges in 1970. While the colleges were not necessarily the same colleges, the data are believed to present an accurate picture of the changes taking place between 1970 and 1974 in programs for low achievers in two-year colleges.

Tabulations are presented as percentages for 1970 and 1974. Items 4 and 5, however, called for rankings; percentages represent respondents selecting the alternatives as either first or second priority. Item 18 was not included in the 1970 questionnaire; therefore, only 1974 data are presented.

1. *The provisions colleges are making for poorly prepared students range all the way from hiring an additional counselor to
developing a full program of recruitment, courses, counseling,
etc. Does your college have any special provisions for students
who do not meet the traditional academic requirements for college work?*

1970	1974	
80%	93%	Yes
20%	7%	No

*If your answer is "No," you need not com-
plete the questionnaire. If, however, you
would like a summary of the data tabulations, please sign your name at the end of
the questionnaire and return it in the enve-
lope provided.*

2. *Please place an* $\boxed{x}$ *in the box by any of the following that
describe special services offered at your college this year.*

64%	82%	Efforts to recruit students who would not ordi-narily seek a college education.
76%	79%	Financial aids designed especially for disadvan-taged students.
61%	72%	Special counseling programs.
92%	98%	Remedial or developmental courses to upgrade verbal or other academic skills.
20%	36%	A total program of recruitment, counseling, courses, etc., with a director.
	16%	Other. _____

3. *If you have a special program for educationally disadvantaged
students, what is its title?*

_____

4. *What do you see as the major obstacle to learning for low-
achieving students? Please rank, using a* $\boxed{1}$ *for the most important,* $\boxed{2}$ *for the next most important, etc.*

7%	7%	Low intelligence.
47%	37%	Poor home background.
42%	49%	Poor elementary and secondary schooling.
49%	28%	Lack of effort; has quit trying.

1970	1974	
22%	31%	Fear of failure.
16%	12%	More interested in nonacademic matters such as car, sports, job.
16%	13%	The necessity of a job prevents adequate time and energy for study.
	6%	Other. _____

5. *Please rank the following broad goals of your college's efforts to educate underprepared students in order of importance.*

58%	57%	To prepare students for regular college work.
54%	51%	To provide skills for job and family responsibilities.
13%	16%	To provide for the needs of minority-group students.
13%	12%	To assist in developing nonacademic talents of the individual.
54%	52%	To change attitudes toward self and school.
	6%	Other. _____

_____

6. *Do you offer any kind of remedial or developmental courses?*

95%	98%	Yes
5%	2%	No *If your answer is "No," skip to question 12.*

7. *Approximately what proportion of the full-time student body is enrolled in remedial courses?*

40%	35%	Less than 10 percent.
39%	51%	Between 10 and 25 percent.
16%	9%	Between 25 and 50 percent.
3%	3%	More than 50 percent.

8. *What proportion of those taking remedial courses are members of ethnic minorities?*

64%	61%	Less than 25 percent.
19%	16%	Between 25 and 50 percent.
10%	12%	Between 50 and 75 percent.
5%	5%	More than 75 percent.

9. *Are remedial courses required for certain students?*

79%	59%	Yes
19%	39%	No

10. *Do remedial courses carry*

1970	1974	
25%	20%	No credit.
29%	42%	Nondegree credit.
32%	53%	Degree credit.

11. *Approximately what proportion of students enrolled in remedial courses later enter regular college courses at your or other institutions?*

11%	9%	Less than 10 percent.
11%	10%	Between 10 and 25 percent.
12%	13%	Between 25 and 50 percent.
45%	51%	More than half.
18%	12%	Don't know.

Special Features of Developmental Efforts

Listed below are some techniques that are frequently used in helping poorly prepared students. Please make an x *in the box by those activities that are in use* this year *at your college.*

12. *Recruitment of students:*

70%	78%	Visits to high schools in disadvantaged areas.
60%	67%	Specific requests to high school counselors.
58%	73%	Work with community agencies and leaders.
52%	61%	Use of students to help in recruiting.
24%	31%	Use of a special recruitment program through external funding.
14%	16%	Other recruitment techniques. _____

13. *Financial aid:*

63%	74%	Available to needy students regardless of academic standing; e.g., may retain grant while on probation.
71%	93%	"Need" used as a major criterion of eligibility for funds.
59%	74%	Use of a federally funded program designed for disadvantaged students.
38%	46%	College has some funds of its own for poorly prepared students.

1970   1974
            9%   Other. _____

14. *Counseling services:*
22%   29%   Separate counseling office for underprepared students.
33%   51%   Use of group interaction or group counseling.
36%   57%   Teacher counselors.
17%   39%   Use of students as counselors.
40%   82%   Diagnostic testing.
12%   18%   Other. _____

15. *Academic adjustments:*
58%   57%   Remedial students carry a lighter course load.
27%   49%   Nonpunitive grading; e.g., pass-no pass.
58%   72%   Remedial classes smaller than regular classes.
            19%   Other. _____

16. *Instructional methods:*
22%   45%   Team teaching.
45%   64%   Emphasis on audiovisual aids.
36%   67%   Skills centers.
36%   65%   Tutoring by fellow students.
44%   74%   Programmed instruction.
 3%   11%   "Guaranteed-success" programs.
 7%   32%   Practicum accompanies academic; e.g., cooperative education.
 5%   8%   Gaming or psychodrama.
21%   39%   Use of materials drawn from black and other ethnic cultures.
31%   68%   "Pacing" methods; i.e., emphasis on achievement regardless of time taken.
 7%   12%   Other. _____

17. *Faculty:*
47%   56%   Instruction of remedial courses restricted to teachers expressing interest.

1970	1974	
50%	61%	Most remedial teachers have some special training for work with underprepared students.
9%	8%	Group sensitivity sessions for faculty.
37%	54%	All expenses paid for attendance at off-campus conferences, workshops, etc.
16%	27%	On-campus in-service training for remedial instructors.
13%	16%	Emphasis on use of ethnic minorities for faculty.
	8%	Other. _____

Experimental Approaches

18. *In recent years, a variety of experimental programs have made an appearance. Please check* any *of the following that have been used at your college.*

[not   52%   Peer counseling.
asked]   73%   Self-paced learning modules.
            23%   Mastery learning.
            22%   Personalized System of Instruction (PSI or the Keller Plan).
            10%   Cognitive mapping-cognitive style measurement.
            25%   T-groups, sensitivity training, or similar small-group sessions.
            25%   Simulation games.
            27%   Microteaching or similar use of videotape feedback of student performance.
            13%   Achievement motivation training.
            23%   Human Potential Seminars.
            16%   Computer-assisted instruction (CAI).
            52%   Media laboratory.
             3%   Internal-External Locus of Control training.

19. *If you have used any of the approaches listed in Question 18 and are especially pleased with them, please indicate which ones.*

[Methods nominated most frequently were self-paced learning modules, peer counseling, and media laboratories.] _____

Comments: ————————————————————————————————

---

20. *If you have tried some of the approaches listed in Question 18 but discontinued their use, please indicate which ones and why you discontinued use.*

[Very few people mentioned dissatisfactions.] ————————————

Statement for ACPA Regarding the Use of Group Experiences in Higher Education

※※※※※※※※※※※※※※※※※※※※※※※※※※※※※※※

Statement of Position (ACPA, 1972)

The American College Personnel Association recognizes the potential of group experience as an effective educational method. It realizes that this method includes potential for both positive and negative outcomes. It does not believe that this condition differs, however, from any other educational method. Therefore, if appropriate structure and supervision is made available, positive effects can be increasingly realized and negative effects can be studied and ultimately eliminated. With this in mind the following statements constitute the position of the

Reprinted by permission of the American Personnel and Guidance Association, Washington, D.C.

Association with regard to the use of group experiences in college and university settings.

1. Any group experience should be purposefully designed to achieve certain basic and explicit goals. Both the goals for the group experience and a general description of the methods and processes to be used should be communicated openly to all potential participants and to any other members of the campus community who may wish to know. Educational outcomes appropriate to the purpose of the setting determine the nature of the group experience, and anyone considering participation can know something of the amount of personal investment [he] may be asked to commit [himself] to in the group. It should always be made clear that group training experiences are not a substitute for psychotherapy unless group psychotherapy is, in fact, the purpose of the group.

2. The decision to involve oneself in any given group experience should be fully voluntary regardless of whether it is a part of the classroom structure or offered apart from academic requirements. Because a basic higher education mission is the development of self-responsibility, the individuals involved must expect to make their own decision about participating based upon their understanding of what they can expect from the group experience. Likewise, the participant should have complete freedom to leave the group at any time.

3. In order to insure that the purposes and practice of group training support and further the educational mission of the individual institution of higher learning, the American College Personnel Association advocates that each institution providing group experiences assure through competent and qualified staff that such experiences are maintained in harmony with its educational purpose and philosophy. Such a staff should include not only qualified trainer/facilitators but also professional consultants to work with participants who may unexpectedly find the group experience too stressful and research consultants to study the results of the group experiences offered. It is essential that those authorizing and/or sponsoring groups have responsibility for diagnosing their situation and designing appropriate group procedures for dealing with the unique needs of the campus and students involved.

4. In view of the powerful effect group experiences may have for people, it is believed that group training/facilitating requires special knowledge and skills and that only those individuals who have acquired such knowledge and skills, as assessed by qualified supervisors, should become involved in the trainer/ facilitator role. As with the purposes, methods, and processes previously discussed, the training and experience of the facilitator/trainer should be available to the public. Also, it is important to dispel the belief that anyone who has simply had a group experience is qualified to be a trainer/facilitator. Although it is recognized that not all preparation need be achieved in a formal manner, there are certain basic elements that can be identified (e.g., knowledge in the behavioral sciences, special knowledge of group dynamics and group laboratory methods, supervised co-training and solo training with groups). It is therefore desirable and necessary for the appropriate and responsible members of the educational community to establish criteria and determine that individuals performing professional trainer/facilitator roles on the campus meet these criteria.

5. It is the position of ACPA that there is need for ethical standards to be developed to guide the practice of trainer/facilitators in conducting group experiences and to protect the community from practices not in its best interest. Decisions involving ethical practice should not be left to individual judgment alone, but practitioners should have available peer-acknowledged ethical standards as a guide for their own practice and for the protection of others involved. Immediate steps to establish such standards are needed.

6. The Association recognizes that the full potential of the group experience has as yet not been fully tested; it encourages greater efforts toward expanding knowledge about the nature and use of this method through research and experimentation. Although success has been demonstrated using group experiences in a variety of learning tasks, particularly in the area of interpersonal and intrapersonal effectiveness, it is recognized that greater knowledge is needed about its use in combination with other educational methods. It is therefore believed that well-designed research by competent practitioners in the field is needed.

Guidelines for Group Facilitators in Higher Education
(ACPA, 1974)

The group facilitator believes in the worth and significance of each human being. He has faith in each person's potentiality to develop personally and interpersonally. He possesses genuine respect for the existence of both positive and negative characteristics within every group, but he believes that every person can achieve quality in his interpersonal encounters with others. The group facilitator protects the integrity and mental health of every person with whom he works and places the welfare of the individual member above the achievement of the group's goals. While demanding the freedom to work professionally, he accepts the responsibility for being a member of the helping professions.

1. *Competency.* Professional competence is a responsibility accepted by any person leading a group.

a. The group facilitator will recognize the limits of his competence and only offer services or use techniques he is trained in or skilled in performing.

b. The group facilitator will remain constant in representing openly and accurately his professional qualifications, affiliations, and purposes.

c. The group facilitator will carefully consider the social climate and moral expectations of the community in which he conducts his work in order to prevent undue controversy that may affect individuals participating in the group.

2. *Publicity.* Announcement of opportunities for group experiences should be made in an appropriate professional manner, giving due consideration to community acceptability, legal standards, and descriptions that are explicit and accurate.

a. Solicitation should not be a motive in the announcements.

b. Special claims should not be made without the availability of scientifically acceptable evidence.

c. Any fee or charges made should be described and clearly stated in the announcement.

3. *Screening.* Adequate procedures shall be utilized for

screening and selecting group members in accordance with the nature and purposes of each group to protect the welfare of individual participants and preserve the integrity of the group's goals.

a. Applicants for a group experience with particular physical health or mental health problems should not be included if there is a likelihood that they may be subjected to unnecessary risk or that because of their particular personal needs they may divert the group from its primary purposes.

b. Applicants receiving help from another professional person should be considered for group membership only after consultation between the group facilitator and the other professional person to consider the appropriateness of the experience for the applicant and the potential impact of the applicant upon the group.

c. Applicants selected for group participation after due consideration of 3a and 3b will be of special concern to the group facilitator in order to protect the welfare of both the individual and the group.

4. *Voluntary participation.* No person should participate in a group other than on a voluntary basis, and the facilitator will protect each member's right of honorable withdrawal from the group without being subjected to undue pressure from other group members.

a. The primal purposes, the basic guidelines, the potential benefits, and the potential risks involved in the group experience should be established and discussed candidly with each prospective member prior to the commencement of the actual group experience.

b. The facilitator will support the individual member's freedom of choice and see that no member is required or unduly urged to participate in any specific activity of the group against his better judgment.

5. *Physical and emotional welfare.* The group facilitator will protect the physical and emotional welfare of individuals in the group.

a. The facilitator will take the responsibility to observe, attend, and intervene on the behalf of a member should it become apparent that emotional stress has developed sufficiently to threaten his well-being.

b. Competent referral sources will be arranged in the event individual members of the group require help beyond the facilitator's present competence.

6. *Respect for the individual.* The group facilitator will strive to establish and maintain a climate of respect within the group for the values, principles, and beliefs of each member participating in the group. When and where appropriate the facilitator will take special care to generate understanding of and respect for international and cultural characteristics of members differing from those which predominate in the group.

7. *Confidentiality.* The group facilitator will respect the confidentiality of information generated about individual members within a group.

a. The facilitator will discuss a group he is facilitating or individuals within the group only with persons clearly concerned with the group and then only for professional purposes.

b. Although assurance cannot be provided by the facilitator, group members will be informed of their mutual responsibility to refrain from revealing outside the group the confidences gained in the group.

c. Audio- or videotapes or other data collected within the group may be utilized only by the group members unless all members of the group give their expressed written permission for its specified use in other circumstances.

d. The use of data generated in a group for classroom teaching or for writing may be done only when the identity of the group and its members is adequately disguised.

8. *Responsibility after termination.* The facilitator's responsibility for the group members does not automatically end with termination of the group experiences.

a. The facilitator will stand ready to deal with individual member needs arising from a terminated group experience or refer the individual to more appropriate sources when he deems that it is beyond his present competence.

b. If the facilitator cannot be readily available after termination of the group experience, competent referral sources will be made available should individual group members have need.

Clear knowledge of their availability will be made known in an appropriate manner to the group members.

9. *Unethical practice.* Group facilitators should actively discourage unethical practices by other persons working with groups. When a group facilitator comes into possession of verified knowledge of specific violations of ethics, informal attempts should be made to rectify the situation. Failure to alleviate the situation in this manner should lead to more formal attempts by the facilitator to correct unethical practices, e.g., established channels of individual institutions. Major consideration should be given to fairness and discretion in such matters but above all the welfare of individuals participating in the group should be primary.

10. *Research.* The group facilitator will attend to the advancement of knowledge in group work by conducting, assisting, or supporting quality-designed and carefully considered research.

Guidelines for the Preparation of Professional Group Facilitators (ACPA, 1975)

Group facilitation is practiced in the service of others and in the presence of others. The goal of the group facilitator is to assist individuals as participants in a group to achieve fuller development as effective human beings. Group facilitation requires special knowledge and skill. Only individuals who have acquired the special knowledge and skill should be involved in the practice of group facilitation.

Following are standards deemed essential for the practice of group facilitation, and they are presented as criteria for preparing group facilitators. How a program of preparation is designed to meet the criteria is the province of those who are responsible for it. It is believed, however, that any program for preparing group facilitators within institutions of higher learning can and should meet these basic criteria.

1. *Personal qualifications.* A group facilitator must demonstrate a high level of personal development. The facilitator should:

a. Be aware of and knowledgeable about his/her needs,

motivations, strengths, weaknesses, problem areas, values, and the impact he/she may have on others.

b. Be able to monitor himself/herself and work through his/her personal problems.

c. Be open to professional criticism and profit from personal feedback.

d. Believe in his/her self-worth and accept responsibility for who he/she is and what he does.

e. Be able to empathize with the feelings of others.

f. Be genuinely concerned for the needs and welfare of others.

2. *Academic preparation.* The professional facilitator should achieve the master's degree or its equivalent in a behavioral science and preferably achieve training in a behavioral science at the post-master's level.

3. *Knowledge and skill.* Knowledge and skill are obtained in a variety of ways. They may be obtained other than through formal course work; however, the normally expected manner to obtain knowledge and skill is by participating in the academic programs provided by accredited institutions. Although course titles, course structures, and program designs may differ considerably from place to place, for group facilitators the following are believed essential:

a. Knowledge and understanding of human behavior.

b. Knowledge and understanding of group dynamics and group behavior.

c. Knowledge about the theory, the research, and the issues in group counseling or the specific type of group(s) one is preparing to facilitate.

d. Knowledge and skill about how to design group experiences and human relation training experiences.

e. Training in specific skills; e.g., listening and other communication skills, nonverbal behavior, therapeutic techniques, evaluation techniques.

f. Knowledge of ethical practice involved with group facilitation.

4. *Group experience.* Prior to accepting the role of facilitator in a group, a person should experience, as a group mem-

ber, similar group experience with a qualified facilitator. More than one group experience prior to facilitating a group, each of sufficient duration to permit the group to achieve maturity, is desirable and may be necessary for facilitators in training.

5. *Supervised experience.* To assure the development of competent group facilitators, supervision is essential during the learning process. Methods of supervision, however, are best left to the professional judgment and skill of each individual facilitator-supervisor.

a. Before becoming self-directed in group facilitation, an individual will facilitate groups under the direct supervision of a qualified group facilitator.

b. An individual will demonstrate to the satisfaction of a qualified supervisor the ability to integrate theory with practice in group facilitation.

c. Before leaving direct supervision an individual will demonstrate competence and confidence in his/her personal approach to group facilitation.

References

Allen, D. W., and Fortune, J. C. "An Analysis of Microteaching: New Procedure in Teacher Education." In D. W. Allen (Ed.), *Microteaching: A Description*. Stanford, Ca.: Stanford University, 1966.

Allen, D. W., and Ryan, K. *Microteaching*. Menlo Park, Ca.: Addison-Wesley, 1969.

Alverno College. *Competence Based Learning at Alverno College*. Milwaukee: Alverno College, 1974.

American College Personnel Association. "A Proposed Statement for American College Personnel Association Regarding the Use of Group Experiences in Higher Education." *Journal of College Student Personnel*, Jan. 1972, *13*, 90-96.

American College Personnel Association. "Addendum I: Guidelines for Group Facilitators in Higher Education." *Journal of College Student Personnel*, March 1974, *15*, 157-159.

American College Personnel Association. "Addendum II: Guidelines for the Preparation of Group Facilitators." *Journal of College Student Personnel*, July 1975, *16*, 342.

American College Testing Program. "Ups and Downs in Education." *ACTivity*, May 1975, *13*, 5.

Anandam, K. *Summary Statements About Students' Evaluation of Courses in Open College.* Interim Report No. 4. Miami, Fla.: Miami-Dade Community College, 1974.

Appley, D. G., and Winder, A. E. *T-Groups and Therapy Groups in a Changing Society.* San Francisco: Jossey-Bass, 1973.

Argyris, C. "On the Future of Laboratory Education." *Journal of Applied Behavioral Science,* 1967, *3*(2), 153-183.

Aspy, D. N. "Reaction to Carkhuff's Articles." *Counseling Psychologist,* 1972, *3*(3), 35-41.

Aspy, D. N. "Empathy: Let's Get the Hell On with It." *Counseling Psychologist,* 1975, *5*(2), 10-14.

Atkin, J. M. "Behavioral Objectives in Curriculum Design: A Cautionary Note." *Science Teacher,* 1968, *35*(5), 27-30.

Atkinson, R. C. "Teaching Children to Read Using a Computer." *American Psychologist,* March 1974, *29*, 169-178.

Back, K. W. *Beyond Words.* New York: Russell Sage, 1972.

Baker, F. B. "Computer-Based Instructional Management Systems: A First Look." *Review of Educational Research,* Feb. 1971, *41*, 51-70.

Bandura, A., and McDonald, F. J. "The Influence of Social Reinforcement and Behavior of Models in Shaping Children's Moral Judgments." *Journal of Abnormal and Social Psychology,* 1963, *67*, 274-281.

Bandura, A., and Walters, R. H. *Social Learning and Personality Development.* New York: Holt, 1963.

Barbee, J. R., and Keil, E. C. "Experimental Techniques of Job Interview Training for the Disadvantaged: Videotape Feedback, Behavior Modification, and Microcounseling." *Journal of Applied Psychology,* 1973, *58*(2), 209-213.

Berger, E. M. "The Relation Between Expressed Acceptance of Self and Expressed Acceptance of Others." *Journal of Abnormal and Social Psychology,* 1952, *47*, 778-782.

Bieri, J. "Complexity-Simplicity as a Personality Variable and Preferential Behavior." In D. W. Fiske and S. R. Maddi (Eds.), *Functions of Varied Experience.* Homewood, Ill.: Dorsey Press, 1961.

Bieri, J., and others. *Clinical and Social Judgment: The Discrimination of Behavioral Information.* New York: Wiley, 1966.

Bird, C. *Effective Study Habits.* New York: Century Co., 1931.

Birnbaum, M. "Sense About Sensitivity Training." *Saturday Review,* Nov. 15, 1969, pp. 82-83 and 96-98.

Bitzer, D. L., and Skaperdas, D. "The Design of an Economically Viable Large-Scale Computer-Based Education System." In S. G. Tickton (Ed.), *To Improve Learning: An Evaluation of Instructional Technology.* Vol. 2. New York: R. R. Bowker, 1971.

Block, J. H. "Introduction." In J. H. Block (Ed.), *Mastery Learning: Theory and Practice.* New York: Holt, 1971a.

Block, J. H. (Ed.) *Mastery Learning: Theory and Practice.* New York: Holt, 1971b.

Block, J. H. "Operating Procedures for Mastery Learning." In J. H. Block (Ed.), *Mastery Learning: Theory and Practice.* New York: Holt, 1971c.

Block, J. H. "Student Learning and the Setting of Mastery Performance Standards." *Educational Horizons,* Summer 1972, *50,* 183-191.

Bloom, B. S. "Affective Consequences of School Achievement." In J. H. Block (Ed.), *Mastery Learning: Theory and Practice.* New York: Holt, 1971a.

Bloom, B. S. "Mastery Learning." In J. H. Block (Ed.), *Mastery Learning: Theory and Practice.* New York: Holt, 1971b.

Borg, W. R. "The Minicourse as a Vehicle for Changing Teacher Behavior: A Three-Year Follow-Up." *Journal of Educational Psychology,* 1972, *63*(6), 572-579.

Born, D. G. "Student Withdrawals in Personalized Instruction Courses and in Lecture Courses." In F. Newman (Chm.), Personalized Instruction: A National Trend Moves into the Rocky Mountain Region. Symposium presented at meeting of Rocky Mountain Psychological Association, Denver, May 1971.

Born, D. G., Gledhill, S. M., and Davis, M. L. "Examination Performance in Lecture-Discussion and Personalized Instruction Courses." In J. G. Sherman (Ed.), *Personalized System of Instruction: 41 Germinal Papers.* Menlo Park, Ca.: W. A. Benjamin, Inc., 1974.

Born, D. G., and Herbert, E. W. "A Further Study of Personalized Instruction for Students in Large University Classes." *Journal of Experimental Education,* Fall 1971, *40.*

Bradford, L. P., Gibb, J. R., and Benne, K. D. (Eds.) *T-Group Theory and Laboratory Method: Innovation in Re-education.* New York: Wiley, 1964.

Breen, P., Donlon, T., and Whitaker, U. "The Learning and Assessment of Interpersonal Skills: Guidelines for Administrators and Faculty." CAEL Working Paper No. 4. Princeton, N.J.: Educational Testing Service, 1975a.

Breen, P., Donlon, T., Whitaker, U. "The Learning and Assessment of Interpersonal Skills: Guidelines for Students." CAEL Working Paper No. 5. Princeton, N.J.: Educational Testing Service, 1975b.

Brown, G. I. *Human Teaching for Human Learning: An Introduction to Confluent Education.* New York: Viking, 1971.

Brudner, H. J. "Computer-Managed Instruction." *Science,* Nov. 29, 1968, *162,* 970-976.

Bruner, J. S., and Tajfel, H. "Cognitive Risk and Environmental Change." *Journal of Abnormal Psychology,* 1961, *62,* 231-241.

Buchanan, P. "Laboratory Training and Organization Development." *Administrative Science Quarterly,* 1969, *40,* 466-480.

Burke, R. L., and Bennis, W. G. "Changes in Perception of Self and Others During Human Relations Training." *Human Relations,* May 1961, *14,* 165-182.

Burton, A. (Ed.) *Encounter.* San Francisco: Jossey-Bass, 1969.

Bushnell, D. D. "Introducing the Docile Technology in Memoriam of CAI." In S. G. Tickton (Ed.), *To Improve Learning: An Evaluation of Instructional Technology.* Vol. 1. New York: R. R. Bowker, 1970.

Calhoun, J. F. "Elemental Analysis of the Keller Method of Instruction." Paper presented at annual meeting of American Psychological Association, Montreal, Canada, 1973.

Campbell, J. P., and Dunnette, M. D. "Effectiveness of T-Group Experiences in Managerial Training and Development." *Psychological Bulletin,* Aug. 1968, *70,* 73-104.

Campeau, P. L. "Selective Review of the Results of Research on the Use of Audiovisual Media to Teach Adults." *AV Communication Review*, Spring 1974, *22*, 5-40.

Canfield, A. A., and Lafferty, J. C. *Learning Styles Inventory.* Plymouth, Mi.: Experiential Learning Methods, 1973.

Carkhuff, R. R. *Helping and Human Relations: A Primer for Lay and Professional Helpers.* 2 vols. New York: Holt, 1969.

Carkhuff, R. R. *The Development of Human Resources: Education, Psychology, and Social Change.* New York: Holt, 1971.

Carkhuff, R. R. "Toward a Technology for Human and Community Resource Development." *Counseling Psychologist*, 1972, *3*(3), 12-30.

Carlson, R. "Identification and Personality Structure in Preadolescents." *Journal of Abnormal and Social Psychology*, 1965, *36*, 659-666.

Carnegie Commission on Higher Education. *New Students and New Places.* New York: McGraw-Hill, 1971.

Carroll, J. B. "A Model of School Learning." *Teachers College Record*, 1963, *64*, 723-733.

Carroll, J. B. "Measurement and Evaluation in Educational Technology." In S. G. Tickton (Ed.), *To Improve Learning: An Evaluation of Instructional Technology.* Vol. 2. New York: R. R. Bowker, 1971a.

Carroll, J. B. "Problems of Measurement Related to the Concept of Learning for Mastery." In J. H. Block (Ed.), *Mastery Learning: Theory and Practice.* New York: Holt, 1971b.

Carron, T. J. "Human Relations Training and Attitude Change: A Vector Analysis." *Personnel Psychology*, 1964, *17*, 403-424.

Cashdan, A., and Lee, V. *Learning Styles.* Bletchley, Buckinghamshire, England: Open University Press, 1971.

Charters, W. W. "Remedial Reading in College." *Journal of Higher Education*, March 1941, *12*, 117-121.

Cheit, E. F. *The Useful Arts and the Liberal Tradition.* New York: McGraw-Hill, 1975.

Chickering, A. W. *Education and Identity.* San Francisco: Jossey-Bass, 1969.

Chickering, A. W. *Commuting Versus Resident Students.* San Francisco: Jossey-Bass, 1974a.

Chickering, A. W. "The Educational Needs of New Learners: Implications for Liberal Arts Colleges." Paper presented at East Central College Consortium Conference on the New Learners, December 1974b.

Chickering, A. W., and McCormick, J. "Personality Development and the College Experience." *Research in Higher Education,* 1973, *1,* 43-70.

Chickering, A. W., McDowell, J., and Campagna, D. "Institutional Differences and Student Development." *Journal of Educational Psychology,* 1969, *60*(4), 315-326.

Coleman, J. S., and others. *Equality of Educational Opportunity.* Washington, D.C.: U.S. Government Printing Office, 1966.

College Entrance Examination Board. *College-Bound Seniors, 1974-75.* New York: College Entrance Examination Board, 1975.

Combs, A. W., Avila, D. L., and Purkey, W. W. *Helping Relationships: Basic Concepts for the Helping Professions.* Boston: Allyn and Bacon, 1971.

Connolly, J. J., and Sepe, T. D. "Individualized Instruction: Are Students Ready?" *Community and Junior College Journal,* March 1973, *43,* 30-31.

Cooley, W. W., and Glaser, R. "The Computer and Individualized Instruction." *Science,* Oct. 31, 1969, *166,* 574-582.

Coulson, J. E. "Computer-Assisted Instruction and Its Potential for Individualizing Instruction." In S. G. Tickton (Ed.), *To Improve Learning: An Evaluation of Instructional Technology.* Vol. 1. New York: R. R. Bowker, 1970.

Craig, R. "Lawrence Kohlberg and Moral Development: Some Reflections." *Educational Theory,* Spring 1974, *24,* 121-129.

Cronbach, L. J. "How Can Instruction Be Adapted to Individual Differences?" In R. M. Gagné (Ed.), *Learning and Individual Differences.* Columbus, Ohio: Merrill, 1967.

Cross, K. P. *Beyond the Open Door: New Students to Higher Education.* San Francisco: Jossey-Bass, 1971.

Cross, K. P. *The Integration of Learning and Earning: Cooperative Education and Nontraditional Study.* Washington, D.C.: American Association for Higher Education, 1973.

Cross, K. P. "The Elusive Goal of Educational Equality." In J. F. Hughes (Ed.), *The Search for Alternatives.* Washington, D.C.: American Council on Education, 1975.

Crowder, N. A. "Automatic Tutoring by Intrinsic Programming." In A. A. Lumsdaine and R. Glaser (Eds.), *Teaching Machines and Programmed Learning.* Washington, D.C.: National Education Association, 1960.

Crutchfield, R. S. "Instructing the Individual in Creative Thinking." In *New Approaches to Individualizing Instruction: A Report of a Conference.* Princeton, N.J.: Educational Testing Service, 1965.

D'Augelli, A. R., and Chinsky, J. M. "Interpersonal Skills and Pretraining: Implications for the Use of Group Procedures for Interpersonal Learning and for the Selection of Nonprofessional Mental Health Workers." *Journal of Consulting and Clinical Psychology,* 1974, *42*(1), 65-72.

Davis, A. R. "Microteaching in a Small Liberal Arts College." *Audiovisual Instruction,* March 1971, *16,* 81-82.

DeLoach, J. F., Dworkin, L., and Wyett, J. L. *The Educational Sciences: An Overview.* Rochester, Minn.: Social Systems Associates, 1971.

de Lone, R. H. "Sketching a Context for Instructional Technology." In S. G. Tickton (Ed.), *To Improve Learning: An Evaluation of Instructional Technology.* Vol. 2. New York: R. R. Bowker, 1971.

Denk, J. R. *The Fear Is Gone: A Study of the Adoption of Computer-Based Curricula in North Carolina's 1973 Institute for Under-Graduate Curricular Reform.* Greensboro, N.C.: University of North Carolina, 1973.

Dessler, A. J. "Teaching Without Lectures." In J. G. Sherman (Ed.), *Personalized System of Instruction: 41 Germinal Papers.* Menlo Park, Ca.: W. A. Benjamin, Inc., 1974.

Dimichael, S. G. "The Transfer Effects of a How-to-Study Course upon Different IQ Levels and Various Academic Subjects." *Journal of Educational Psychology,* March 1943, *24,* 166-175.

DiStefano, J. J. "Interpersonal Perceptions of Field-Independent and Field-Dependent Teachers and Students." Unpublished doctoral dissertation, Cornell University, 1969.

Doty, R. B. "Personalized Laboratory Instruction in Microbiology: The Audio-Tutorial Approach." *Educational Technology*, Jan. 1974, *14*, 36-39.

Dunnette, M. D., and Campbell, J. P. "Laboratory Education: Impact on People and Organizations." *Industrial Relations*, 1968, *8*(1), 1-27.

Edwards, C. H. "Sensitivity Training and Education: A Critique." *Educational Leadership*, Dec. 1970, *28*, 258-261.

Ehrle, E. B. "Avoiding the Audio-Tutorial Mistake." *BioScience*, Jan. 15, 1970, p. 103.

Elliott, R., and McMichael, R. E. "Effects of Specific Training on Frame Dependence." *Perceptual and Motor Skills*, 1963, *17*, 363-367.

Ely, D., and Minars, E. "The Effects of a Large Scale Mastery Environment on Students' Self-Concept." *Journal of Experimental Education*, Summer 1973, *41*, 20-22.

Entwisle, D. R. "Evaluations of Study-Skills Courses: A Review." *Journal of Educational Research*, March 1960, *53*, 243-251.

Erickson, S. *Learning Theory and the Teacher. IV: The Reinforcement Principle.* Memo to the Faculty, No. 48. Ann Arbor: Center for Research on Learning and Teaching, University of Michigan, 1972.

Erikson, E. H. *Childhood and Society.* New York: Norton, 1950.

Evans, H. M., and Dubois, E. E. "Community/Junior College Remedial Programs—Reflections." *Journal of Reading*, Oct. 1972, *16*, 38-45.

Farmer, J., and others. "The Role of Proctoring in Personalized Instruction." *Journal of Applied Behavior Analysis*, Winter 1972, *5*, 401-404.

Feldman, K. A., and Newcomb, T. M. *The Impact of College on Students.* Volume I: *An Analysis of Four Decades of Research.* San Francisco: Jossey-Bass, 1969.

Ferster, C. B. "Individualized Instruction in a Large Introductory Psychology College Course." In J. G. Sherman (Ed.), *Personalized System of Instruction: 41 Germinal Papers.* Menlo Park, Ca.: W. A. Benjamin, Inc., 1974.

Fine, S. A., and Wiley, W. W. *An Introduction to Functional Job Analysis.* Methods for Manpower Analysis, No. 4. Kalamazoo, Mi.: W. E. Upjohn Institute for Employment Research, 1971.

Flanagan, J. C. "The Goals of Project PLAN." In R. A. Weisgerber (Ed.), *Developmental Efforts in Individualized Learning.* Itasca, Ill.: F. E. Peacock, 1971.

Flanders, N. A. "Introduction." In D. Allen and K. Ryan, *Microteaching.* Menlo Park, Ca.: Addison-Wesley, 1969.

Frank, J. D. "Training and Therapy." In L. P. Bradford, J. R. Gibb, and K. D. Benne (Eds.), *T-Group Theory and Laboratory Method: Innovation in Re-education.* New York: Wiley, 1964.

Gallup, H. F. "Problems in the Implementation of a Course in Personalized Instruction." Paper presented at American Psychological Association meeting, Sept. 6, 1971 (Personalized Instruction: A Symposium in Honor of Fred Keller).

Gardner, J. *Excellence: Can We Be Equal and Excellent Too?* New York: Harper, 1961.

Gardner, R. W., Holzman, P. S., and others. "Cognitive Control: A Study of Individual Consistencies in Cognitive Behavior." *Psychological Issues,* 1959, *1*(4).

Gardner, R. W., and Long, R. I. "Control, Defense, and Centration Effect: A Study of Scanning Behavior." *British Journal of Psychology,* 1962, *53,* 129-140.

Gardner, R. W., and Schoen, R. A. "Differentiation and Abstraction In Concept Formation." *Psychological Monographs,* 1962, *76*(41).

Gassner, S. M., Gold, J., and Snadowsky, A. M. "Changes in the Phenomenal Field as a Result of Human Relations Training." *Journal of Psychology,* 1964, *58,* 33-41.

Gazda, G. M., and others. *Human Relations Development: A Manual for Educators.* Boston: Allyn and Bacon, 1973.

Gibb, G. "CCTV: Some Guide Lines for the Future Use of Videotapes in Professional Training." *Education for Teaching,* Spring 1970, *81,* 51-56.

Gibb, J. R. "The Present Status of T-Group Theory." In L. P. Bradford, J. R. Gibb, and K. D. Benne (Eds.), *T-Group Theory and Laboratory Method: Innovation in Re-education.* New York: Wiley, 1964.

Gibb, J. R. "The Effects of Human Relations Training." In A. E. Bergin and S. L. Garfield (Eds.), *Handbook of Psychotherapy and Behavior Change.* New York: Wiley, 1971.

Gibb, J. R., and Gibb, L. M. "Humanistic Elements in Group Growth." In J. F. T. Bugental (Ed.), *Challenges of Humanistic Psychology.* New York: McGraw-Hill, 1967.

Gilligan, J. F. "Personality Characteristics of Selectors and Nonselectors of Sensitivity Training." *Journal of Counseling Psychology,* 1973, *20*(3), 265-268.

Glasser, W. *Schools Without Failure.* New York: Harper, 1969.

Golden West College. *Computer Assisted Instruction at Golden West College: A Description and Evaluation.* Huntington Beach, Ca.: Golden West College, undated.

Goldman, R. M., Wade, S., and Zegar, D. "Students Without Harness: The 'SUM' Experiment in Self-Paced Learning." *Journal of Higher Education,* March 1974, *45,* 197-210.

Goodenough, D. R., and Karp, S. A. "Field Dependence and Intellectual Functioning." *Journal of Abnormal and Social Psychology,* 1961, *63*(2), 241-246.

Goodlad, J. I. "Education and Technology. ' In S. G. Tickton (Ed.), *To Improve Learning: An Evaluation of Instructional Technology.* Vol. 2. New York: R. R. Bowker, 1971.

Goodstein, L. D., and Crites, J. O. "Brief Counseling with Poor College Risks." *Journal of Counseling Psychology,* 1961, *8*(4), 318-321.

Gordon, E. W., and Wilkerson, D. A. *Compensatory Education for the Disadvantaged.* New York: College Entrance Examination Board, 1966.

Grant, W. H. "Student Development in the Community College." In T. O'Banion and A. Thurston (Eds.), *Student Development Programs in the Community Junior College.* Englewood Cliffs, N.J.: Prentice-Hall, 1972.

Grater, M. "Changes in Self and Other Attitudes in a Leadership Training Group." *Personnel and Guidance Journal,* 1959, *37,* 493-496.

Green, B. A., Jr. "Fifteen Reasons Not to Use the Keller Plan." In J. G. Sherman (Ed.), *Personalized System of Instruction: 41 Germinal Papers.* Menlo Park, Ca.: W. A. Benjamin, Inc., 1974.

Guinan, J. F., Foulds, M. L., and Wright, J. C. "Do the Changes Last? A Six-Month Follow-Up of a Marathon Group." *Small Group Behavior,* May 1973, *4,* 117-180.

Hall, K. A. "Computer-Assisted Instruction: Problems and Performance." *Phi Delta Kappan,* June 1971, *52,* 628-631.

Hall, K. A., Cartwright, G. P., and Mitzell, H. E. "A Triumph for CAI." *Phi Delta Kappan,* Sept. 1974, *56,* 70-72.

Hammond, A. L. "Plato and Ticcit: CAI in Action." *College and University Business,* Oct. 1972.

Hampton, W. "Audiovisual Technology." *College and University Business,* Feb. 1972.

Hansen, D. N., Dick, W., and Lippert, H. T. *Research and Implementation of Collegiate Instruction of Physics via Computer-Assisted Instruction.* Vol. 1. Technical Report No. 3. Tallahassee: Florida State University, Computer-Assisted Instruction Center, 1968.

Harris, M. B., and Liguori, R. A. "Some Effects of a Personalized System of Instruction in Teaching College Mathematics." *Journal of Educational Research,* Oct. 1974, *68,* 62-66.

Hartley, J. R. "An Experiment Showing Some Student Benefits Against Behavioral Costs in Using Programmed Instruction." *Programmed Learning and Educational Technology,* 1968, *5,* 219-229.

Hartley, J. R. "Aspects of Programmed Learning." *Trends in Education,* Oct. 1973, *32,* 30-35.

Hartshorne, H., and May, M. A. *Studies in the Nature of Character.* Vol. 1: *Studies in Deceit.* Vol. 2: *Studies in Service and Self-Control.* Vol. 3: *Studies in Organization of Character.* New York: Macmillan, 1928-1930.

Harvey, O. J., Hunt, D. E., and Schroder, H. M. *Conceptual Systems and Personality Organization.* New York: Wiley, 1961.

Hausman, L. "The ABC's of CAI." *American Education,* Nov. 1967.

Heath, R. *The Reasonable Adventurer.* Pittsburgh: University of Pittsburgh Press, 1964.

Hedges, W. D. "Computer-Assisted Instruction and the Schools." *Educational Leadership,* Jan. 1973, *30,* 361-365.

Hess, R. D., and Tenezakis, M. D. *Selected Findings from "The Computer as a Socializing Agent: Some Socioaffective Outcomes of CAI."* Stanford, Ca.: Center for Research and Development in Teaching, Stanford University, 1971.

Hilgard, E. R. "The Psychological Heuristics of Learning." In S. G. Tickton (Ed.), *To Improve Learning: An Evaluation of Instructional Technology.* Vol. 2. New York: R. R. Bowker, 1971.

Hill, J. E. *The Educational Sciences.* Bloomfield Hills, Mi.: Oakland Community College Press, 1971.

Himber, C. "Evaluating Sensitivity Training for Teen-Agers." *Journal of Applied Behavioral Science,* 1970, *6*(3), 307-322.

Hoberock, L. L., and others. "Theory of PSI Evaluated for Engineering Education." In J. G. Sherman (Ed.), *Personalized System of Instruction: 41 Germinal Papers.* Menlo Park, Ca.: W. A. Benjamin, Inc., 1974.

Hodge, F. P. (Ed.) *Cognitive Style Research: A Report of a Seminar.* Albany: Two-Year College Development Center, State University of New York at Albany, 1974.

Hodgkinson, H. L. "Adult Development: Implications for Faculty and Administrators." *Educational Record,* Fall 1974, *55,* 263-274.

Holzman, P. S. "The Relation of Assimilation Tendencies in Visual, Auditory, and Kinesthetic Time-Error to Cognitive Attitudes of Leveling and Sharpening." *Journal of Personality,* 1954, *22,* 375-394.

Holzman, P. S. "Scanning: A Principle of Reality Contact." *Perceptual and Motor Skills,* 1966, *23,* 835-844.

Holzman, P. S., and Klein, G. S. "Cognitive System Principles of Leveling and Sharpening: Individual Differences in Assimilation Effects in Visual Time-Error." *Journal of Psychology,* 1954, *37,* 105-122.

House, R. J. "T-Group Education and Leadership Effectiveness: A Review of the Empiric Literature and a Critical Evaluation." *Personnel Psychology,* 1967, *20,* 1-32.

Hoyt, D. P. *The Relationship Between College Grades and Adult Achievement: A Review of the Literature.* Research Report No. 7. Iowa City, Ia.: American College Testing Program, 1965.

Huck, S. W., and Long, J. D. "The Effect of Behavioral Objectives on Student Achievement." *Journal of Experimental Education,* Fall 1973, *42,* 40-41.

Huckfeldt, V. E. *A Forecast of Changes in Postsecondary Education.* Boulder, Co.: National Center for Higher Education Management Systems, Western Interstate Commission for Higher Education, 1972.

Huther, J. "Behavioral Objectives and Guaranteed Learning: Equality Carried to Its Final Extreme." *Community College Review,* July 1973, *1,* 30-36.

Ivey, A. E. *Microcounseling.* Springfield, Ill.: Thomas, 1971a.

Ivey, A. E. "Review of R. R. Carkhuff's *Helping and Human Relations.*" *Personnel and Guidance Journal,* 1971b, *49,* 408-411.

James, C. D. R. "A Cognitive Style Approach to Teacher-Pupil Interaction and the Academic Performance of Black Children." Unpublished master's thesis, Rutgers University, 1973.

Jamison, D., Suppes, P., and Wells, S. *The Effectiveness of Alternative Instructional Media: A Survey.* Princeton, N.J.: Educational Testing Service, 1973.

Janis, I. L., and King, B. T. "The Influence of Role Playing on Opinion Change." *Journal of Abnormal and Social Psychology,* 1954, *49,* 211-218.

Johnson, D. W., and Johnson, F. P. *Joining Together.* Englewood Cliffs, N.J.: Prentice-Hall, 1975.

Joyce, B., and Weil, M. *Models of Teaching*. Englewood Cliffs, N.J.: Prentice-Hall, 1972.

Kagan, J. "Reflection-Impulsivity and Reading Ability in Primary Grade Children." *Child Development,* 1965, *36,* 609-628.

Kagan, J., Moss, H. A., and Sigel, I. E. "Conceptual Style and the Use of Affect Labels." *Merrill-Palmer Quarterly,* 1960, *6,* 261-278.

Kagan, J., Moss, H. A., and Sigel, I. E. "Psychological Significance of Styles of Conceptualization." In J. C. Wright and J. Kagan (Eds.), *Basic Cognitive Progresses in Children*. New York: Society for Research in Child Development, 1963.

Kagan, J., Rosman, B. L., and others. "Information Processing and the Child: Significance of Analytic and Reflective Attitudes." *Psychological Monographs,* 1964, *78*(58).

Kallenbach, W. W., and Gall, M. D. "Microteaching Versus Conventional Methods in Training Elementary Intern Teachers." *Journal of Educational Research,* 1969, *63*(3), 136-141.

Keen, P. G. W. *Cognitive Style and the Problem-Solving Process*. Cambridge: Massachusetts Institute of Technology, 1974.

Keller, F. S. "Goodbye, Teacher." *Journal of Applied Behavior Analysis,* 1968, *1,* 79-89.

Keller, F. S. "The Basic System." In F. S. Keller and J. G. Sherman, *The Keller Plan Handbook*. Menlo Park, Ca.: W. A. Benjamin, Inc., 1974a.

Keller, F. S. "PSI and Reinforcement Theory." In F. S. Keller and J. G. Sherman, *The Keller Plan Handbook*. Menlo Park, Ca.: W. A. Benjamin, Inc., 1974b.

Keller, F. S. "PSI Is Not for Everyone." In F. S. Keller and J. G. Sherman, *The Keller Plan Handbook*. Menlo Park, Ca.: W. A. Benjamin, Inc., 1974c.

Keller, F. S., and Sherman, J. G. "Afterthoughts and Leftovers." In F. S. Keller and J. G. Sherman, *The Keller Plan Handbook*. Menlo Park, Ca.: W. A. Benjamin, Inc., 1974a.

Keller, F. S., and Sherman, J. G. *The Keller Plan Handbook*. Menlo Park, Ca.: W. A. Benjamin, Inc., 1974b.

Kelley, A. C. "An Experiment with TIPS: A Computer Aided Instructional System for Undergraduate Education." *American Economic Review,* 1968, *58,* 446-457.

Kelly, G. A. *The Psychology of Personal Constructs.* Vol. 1. New York: Norton, 1955.

Keogh, B. K., and Donlon, G. McG. "Field Dependence, Impulsivity, and Learning Disabilities." *Journal of Learning Disabilities,* June-July 1972, *5,* 16-21.

King, M., Payne, D. C., and McIntire, W. G. "The Impact of Marathon and Prolonged Sensitivity Training on Self-Acceptance." *Small Group Behavior,* Nov. 1973, *4,* 414-423.

Klaw, S. "Inside a T-Group." *Think,* Nov.-Dec. 1965, *31,* 26-30.

Kleemann, J. L. "The Kendall College Human Potential Seminar Model: Research." *Journal of College Student Personnel,* March 1974, *15,* 89-95.

Klein, G. S. "Need and Regulation." In M. R. Jones (Ed.), *Nebraska Symposium on Motivation.* Lincoln: University of Nebraska Press, 1954.

Klein, G. S., Gardner, R. W., and Schlesinger, H. J. "Tolerance for Unrealistic Experiences: A Study of the Generality of a Cognitive Control." *British Journal of Psychology,* 1962, *53,* 41-55.

Kogan, N. "Educational Implications of Cognitive Styles." In G. S. Lesser (Ed.), *Psychology and Educational Practice.* Glenview, Ill.: Scott, Foresman, 1971.

Kogan, N., and Wallach, M. A. *Risk Taking.* New York: Holt, 1964.

Kohlberg, L. "The Development of Moral Stages: Uses and Abuses." *Proceedings of the 1973 Invitational Conference on Testing Problems.* Princeton, N.J.: Educational Testing Service, 1973.

Kohlberg, L., and Mayer, R. "Development as the Aim of Education." *Harvard Educational Review,* Nov. 1972, *42,* 449-496.

Kohlberg, L., and Turiel, E. "Moral Development and Moral Education." In G. S. Lesser (Ed.), *Psychology and Educational Practice.* Glenview, Ill.: Scott, Foresman, 1971.

Kornrich, M. (Ed.) *Underachievement*. Springfield, Ill.: Thomas, 1965.

Kulik, J. A., Kulik, C. L., and Carmichael, K. "The Keller Plan in Science Teaching." *Science,* Feb. 1, 1974, *183,* 379-383.

LaGuardia Community College. *A Self-Study. Prepared for the Middle States Association of Colleges and Secondary Schools.* New York: LaGuardia Community College, 1974.

Lakin, M. "Some Ethical Issues in Sensitivity Training." *American Psychologist,* Oct. 1969, *24,* 923-928.

Lange, P. C. *Today's Education.* Washington, D.C.: National Education Association, 1972, *61,* 59.

Lavin, D. E. "Open Admissions at CUNY: An Overview of Policy and Research." Paper presented to the American Psychological Association Symposium, Sept. 1971.

Lecky, P. *Self-Consistency: A Theory of Personality.* Long Island, N.Y.: Island Press, 1945.

Legge, W. B., and Asper, L. "The Effect of Videotaped Microteaching Lessons on the Evaluative Behavior of Pre-Student-Teachers." *Journal of Teacher Education,* Fall 1972, *23,* 363-366.

Lesnick, M. "Reading and Study Behavior Problems of College Freshmen." *Reading World,* May 1972, *11,* 296-319.

Levinson, D. J., and others. "The Psychosocial Development of Men in Early Adulthood and the Mid-Life Transition." In D. F. Ricks (Ed.), *Life History Research in Psychopathology.* Minneapolis: University of Minnesota Press, 1974.

Lewin, K. *Field Theory in Social Science.* New York: Harper, 1951.

Lewin, K. "Studies in Group Decision." In D. Cartwright and A. Zander (Eds.), *Group Dynamics: Research and Theory.* New York: Harper, 1953.

Licklider, J. C. R. "Programmed Instruction." In S. G. Tickton (Ed.), *To Improve Learning: An Evaluation of Instructional Technology.* Vol. I, Appendix A. New York: R. R. Bowker, 1970.

Lieberman, M. A., Yalom, I. D., and Miles, M. B. "The Impact of Encounter Groups on Participants: Some Preliminary Findings." *Journal of Applied Behavioral Science,* 1972, *8*(1), 29-50.

Lieberman, M. A., Yalom, I. D., and Miles, M. B. *Encounter Groups: First Facts.* New York: Basic Books, 1973.

Loevinger, J. *The Meaning and Measurement of Ego Development.* San Francisco: Jossey-Bass, 1970.

Ludwig, T. G. "The Human Development Course in the Community Junior College: Towards a Model." Unpublished doctoral dissertation, University of Illinois, Urbana, 1973.

Maeroff, G. I. "Students' Scores Again Show Drop." *New York Times,* Dec. 16, 1973.

Majer, K., Hansen, D., and Dick, W. "Note on Effects of Individualized Verbal Feedback on Computer-Assisted Learning." *Psychological Reports,* 1971, *28,* 217-218.

Markle, S. M. "Programming and Programmed Instruction." In S. G. Tickton (Ed.), *To Improve Learning: An Evaluation of Instructional Technology.* Vol. I. New York: R. R. Bowker, 1970.

Marshall, S. A. "Sensitivity Training: A Report." *Educational Leadership,* Dec. 1970, *28,* 250-253.

Martens, K. *Cognitive Style: A Bibliography of Selected Introductory Readings.* Albany: Two-Year College Development Center, State University of New York at Albany, 1975.

Maslow, A. H. *Toward a Psychology of Being.* New York: Van Nostrand, 1962.

Maslow, A. H. "Self-Actualization and Beyond." In J. F. T. Bugental (Ed.), *Challenges of Humanistic Psychology.* New York: McGraw-Hill, 1967.

Maslow, A. H. (Ed.) *Motivation and Personality.* (2nd ed.) New York: Harper, 1970.

Maxwell, M. J. "The Role of Attitudes and Emotions in Changing Reading and Study Skills Behavior of College Students." *Journal of Reading,* March 1971, *14*(6), 359-423.

McCausland, D. F., and Stewart, N. E. "Academic Aptitude,

Study Skills, and Attitudes and College GPA." *Journal of Educational Research*, April 1974, *67*, 354-357.

McClelland, D. C. "Testing for Competence Rather Than for 'Intelligence.'" *American Psychologist*, Jan. 1973, *28*, 1-14.

McDonald, A. S. "Influence of a College Reading Improvement Program on Academic Performance." *Journal of Educational Psychology*, 1957, *48*, 171-181.

McDonald, R. L., and Dodge, R. A. "Audio-Tutorial Packages at Columbia Junior College." In J. G. Creager and D. L. Murray (Eds.), *The Uses of Modules in College Biology Teaching*. Commission on Undergraduate Education in the Biological Sciences, 1971.

McHolland, J. D. "From Stress to the Release of Human Potential." Speech delivered at Illinois College Personnel Association, Chicago, 1968.

McIntyre, C. J. "Acceptance by Others and Its Relation to Acceptance of Self and Others." *Journal of Abnormal and Social Psychology*, 1952, *47*, 624-625.

McKeachie, W. J. *Teaching Tips: A Guidebook for the Beginning College Teacher*. Lexington, Ma.: Heath, 1969.

McKeachie, W. J. "Instructional Psychology." In M. R. Rosenzweig and L. W. Porter (Eds.), *Annual Review of Psychology*. Vol. 25. Palo Alto, Ca.: Annual Reviews, Inc., 1974.

McKenney, J. L., and Keen, P. G. W. "How Managers' Minds Work." *Harvard Business Review*, May-June 1974, *52*, 79-90.

McKnight, P. C. "Microteaching in Teacher Training: A Review of Research." *Research in Education*, Nov. 1971, *6*, 24-38.

McLeish, J. *The Lecture Method*. Cambridge Monographs on Teaching Methods, No. 1. Cambridge, England: Cambridge Institute of Education, 1968.

McMichael, J. S., and Corey, J. R. "Contingency Management in an Introductory Psychology Course Produces Better Learning." *Journal of Applied Behavior Analysis*, 1969, *2*, 79-83.

Meister, M., Tauber, A., and Silverman, S. "Operation Second Chance." *Junior College Journal*, Oct. 1962, *33*, 78-88.

Messick, S. "The Criterion Problem in the Evaluation of Instruc-
    tion: Assessing Possible, Not Just Probable, Intended
    Outcomes." In M. C. Wittrock and D. E. Wiley (Eds.),
    The Evaluation of Instruction: Issues and Problems. New
    York: Holt, 1970.
Messick, S., and Kogan, N. "Differentiation and Compartment-
    alization in Object-Sorting Measures of Categorizing
    Style." *Perceptual and Motor Skills,* 1963, *16,* 47-51.
Mesthene, E. G. "Instructional Technology and the Purpose of
    Education." In S. G. Tickton (Ed.), *To Improve Learn-
    ing: An Evaluation of Instructional Technology.* Vol. 2.
    New York: R. R. Bowker, 1971.
Miles, M. B. "Human Relations Training: Processes and Out-
    comes." *Journal of Counseling Psychology,* 1960, *7*(4),
    301-306.
Milton, O. "The Changing Nature of Instruction." *Journal of
    Research and Development in Education,* Winter 1973, *6,*
    115-125.
Morman, S. J. "An Audio-Tutorial Method of Instruction vs.
    the Traditional Lecture-Discussion Method." *Two-Year
    College Mathematics Journal,* Fall 1971, *4,* 56-61.
Morris, C. J., and Kimbrell, G. M. "Performance and Attitudinal
    Effects of the Keller Method in an Introductory Psychol-
    ogy Course." *Psychological Record,* Fall 1972, *22,*
    523-530.
Morris, S. B., Pflugrath, J. C., and Taylor, B. "Encounter in
    Higher Education." In A. Burton (Ed.), *Encounter.* San
    Francisco: Jossey-Bass, 1969.
Mosher, R. L., and Sprinthall, N. A. "Psychological Education:
    A Means to Promote Personal Development During Ado-
    lescence." *Counseling Psychologist,* 1971, *2*(4), 3-82.
Mouly, G. J. "A Study of the Effects of a Remedial Reading
    Program on Academic Grades at the College Level." *Jour-
    nal of Educational Psychology,* Dec. 1952, *43,* 459-466.
Munday, L. A., and Davis, J. C. *Varieties of Accomplishment
    After College: Perspectives on the Meaning of Academic
    Talent.* Iowa City, Ia.: American College Testing Pro-
    gram, 1974.
Myers, G. E., and others. "Effect of Feedback on Interpersonal

Sensitivity in Laboratory Training Groups." *Journal of Applied Behavioral Science,* 1969, *5*(2), 175-185.

Myers, W. A. "Operant Learning Principles Applied to Teaching Introductory Statistics." In J. G. Sherman (Ed.), *Personalized System of Instruction: 41 Germinal Papers.* Menlo Park, Ca.: W. A. Benjamin, Inc., 1974.

Nagle, R. M. "Personality Differences Between Graduate Students in Clinical and Experimental Psychology at Varying Experience Levels." Unpublished doctoral dissertation, Michigan State University, 1967. Ann Arbor: University Microfilms, 1968. No. 68-11,081.

Nelson, K. H. *A Bibliography of Cognitive Style Research.* Cambridge: Harvard Business School, Harvard University, 1973.

Nelson, T. F., and Scott, D. W. "Personalized Instruction in Educational Psychology." In J. G. Sherman (Ed.), *Personalized System of Instruction: 41 Germinal Papers.* Menlo Park, Ca.: W. A. Benjamin, Inc., 1974.

Newkirk, R. L. "A Comparison of Learner Control and Machine Control Strategies for Computer-Assisted Instruction." *Programmed Learning and Educational Technology,* March 1973, *10,* 82-91.

Newman, J. H. *The Idea of a University.* New York: American Press, 1941. Originally published 1852.

Novak, J. *The Future of Modular Instruction.* CIUE Notes, No. 6. Ithaca, N.Y.: Center for Improvement of Undergraduate Education, Cornell University, 1973.

O'Banion, T., Thurston, A., and Gulden, J. "Junior College Student Personnel Work: An Emerging Model." In T. O'Banion and A. Thurston (Eds.), *Student Development Programs in the Community Junior College.* Englewood Cliffs, N.J.: Prentice-Hall, 1972.

Olch, D. S., and Snow, D. L. "Personality Characteristics of Sensitivity Group Volunteers." *Personnel and Guidance Journal,* 1970, *48,* 848-850.

Ornstein, J. "New Accents in Foreign Language Teaching." *Intellect,* March 1975, *103,* 395-398.

Osipow, S. H. "Cognitive Styles and Educational-Vocational

Preferences and Selection." *Journal of Counseling Psychology,* Nov. 1969, *16,* 534-546.

Panos, R. J. "Criteria of Student Development." *Journal of College Student Personnel,* Sept. 1968, *9,* 308-311.

Papke, D. R. "An Experiment in Self-Paced Physics." *Change,* Nov. 1973, *5,* 19-20.

Parkus, L. "The Computer." In S. G. Tickton (Ed.), *To Improve Learning: An Evaluation of Instructional Technology.* Vol. 1, Appendix A. New York: R. R. Bowker, 1970.

Perry, W. G., Jr. *Forms of Intellectual and Ethical Development in the College Years.* New York: Holt, 1970.

Peterson, R. E. *Goals for California Higher Education: A Survey of 116 College Communities.* Princeton, N.J.: Educational Testing Service, 1973.

Pettigrew, T. F. "The Measurement and Correlates of Category Width as a Cognitive Variable." *Journal of Personality,* 1958, *26,* 532-544.

Pittman, J. A. "A Study of the Academic Achievement of 415 College Students in Relation to Remedial Courses Taken." *Journal of Negro Education,* 1960, *29,* 426-437.

Postlethwait, S. N. "Independent Study in Biology." In R. A. Weisgerber (Ed.), *Developmental Efforts in Individualized Learning.* Itasca, Ill.: F. E. Peacock, 1971.

Postlethwait, S. N. "Minicourses: A Concern for Individualization." In National Conference on Open Learning in Higher Education, *Proceedings.* Lincoln: State University of Nebraska, 1974.

Postlethwait, S. N., Novak, J., and Murray, H. T., Jr. *The Audio-Tutorial Approach to Learning: Through Independent Study and Integrated Experiences.* (2nd ed.) Minneapolis: Burgess, 1969.

Protopapas, P. "A Report on the Use of the Keller Plan in a General Biology Course at Lowell State College." In J. G. Sherman (Ed.), *Personalized System of Instruction: 41 Germinal Papers.* Menlo Park, Ca.: W. A. Benjamin, Inc., 1974.

Quinlan, D. M., and Blatt, S. J. "Field Articulation and Performance Under Stress: Differential Predictions in Surgical and Psychiatric Nursing Training." *Journal of Consulting and Clinical Psychology,* 1972, *39.*

Rappaport, W. "TICCIT-CAI in the Community College." *Community and Junior College Journal,* March 1974, *44,* 72-73.

Reddy, W. B. "The Impact of Sensitivity Training on Self-Actualization: A One-Year Follow-Up." *Small Group Behavior,* Nov. 1973, *4,* 407-413.

Reed, F. C., Ertel, P. Y., and Collart, M. E. "A Model for the Development of Computer Assisted Instruction Programs." *Educational Technology,* March 1974, *14,* 12-20.

Reed, R. *Peer-Tutoring Programs for the Academically Deficient Student in Higher Education.* Berkeley: Center for Research and Development in Higher Education, University of California, 1974.

Rennels, M. R. "The Effects of Instructional Methodology in Art Education upon Achievement on Spatial Tasks by Disadvantaged Negro Youths." *Journal of Negro Education,* 1970, *39,* 116-123.

Renzi, N. B. "A Study of Some Effects of Field Dependence-Independence and Feedback on Performance Achievement." Unpublished doctoral dissertation, Hofstra University, 1974. *Dissertation Abstracts International,* 1974, *35,* 2059A. (University Microfilms No. 74-21, 861.)

Rest, J. "Developmental Psychology as a Guide to Value Education: A Review of 'Kohlbergian' Programs." *Review of Educational Research,* Spring 1974, *44,* 241-259.

Richason, B. F., Jr. "Independent Study in Geography." In R. S. Weisgerber (Ed.), *Developmental Efforts in Individualized Learning.* Itasca, Ill.: F. E. Peacock, 1971.

Riechmann, S. W., and Grasha, A. F. "A Rational Approach to Developing and Assessing the Construct Validity of a Student Learning Style Scales Instrument." *Journal of Psychology,* 1974, *87,* 213-223.

Riesman, D., Gusfield, J., and Gamson, Z. *Academic Values and Mass Education: The Early Years of Oakland and Monteith.* Garden City, N.Y.: Doubleday, 1970.

Robinson, H. A. "A Note on the Evaluation of College Remedial Reading Courses." *Journal of Educational Psychology*, Feb. 1950, *41*, 83-96.

Rogers, C. R. *Client-Centered Therapy*. Boston: Houghton Mifflin, 1951.

Rogers, C. R. "The Necessary and Sufficient Conditions of Therapeutic Personality Change." *Journal of Consulting Psychology*, 1957, *21*, 95-103.

Rogers, C. R. *On Becoming a Person: A Therapist's View of Psychotherapy*. Boston: Houghton Mifflin, 1961.

Rogers, C. R. "The Increasing Involvement of the Psychologist in Social Problems: Some Comments, Positive and Negative." *Journal of Applied Behavioral Science*, 1969, *5*(1), 3-7.

Rogers, C. R. *Encounter Groups*. New York: Harper, 1970.

Rogers, C. R. "Empathic: An Unappreciated Way of Being." *Counseling Psychologist*, 1975, *5*(2), 2-10.

Rosenthal, R. "Self-Fulfilling Prophecy." *Psychology Today*, 1968, *2*.

Roth, C. H. "Continuing Effectiveness of Personalized Self-Paced Instruction in Digital Systems Engineering." *Engineering Education*, 1973, *63*(6), 447-450.

Roueche, J. E. "The Open-Door College: The Problem of the Low Achiever." *Journal of Higher Education*, Nov. 1968a, *39*, 453-456.

Roueche, J. E. *Salvage, Redirection, or Custody?* Washington, D.C.: American Association of Junior Colleges, 1968b.

Roueche, J. E. "Accommodating Individual Differences." *Community College Review*, July-Aug. 1973, *1*, 24-29.

Roueche, J. E., and Kirk, R. W. *Catching Up: Remedial Education*. San Francisco: Jossey-Bass, 1973.

Roueche, J. E., and Wheeler, C. L. "Instructional Procedures for the Disadvantaged." *Improving College and University Teaching*, Summer 1973, *21*, 222-225.

Rubin, I. "The Re-education of Prejudice Through Laboratory Training." *Journal of Applied Behavioral Science*, 1967, *3*(1), 29-50.

Ruskin, R. S. *The Personalized System of Instruction: An Educational Alternative.* Washington, D.C.: American Association of Higher Education, 1974.

Sanford, N. *Where Colleges Fail: A Study of the Student as a Person.* San Francisco: Jossey-Bass, 1969.

Santeusanio, R. P. "Do College Reading Programs Serve Their Purpose?" *Reading World,* May 1974, *13,* 258-271.

Saturday Review—Education. "Do the First Two Years Matter? A Conversation with Jerome Kagan." April 1973, *1*(3), 41-43.

Sax, S. E. *Computer-Assisted Instruction and the New Student.* Berkeley: Center for Research and Development in Higher Education, University of California, 1972.

Schein, E. H., and Bennis, W. G. *Personal and Organizational Change Through Group Methods: The Laboratory Approach.* New York: Wiley, 1965.

Schlesinger, H. J. "Cognitive Attitudes in Relation to Susceptibility to Interference." *Journal of Personality,* 1954, *22,* 354-374.

Schoen, H. L. "A Comparison of Types of Feedback to Student Responses in a CAI Unit." In *Proceedings of the 1972 Conference on Computers in Undergraduate Curricula.* Atlanta: Georgia Institute of Technology, 1972.

Schwen, T. M. "The Effect of Cognitive Styles and Instructional Sequences on Learning a Hierarchical Task." Unpublished doctoral dissertation, Indiana University, 1970. *Dissertation Abstracts International,* 1970, *31,* 2797A-2798A. (University Microfilms No. 70-23, 380.)

Scott, W. A. "Conceptualizing and Measuring Structural Properties of Cognition." In O. J. Harvey (Ed.), *Motivation and Social Interaction.* New York: Ronald Press, 1963.

Seldman, M. L., McBrearty, J. F., and Seldman, S. L. "Deification of Marathon Encounter Group Leaders." *Small Group Behavior,* Feb. 1974, *5,* 80-91.

Sharon, A. T. "Assessing the Effectiveness of Remedial College Courses." *Journal of Experimental Education,* Winter 1972, *41,* 60-62.

Sharp, S. L. "Effective Study Methods." *Journal of Higher Education,* May 1943, *14,* 271-272.

Sheppard, W. C., and MacDermot, H. G. "Design and Evaluation of a Programmed Course in Introductory Psychology." *Journal of Applied Behavior Analysis,* 1970, *3,* 5-11.

Sherman, J. G. "A Permutation on an Innovation." Paper presented at meeting of American Psychological Association, Sept. 6, 1971.

Sherman, J. G. "Afterthoughts and Leftovers: That's Fine for Rote Learning—But What About Creativity?" In F. S. Keller and J. G. Sherman, *The Keller Plan Handbook.* Menlo Park, Ca.: W. A. Benjamin, Inc., 1974a.

Sherman, J. G. "Logistics." In F. S. Keller and J. G. Sherman, *The Keller Plan Handbook.* Menlo Park, Ca.: W. A. Benjamin, Inc., 1974b.

Sherman, J. G. (Ed.) *Personalized System of Instruction: 41 Germinal Papers.* Menlo Park, Ca.: W. A. Benjamin, Inc., 1974c.

Sherman, J. G. "Problems." In J. G. Sherman (Ed.), *Personalized System of Instruction: 41 Germinal Papers.* Menlo Park, Ca.: W. A. Benjamin, Inc., 1974d.

Sherman, J. G. "PSI: Some Notable Failures." In J. G. Sherman (Ed.), *Personalized System of Instruction: 41 Germinal Papers.* Menlo Park, Ca.: W. A. Benjamin, Inc., 1974e.

Sherman, J. G. "PSI Today." In F. S. Keller and J. G. Sherman, *The Keller Plan Handbook.* Menlo Park, Ca.: W. A. Benjamin, Inc., 1974f.

Silberman, H. F. "Characteristics of Some Recent Studies of Instructional Methods." In J. E. Coulson (Ed.), *Programmed Learning and Computer-Based Instruction.* New York: Wiley, 1962.

Skinner, B. F. "Teaching Machines." *Science,* 1958, *128,* 969-977.

Smith, R. L., and Walz, G. R. (Eds.) *Developing Students' Potentials.* Washington, D.C.: Education Resources Division Capitol Publications, undated.

Sperry, L. *Learning Performance and Individual Differences:*

Essays and Readings. Glenview, Ill.: Scott, Foresman, 1972.

Spotts, J. V., and Mackler, B. "Relationships of Field-Dependent and Field-Independent Cognitive Styles to Creative Test Performance." *Perceptual and Motor Skills,* 1967, *24,* 239-268.

Sprinthall, N. A. "Humanism: A New Bag of Virtues for Guidance?" *Personnel and Guidance Journal,* Jan. 1972a, *50,* 349-356.

Sprinthall, N. A. "Human Resource Training: A Response." *Counseling Psychologist,* 1972b, *3*(3), 56-61.

Sprinthall, N. A., and Erickson, V. L. "Learning Psychology by Doing Psychology: Guidance Through the Curriculum." *Personnel and Guidance Journal,* Feb. 1974, *52,* 396-405.

Steinfeld, S. L. "Level of Differentiation and Age as Predictors of Reinforcer Effectiveness." Unpublished doctoral dissertation, Hofstra University, 1973. *Dissertation Abstracts International,* 1973, *34,* 2912B-2913B. (University Microfilms No. 73-25, 324.)

Steinzor, B. "On N+1 Person Groups." In A. Burton (Ed.), *Encounter.* San Francisco: Jossey-Bass, 1969.

Stickgold, A. "Policy Implications of Changing Student Values in the Collegiate Culture." *Liberal Education,* May 1975, *61,* 173-186.

St. John-Brooks, C., and Spelman, B. "Microteaching." *Trends in Education,* July 1973, *31,* 14-19.

Stock, D. "Factors Associated with Change in Self-Percept." In D. Stock and H. A. Thelen (Eds.), *Emotional Dynamics and Group Culture.* New York: New York University Press, 1958.

Stock, D. "A Survey of Research on T Groups." In L. P. Bradford, J. R. Gibb, and K. D. Benne (Eds.), *T-Group Theory and Laboratory Method: Innovation in Re-education.* New York: Wiley, 1964.

Stolurow, L. M. "Programmed Instruction." In R. L. Ebel (Ed.), *Encyclopedia of Educational Research.* (4th ed.) Washington, D.C.: American Educational Research Association, 1969.

Strauss, G., and Sayles, L. R. *Personnel: The Human Problems of Management.* (3rd ed.) Englewood Cliffs, N.J.: Prentice-Hall, 1972.

Stuart, I. R. "Perceptual Style and Reading Ability: Implications for an Instructional Approach." *Perceptual and Motor Skills,* 1967, *24,* 135-138.

Suppes, P. "The Use of Computers in Education." *Scientific American,* Sept. 1966, pp. 207-220.

Sutter, E. M. "Individual Differences and Social Conditions as They Affect Learning by Computer-Assisted Instruction." Unpublished doctoral dissertation, University of Texas, 1967.

Szydlik, P. P. "Results of a One-Semester Self-Paced Physics Course at the State University College, Plattsburgh, New York." In J. G. Sherman (Ed.), *Personalized System of Instruction: 41 Germinal Papers.* Menlo Park, Ca.: W. A. Benjamin, Inc., 1974.

Taylor, C. W. "Cultivating New Talents: A Way to Reach the Educationally Deprived." *Journal of Creative Behavior,* Spring 1968, *2,* 83-90.

Thorndike, E. L. *Education, A First Book.* New York: Macmillan, 1912.

Tinker, I. "The Response of American Colleges to the Underprepared Students." Part II. In C. O. Atkinson, A. Etzioni, and I. Tinker (Eds.), *Post-Secondary Education and the Disadvantaged: A Policy Study.* New York: Center for Policy Research, 1969.

Torshen, K. "The Relation of Classroom Evaluation to Students' Self-Concepts and Mental Health." Unpublished doctoral dissertation, University of Chicago, 1969.

Trent, J. W., and Medsker, L. L. *Beyond High School.* San Francisco: Jossey-Bass, 1968.

Tresselt, M. E., and Richlin, M. "Differential Prognosis in a College Study Methods Course." *Journal of Psychology,* Jan. 1951, *31,* 81-89.

Triggs, F. O. "Remedial Reading Programs: Evidence of Their Development." *Journal of Educational Psychology,* Dec. 1942, *33,* 678-685.

Trotzer, J. P., and Sease, W. A. "The Effect of Group-Centered and Topic-Centered Methods on Volunteer College Students' Self-Concepts." *Journal of College Student Personnel,* July 1971, *12,* 292-296.

Truax, C. B., and Carkhuff, R. R. *Toward Effective Counseling and Psychotherapy: Training and Practice.* Chicago: Aldine, 1967.

Trueblood, R. W., and McHolland, J. D. *Self-Actualization and the Human Potential Group Process.* Evanston, Ill.: Kendall College, 1970.

United States Department of Labor. *Dictionary of Occupational Titles.* 2 vols. (3rd ed.) Washington, D.C.: U.S. Government Printing Office, 1965.

University of Michigan, Center for Research on Learning and Teaching. *Memo to the Faculty.* No. 55. Ann Arbor: University of Michigan, 1975.

Vinsonhaler, J. F., and Bass, R. K. *Ten Major Studies of the Evaluation of CAI Drill and Practice.* Information Systems Laboratory Report No. 21. Lansing: Michigan State University, 1971.

Wagner, A. C. "Changing Teaching Behavior: A Comparison of Microteaching and Cognitive Discrimination Training." *Journal of Educational Psychology,* 1973, *64*(3), 299-305.

Wallace, W. L. *Peer Groups and Students' Achievement.* Chicago: Aldine, 1965.

Wells, H. C. "To Get Beyond the Words." *Educational Leadership,* Dec. 1970, *28,* 241-244.

White, J. "The Human Potential Laboratory in the Community College." *Journal of College Student Personnel,* March 1974, *15,* 96-100.

Wiggins, T. W. "Sensitivity Training: Salvation or Conspiracy?" *Educational Leadership,* Dec. 1970, *28,* 254-257.

Wilson, P. M. "Do Students Learn from and Like an Audio-Tutorial Course in Freshman Mathematics?" *Two-Year College Mathematics Journal,* Fall 1972, *3,* 37-41.

Wilson, R. C., and others. *College Professors and Their Impact on Students.* New York: Wiley, 1975.

Wineman, J. H. "Cognitive Style and Reading Ability." *California Journal of Educational Research,* March 1971, *22,* 74-79.

Withey, S. B. *A Degree and What Else? Correlates and Consequences of a College Education.* Prepared for the Carnegie Commission on Higher Education. New York: McGraw-Hill, 1971.

Witkin, H. A. *The Role of Cognitive Style in Academic Performance and in Teacher-Student Relations.* Princeton, N.J.: Educational Testing Service, 1973.

Witkin, H. A., and Berry, J. W. *Psychological Differentiation in Cross-Cultural Perspective.* Princeton, N.J.: Educational Testing Service, 1975.

Witkin, H. A., and Cox, P. W. "Cognitive Styles and Career Guidance." *Findings* (a quarterly newsletter of Educational Testing Service), 1975, *2*(3), 1-4.

Witkin, H. A., Cox, P. W., and others. *Field Dependence-Independence and Psychological Differentiation: Bibliography with Index.* Princeton, N.J.: Educational Testing Service, 1974.

Witkin, H. A., Dyk, R. B., and others. *Psychological Differentiation.* New York: Wiley, 1962.

Witkin, H. A., Lewis, H. B., and others. *Personality Through Perception.* New York: Harper, 1954. (Republished: Westport, Conn.: Greenwood Press, 1972.)

Witkin, H. A., and Moore, C. A. "Cognitive Style and the Teaching-Learning Process." Paper presented at annual meeting of American Educational Research Association, Chicago, April 15-20, 1974.

Witkin, H. A., Moore, C. A., and others. *Field-Dependent and Field-Independent Cognitive Styles and Their Educational Implications.* Princeton, N.J.: Educational Testing Service, 1975.

Witkin, H. A., Oltman, P. K., and others. *Field Dependence-Independence and Psychological Differentiation: A Bibliography Through 1972 with Index.* Princeton, N.J.: Educational Testing Service, 1973.

Wragg, E. C. "The Influence of Feedback on Teachers'

Performance." *Educational Research,* June 1971, *13,*
218-221.

Wylie, R. C. *The Self-Concept.* Lincoln: University of Nebraska
Press, 1961.

Zinn, K. L. "Computers in the Instructional Process: Directions
for Research and Development." *Communications of the
ACM,* July 1972, *15,* 648-651.

Zoll, E. J. "Research in Programmed Instruction in Mathematics." *Mathematics Teacher,* 1969, *62,* 103-110.

Index

✳✳✳✳✳✳✳✳✳✳✳✳✳✳✳✳✳✳✳✳✳✳✳✳✳✳✳✳✳✳✳✳✳✳✳

A

281